International Human Resource Management

Theory and Practice

Edited by

Mustafa Özbilgin

WITHDRAWN
UTSA LIBRARIES

Selection, editorial matter and his own chapters © Mustafa Özbilgin 2005
Individual chapters and case studies © individual contributors 2005

All rights reserved. No reproduction, copy or transmission of this
publication may be made without written permission.

No paragraph of this publication may be reproduced, copied or transmitted
save with written permission or in accordance with the provisions of the
Copyright, Designs and Patents Act 1988, or under the terms of any licence
permitting limited copying issued by the Copyright Licensing Agency, 90
Tottenham Court Road, London W1T 4LP.

Any person who does any unauthorized act in relation to this publication
may be liable to criminal prosecution and civil claims for damages.

The authors have asserted their rights to be identified as the authors of
this work in accordance with the Copyright, Designs and Patents Act 1988.

First published 2005 by
PALGRAVE MACMILLAN
Houndmills, Basingstoke, Hampshire RG21 6XS and
175 Fifth Avenue, New York, N.Y. 10010
Companies and representatives throughout the world

PALGRAVE MACMILLAN is the global academic imprint of the Palgrave
Macmillan division of St. Martin's Press, LLC and of Palgrave Macmillan Ltd.
Macmillan® is a registered trademark in the United States, United Kingdom
and other countries. Palgrave is a registered trademark in the European
Union and other countries.

ISBN 0–333–99323–3

This book is printed on paper suitable for recycling and made from fully
managed and sustained forest sources.

A catalogue record for this book is available from the British Library.

Library of Congress Cataloging-in-Publication Data
International human resource management: theory and practice / edited by Mustafa Özbilgin
    p. cm.
  Includes bibliographical references and index.
  ISBN 0–333–99323–3 (pbk.)
    1. International business enterprises— Personnel management. I. Özbilgin, Mustafa.
  HF5549.5.E451578 2005
  658.3—dc22

                                                                    2004051636

10   9   8   7   6   5   4   3   2   1
14 13 12 11 10 09 08 07 06 05

Printed and bound in China

Library
University of Texas
at San Antonio

Contents

List of Case Studies

Preface

This book offers an introduction to the theory and practice of international human resource management. Taking readers through the journey of the development of mainstream human resource management, the book identifies the significance of the study of international contexts, processes and issues pertaining to effective employment of people. The aim of the book is to provide insights into developments in the field of international human resource management from both practitioner and academic perspectives. The explanatory, analytic and critical evaluations in each chapter are supplemented by discussion questions as well as case studies, reflecting on lived experience relevant to each aspect of international human resource management under study.

The book is suitable for both postgraduate and undergraduate study, as well as for management practitioners. Although the text would be most useful for students who are studying international human resource management for the first time, the book is designed to address the needs of students with diverse levels of skills and educational backgrounds. The examples and questions in the book capture the internationalization of the interest for human resource management, encouraging readers to draw on their experiences from their unique cultural backgrounds. The distinctive developmental approach of the book also ensures that each chapter examines competing definitions of the concepts, and offers analytical, critical as well as practical insights, recognizing the different skill levels and learning needs of readers.

This is also a useful text for practitioners of management, as it offers an analytical framework for examination of international employment practice, dissecting the field into its main components and exploring each aspect in a different chapter. The most appealing aspect of the book for management practitioners is its review of careers and competencies, as relevant to international management of people, and its structured way of identifying macro, meso and micro contexts and key influences and considerations at these levels for effective management of both international teams and operations.

The field of international human resource management is ripe with high-level inaccessible texts, which mainly offer critical examinations of academic perspectives on the subject. This book is unique in that it provides a clear analytical framework of the key aspects of international human resource management, introducing and developing each of these in a separate chapter in an accessible style.

The book has 10 chapters. The first chapter introduces the concept of human resource management, examining its historical development as a field of study and professional practice. The chapter highlights where the mainstream human resource practices and theory fail to offer tools for effective management of international teams and operations. Following this, the chapter explains the emergence of the notion of international human resource management, accounting for the key factors contributing to its current popularity.

Chapter 2 introduces the key aspects of international human resource management, offering a unifying framework of its components. This framework determines the structure of the book, with each chapter exploring one aspect in the framework. Each aspect of international human resource management is introduced and its key tenets are examined in this chapter. The book adopts a funnelling approach and starts with the study of macro-international aspects and continues with the study of the meso-national context and concludes with micro-individual issues as relevant to international human resource management. Thus subsequent chapters follow this logical flow from macro to meso and micro perspectives.

Chapter 3 of the book elaborates on the nature of the global workforce, identifying its key demographic attributes. The chapter broadly examines the concept of globalization, its uneven impact on employment practices as well as its implications for international employment practice, also identifying key institutions of regulation of the global labour force.

Chapter 4 examines the international context in which international and multinational organizations operate. The chapter explores the convergence and divergence of human resource management practices and the key concerns for multinational companies and their management of employees in different national contexts as well as in diverse teams.

Chapter 5 moves from the international to the national context of international human resource management, identifying institutions such as trade unions, employers' associations and professional bodies that impact on the regulation of employment practices in national settings. It also explores the changing nature of voice and representation, linking these with international human resource management.

Strategic management has become a key concern for organizations as a method for achieving improved performance outcomes, and in recognition of this Chapter 6 explores the strategic aspects of international human resource management, identifying differences between domestic and international strategic concerns. The chapter analyses different strategic options for MNCs regarding issues of choice of location, management of cultural diversity and international transfers as well as mergers and acquisitions.

Chapter 7 is concerned with the operational aspects of international human resource management, such as recruitment and selection, with insights into methods and approaches for eliminating discrimination and bias. The chapter explores the significance of training as a method of human resource development and examines particular operational concerns for management of expatriate staff.

Chapter 8 defines career and examines the specific attributes of international careers. The chapter provides some conceptual frameworks for understanding career processes and dynamics in the global context. It elaborates on a range of strategic options for expatriation and repatriation, highlighting the significance of career management at the international level for attracting and retaining best talent.

Defining the concept of competencies as skills and experiences necessary for staff to perform their tasks effectively, Chapter 9 identifies the spectrum of professional competencies of an international human resource manager. The chapter then refocuses, from an individual perspective, on the complexities involved in managing human resources in an international context.

Focusing on the main challenges facing international human resource management, chapter 10 notes the significance of social responsibility and management of diversity in the context of increased globalization. The chapter also refers to a number of puzzles in international human resource management practice and discourse, identifying these as the key challenges facing international human resource management theory and practice today.

Mustafa Özbilgin

Notes on the Contributors

Mustafa Özbilgin is a Senior Lecturer in Human Resource Management at Queen Mary, University of London. He previously worked at the Universities of Surrey and Hertfordshire. His research is in the field of comparative and cross-national study of employment relations, diversity, discrimination and ethics in organizations. He holds a post of Visiting Fellow at the School of Industrial and Labor Relations (ILR) of Cornell University, USA, and was an IRISS fellow at CEPS-INSTEAD in Luxembourg in 2002. He has recently co-authored and co-edited two books respectively titled, *Gender and Banking* (Palgrave, IB Tauris) and *Arts Marketing* (Butterworth & Heineman, Elsevier Press), and his papers are published in journals such as *Journal of Vocational Behavior, Personnel Review, Gender, Work and Organization, Career Development International* and *Management International*.

Yehuda Baruch is Professor of Management at the University of East Anglia (UEA) Norwich, UK, and formerly a visiting Associate Professor at the University of Texas at Arlington, USA, and a visiting Research Fellow at London Business School. He holds a BSc in Electronic Engineering (Ben Gurion, Israel), MSc and DSc in Management and Behavioral Sciences (The Technion, Israel). After working as a project manager in high-technology industry, he is now pursuing a career in academia. His research interests are careers, strategic and global HRM, and the impact of technology on management. He has published more than 60 papers in these fields in a number of journals, including *Human Relations, Human Resource Management, Organizational Dynamics, Journal of Vocational Behavior* and *Organization Studies* and a book titled *Managing Career: Theory and Practice*. Professor Baruch is the Editor of *Career Development International* and the Elected Chair for the Career Division of the Academy of Management, 2003.

Moira Calveley is a visiting Research Fellow at the University of Hertfordshire. She is a specialist in public-sector employment and trade unions, and has completed a PhD in 'Workplace Industrial Relations in a "Failing" School'. She has presented papers in national and international conferences and her most recent publication appeared in the *British Journal of Industrial Relations*. She worked in the insurance sector as a research manager for a number of years, and is a full member of the Chartered Institute of Personnel and Development. She has taught postgraduate and undergraduate modules in the field of industrial relations and human resource management.

K. Zeynep Girgin is Instructor in Human Resource Management and Organizational Behaviour at Bilkent University, Turkey. She is currently in the process of completing her PhD dissertation titled, 'Transferability of Human Resource Policies and Practices: American Multinationals in Turkey', at De Montfort University, Leicester, UK. Her research interests include international and comparative human resource management, reflective practice and the scholarship of teaching. Her research is published in *Innovations in Education* and *Training International*.

Geraldine Healy is Professor of Employment Relations at Queen Mary, University of London. Previously, she was Director of the Centre for Research in Employment Studies (CRES) at the University of Hertfordshire. She has published extensively on gender, career and employment relations. Her current research projects include minority ethnic women in trade unions (an ESRC Future of Work Project with Bristol University), contemporary approaches to equality and careers in academia in Turkey and internationally.

Mine Karataş-Özkan is a Lecturer in Entrepreneurship at the University of Southampton, currently conducting a doctoral research project at the Derbyshire Business School, University of Derby. Her main research interests are the learning and managing experiences of venture teams, managing diversity in a venture-team context, university–industry collaboration, university incubators and gender structures of the human resources profession. Together with colleagues, she has published and presented papers at conferences in these areas. Previously, Mine pursued a career in corporate banking.

Olympia Kyriakidou is a Chartered Psychologist and Lecturer in Organizational Behaviour in the School of Management, University of Surrey. She received her PhD in organizational psychology from the University of Surrey where she specialized in the field of employees' sensemaking and enactment of organizational change. Her research interests are in the application of psychology to organizational issues, organizational change and development, the social psychology of networks, organizational culture and sensemaking, knowledge management and shared cognition as well as virtual teams and measurement of effectiveness. Olympia currently works on the development of a relational perspective in the conceptualization of organizational studies. In the past, she was involved in the Department of Trade and Industry (DTI) Industry Forum Adaptation Programme exploring issues of organizational culture and employee retention in SMEs and QinetiQ exploring new conceptualizations of the digitized organization.

Peter Xu Lu has been working as a Research Associate at the Centre for Cross-Cultural Management Research, EAP European School of Management in Oxford, for the past four years. He also taught Business Studies at Oxford Brookes University Business School as an Associate Lecturer (part-time). Prior to coming to the UK, he worked as an Assistant General Manager in a large private enterprise in China.

Ayşe Saka is an Assistant Professor at the Department of Management, University of Mugla, Turkey. Having earned a PhD from Warwick Business School, University of Warwick, she worked as a Research Fellow between 2001 and 2003 at the Department of International Economics and Business, University of Gröningen, the Netherlands. Her research interests include comparative knowledge diffusion processes in cross-national settings, organizational learning within the MNC context, and institutional change processes. Her current research focuses on the characteristics of industrial districts and their performance implications in the Turkish textile industry. Her most recent publication appeared in *Organization Studies*.

Niccola Swan joined Barclays Bank in 1980. She has spent time as a business relationship manager, a credit risk manager, operations director, area director, regional sales director and head of mortgages operations. Barclays operates in 60 countries (including as Barclaycard) and employs around 75,000 people around the globe. Niccola was appointed in November 2001 to her current position as Director of Equality and Diversity at Barclays. She and her team have drawn up and published the diversity strategy for Barclays and have agreed with the Barclays Board externally published demanding objectives and action plans. These cover all aspects of diversity (including gender, race, disability, age, sexual orientation, religion and working patterns) for employees, customers, suppliers and the community. Her team is now working with all the Barclays businesses around the world to ensure that diversity practices are integrated into day-to-day business activity. Niccola lives in Yorkshire, is married and has two teenage children. As her office is in London, she is a role model for flexible working.

Ahu Tatlı is pursuing a doctoral study on 'Equal Opportunities and Diversity Management in Employment in Europe' at the University of Surrey, School of Management. She holds a BSc degree in Sociology from the Middle East Technical University in Turkey. She has an MA in Political Science from Bilkent University in Turkey with a thesis titled 'Islamist Women in the post-1980s' Turkey: Ambivalent Resistance'. Previously, she worked as a project coordinator in a women's NGO, 'The Flying Broom' in Turkey. Her research interests are in the areas of sociology of the Middle East, women and Islam, feminist methodology, equal opportunities and diversity management.

Chapter one

Introducing International Human Resource Management

Mustafa Özbilgin

Case study by Ayşe Saka

Learning outcomes

After reading this chapter, you should be able to:

■ Define the concept of human resource management.
■ Identify distinct theoretical contributions in the field of HRM.
■ Discuss the usefulness of these dominant mainstream approaches to HRM in an international context.
■ Define the concept of international human resource management and its key elements.
■ Understand the main models and themes of international human resource management.

INTRODUCTION

The increased speed of change in communication and transportation technologies, expansion of economic markets, desire to access better pools of resources, the challenge of competition, and improved mobility of people have fostered internationalization of the context of business (Griffin and Pustay 1998). The advent of communication and transportation technologies continues to widen the geographic imagination and reach of businesses beyond their traditional geographically constrained scope. Thriving on these favourable conditions, international, transnational and multinational companies have been achieving unprecedented economic and political success, whilst facing similarly major challenges in the process of becoming international players, particularly in the last three decades.

What kind of evidence can you provide for increased internationalization of business in your country?

How does your country compare to other countries in terms of internationalization of its business practices?

The challenges of the international context have encouraged international companies to develop new ways of doing business or to transfer their established practices between their home and host countries. While some companies have adopted ethno-centric approaches, choosing to transfer their home-country practices to their international operations, others have diversified or localized their business practices to the specific conditions of the host countries (Adler 1991). At the operational level these strategic choices are translated into choices for functional areas in business, including human resource management.

This chapter seeks to explore the theory and practice of human resource management in this increasingly internationalizing context. The chapter introduces and defines the concept of human resource management, highlighting the reasons behind the emergence and quick take-up of this concept in the industrialized countries. Based on a review of the main theoretical contributions of various schools of management to the academic development of this field, the chapter goes on to explain the rapid change and increased theoretical closure of mainstream conceptual frameworks and approaches to human resource management. The limited nature of the geographic and cultural relevance of mainstream writing and theory-making in this field is problematized and it is argued that the limitations of mainstream human resource management theory warrants further attention to international issues in this field, and to the study of international human resource management. The chapter goes on to explore the concept and practice of international human resource management, identifying its emerging and key themes and issues.

DEFINING HUMAN RESOURCE MANAGEMENT

The definitions and meanings attributed to academic concepts evolve over time, different authors offer differing definitions for the same concept. While some emerging definitions gain currency, others are deemed obsolete in time. Therefore, it is often possible to identify a number of 'competing definitions' of academic concepts at any given time. Reportedly, the definitions of human resource management (HRM) have also evolved over time, gaining a number of competing meanings. In its contemporary form, human resource management can be defined as a range of management activities which aim to achieve organizational objectives through effective use of employees.

The statement, which became the cliché of our times, that 'people are the most important resource in business' informs this definition (Taylor *et al.* 1996). Recognizing human resources as one of the main organizational resources, on a par with or even more significant than financial, technological and physical resources, marks a radical departure from earlier approaches and definitions of people management which considered it as a secondary business concern to management of other resources of organizations.

GROUP ACTIVITY

Identify different names given to activities associated with people-management in your country. Define and discuss these different names and professional activities associated with each of them. Based on this discussion, identify contemporary and competing definitions of the concept of human resource management.

Exploring the historical development of human resources can shed some light on our understanding of its current definition and practice. Human resource management has a complex and elusive history; it is complex because the rhetoric and practice of HRM have different historical paths of development. While the practice of various methods and techniques of HRM has a history as old and complex as the history of work and organization, human resource management as an academic area of work or as discourse is claimed to have originated only in the 1950s with the works of Drucker (1954) and McGregor (1957). In his seminal book, *The Practice of Management*, Peter Drucker coined the term human resources. However, the concept gained wider international recognition in academic and practitioner circles by the 1980s, particularly in the Anglo-Saxon world (Sparrow and Hiltrop 1994).

It is important to make a distinction between academic rhetoric and managerial practice of human resource management. Although the functions and operational aspects of human resource management have been practiced since much earlier internationally, the rhetoric as coined in North America and espoused by both American and British academics and in Western Europe generally has been enjoying wider popularity and international recognition only in the last two decades. The 1990s has also seen the wider adaptation of this concept in developing and less-developed countries.

GROUP ACTIVITY

Based on a review of the national and international literature, explore the theoretical and professional development of human resource management in your country. How does this compare to the theoretical and professional development of the concept in neighbouring countries?

The history of human resource management is also elusive because of a series of seamless changes in name and strategic direction. This has encouraged academic debate on what constitutes human resource management and if and how this 'new' concept differs from its predecessors such as personnel management, manpower management and welfare management. The change from personnel management to human resource management in particular is considered as the most significant turning point in the historical development of people-management discourses. This attracted a spectrum of critical evaluations, considering it merely as a change of name, simply an attempt at reviving a weakening area of work with a new buzz phrase, or a change of strategic direction recognizing human resources as one of the strategically important resources of an organization. Legge (1995) explains that the hype of changing the name from personnel management to human resource management was indeed an inevitable outcome of the political economy and market conditions of the 1980s.

Furthermore, Sisson and Storey (1998) argue that human resource management is a controversial concept, attributing its controversy to problems with its definition, divergence in implementation and discourse, and unexpected consequences of its implementation. Although the theory and implementation of HRM is in need of demystification, HRM is a clearly interdisciplinary and fast-changing area of study and work, encompassing earlier notions of welfare, manpower and personnel management and being in close association with employee and industrial relations as well as sociology and psychology of work. Despite its interdisciplinary and eclectic nature, the overwhelming majority of the earlier theoretical works on human resource management originate from North America and the United Kingdom. The mainstream literature continues to rely heavily on contributions from industrialized countries. The next section outlines these contributions, problematizing their contextual specificity.

THEORETICAL DEVELOPMENT OF HRM

Several schools of management in the USA and the UK have made significant contributions to the development of the mainstream theory of HRM. The Michigan Model was developed by Fombrun, Tichy and Devanna (1984), who proposed that in order to improve their performance, companies must build a direct link between their corporate and human resource strategies and structures (Mabey *et al.* 1998). Their formulation aimed at promoting an instrumental use of human resources in order to realize corporate objectives. In the same period, a group of academics from Harvard Business School argued for a broader framework for HRM decisions and strategy. The Harvard Model, formulated by Beer *et al.* (1985), suggested that HRM decisions should be informed by both stakeholder interests and also a set of situational factors. The model illustrates the influence of situational factors on stakeholder interests, and their impact on human resource policy choices which are destined to deliver a raft of predetermined human resource outcomes such as commitment, competence, congruence and cost-effectiveness. These outcomes consequently produce long-term and sustainable benefits for the individual, the organization and society. This is a highly prescriptive model of HRM which emphasizes a number of presumed long-term benefits of acting on stakeholder interests and situational factors, assuming that there is a set of predetermined and 'superior' human resource policy choices (Sisson and Timperlet 1996, p. 163). The Michigan and Harvard models were often compared and contrasted in terms of their approaches to the use of human resources. While the Michigan model accentuates the strategic resource aspect of human *resources*, the Harvard model emphasizes the human element in the *human* resource formulations.

These two classical models of HRM have underpinned the 'hard' and 'soft' variants of HRM, respectively. The 'hard' variant considers employees as one of the key resources of organizations, arguing in this tradition that human resources should be used effectively in order to achieve organizational goals. On the other hand, the 'soft' variant considers employees first and foremost as human beings who contribute to the organization (Maund 2001). These two distinctively different approaches to HRM have been classically used to account for differences in management of people in organizations. The debate on the relative and context-specific usefulness of these two approaches continues. Based on a recognition of the significance of both approaches, more contemporary formulations of HRM incorporate and display a combination of soft and hard attributes, rather than rejecting one for the other.

Focusing on the theme of the strategic relevance of HRM, which was also evident in the Michigan model, the New York Model has introduced and illustrated the concept of 'strategic fit' between corporate and human resource strategy. The New York model was formulated by Schuler and Jackson (1987) and advocated that a range of 'needed role behaviours' could be deduced from Porter's earlier works on competitive strategies, and these could provide a set of prescriptions for desirable strategic choices for HRM and industrial relations functions. The Harvard, Michigan and New York models share a common attribute. As Sparrow and Hiltrop (1994) so succinctly explain it, these three models could be named as 'matching models' of HRM, because of their common aim to match the human resources strategy with that of the corporation.

The MIT Model, which was introduced by Kochan *et al.* (1986), provided a framework accounting for the development of industrial relations in the USA. The model describes three phases of development: the 'New Deal' phase attributed to high levels of regulation in the workplace and the 'non-union' phase identifiable by extensive HRM policies designed to promote individual commitment. The authors argue that these two phases could be incorporated into what they call, the 'new industrial relations' phase, which assumes that joint consultation between employees and employers, and increased levels of cooperation and flexibility in the workplace will provide companies with adaptability and representation which were evidently missing from the other two phases. However, Sisson and Timperlet (1986, p. 164) from the UK argued that this model, similar to the Harvard model, has a prescriptive approach, advocating the use of the 'New industrial relations' phase as an ideal, and that it fails to provide evidence for its wider international applicability.

The Warwick Model was developed by Storey (1992) in the UK. It contrasted attributes of personnel management and HRM and examined evidence of their practice in the UK. This model provided a number of key attributes and indicators of people management and highlighted the differentiation between personnel and HRM approaches.

Despite an apparent domination of the mainstream HRM literature by models, theories and concepts developed in North America and the UK, the Aix Model from France was able to gain mainstream recognition in texts. The model, which underlines the significance of social and educational systems in the management of human resources, was propagated by Maurice *et al.* (1980, 1986). Another similar model outside the English-speaking world was the Japanese Model of HRM (Tung 1984), introduced in the 1980s, that emphasized how quality considerations can be integrated into people-management techniques.

GROUP ACTIVITIES

Examine the HRM system of a company that you know, such as your current educational institution or workplace, and discuss if their human resource management approach conforms to any of the theoretical models identified above.

Discuss the reasons why your company of choice formulated their human resource approach in its current form.

DEVELOPMENT OF INTERNATIONAL HRM

The mainstream HRM theories, which were overwhelmingly formulated in management schools in North America and the UK in the 1980s, have quickly found their way to other developed and developing countries and gained much wider international recognition in the 1990s. The take up of HRM principles and techniques in industrialized countries owes much to a number of changes in the composition and nature of their key industries and labour market conditions. First, early experiences of industrialization in Western Europe and North America required their workforces to be organized and supervised differently to the previous era, and scientific management techniques were formulated in the rapidly growing manufacturing sectors in these regions. However, more recently the industrial composition in the industrialized countries has been changing from manufacturing to service industries, the latter slowly replaced manufacturing as the main employer of labour in advanced economies. Faced with changes in their key industries, industrialized countries have sought to develop new and effective methods of managing human resources in their emerging industries.

Secondly, due to their higher rates of employment and economic development, and their ageing populations, the labour markets in industrialized societies have been experiencing skills shortages in many areas of employment and work. This is best evidenced in the changing nature of competitive migration policies some developed countries such as the USA, Canada, Australia and Germany are pursuing in order to seek cover for skills shortages in their labour forces. These demographic circumstances in the developed countries have been boosting demand for skilled labour and encouraging competitive people-management techniques for more effective ways of managing the limited supply of national human resources.

GROUP ACTIVITY

Examine the labour market conditions in your country, comparing it with two other countries. How do these conditions impact on the agendas of human resource managers in your selected countries?

These two specific circumstances may partly account for the rapid development and spread of HRM discourse and practice in developed countries. However, the similarly rapid spread of human resource practices to developing and less-developed countries warrants further elaboration. The spread of the HRM philosophy and techniques beyond the developed regions of the world can be attributed to the following reasons:

1 Scientific knowledge on HRM has been taken up by management schools internationally. There are now professional bodies in developed as well as developing countries providing support and education on management issues. Transfer of professional and academic knowledge from developed to developing and less-developed countries has enabled a wider take-up of this business concept.

2 International companies contribute to the transfer of HRM techniques and practices to developing and less-developed countries, through their branches or other business associations.

3   Managers in developing and less-developed countries also experience skills short-
    ages in certain areas of work and employment, and seek effective ways of manag-
    ing the short supply of human resources. In search of increased efficiency and
    effectiveness, human resource philosophies, originating from North America and
    Western Europe, are adopted and developed by practitioners and academics in
    developing countries.

Although the geographic reach of the concept of HRM has broadened at an unprecedented rate over the last two decades, this development was not always welcome.
Crossing national borders, the theory and practice of HRM was met with considerable
resistance and challenge. The main sources of trepidation in importing HRM techniques were international variations in philosophies, approaches and structures of
employment relations, trade unions, employment law, management systems, and
societal and organizational cultures.

   A consensus has emerged during the last three decades that the mainstream human
resource approaches and theories are inadequate in addressing the human resource
issues facing international and multinational companies (MNCs). Out of this recognition, and also as a direct outcome of the MNCs pursuit of effective ways of managing
their international human resources (Taylor *et al.* 1996), international human resource
management (IHRM) has emerged as a new area of academic study and management
practice. The theory of IHRM has been receiving growing recognition only since the
late 1980s (Scullion and Starkey 2000). Caliguiri (1999) with her study of academic
journals in the field of IHRM identified that IHRM has established itself as a
respectable scholarly interest between the disciplines of international management
and HRM. She contends that the interest in the field of IHRM is not a passing fad, but
is set to grow further due to the relevance of issues such as cross-national comparative
human resources, expatriate management and cross-cultural diversity within multinational enterprises to the effective management of human resources internationally.

DEFINING INTERNATIONAL HUMAN RESOURCE MANAGEMENT

Although the studies on IHRM provide insights into various techniques, approaches,
themes and principles of HRM in an international context, they have hardly
attempted to provide a standalone definition of the concept. IHRM can be defined as
a range of people management functions, processes and activities which involve
consideration of more than one national context (Taylor *et al.* 1996). 'Involvement of
more than one national context' implies three levels of practice and study of IHRM,
identified by Jain, Lawler and Morishima (1998) as:

1   Single-country human resource activities often involve considerations of interna-
    tional human resource issues. For example, skills shortages in a country may
    encourage recruitment of migrant labour, and this practice requires national
    companies to take into account the international aspects of HRM such as growing
    competition for international labour. Similarly, there are studies of HRM issues in
    a single-country context that provide insights into national systems, structures
    and approaches of people management, allowing cross-national comparisons and
    contributing to our understanding of convergence and divergence of employment
    systems, management approaches and other human resource issues. There is an
    extensive body of literature on single-country studies of HRM.

2 Companies operating in more than one country may carry out IHRM activities at another level. For example, management of international assignments, expatriates and the process of repatriation require such considerations. There are for example studies involving management of expatriate workers in MNCs that explore the strategic role of the corporate human resource function in MNCs. The corporate function performs personnel roles such as the management of succession, career development, strategic staffing, international management mobility and training, and repatriation of international workers. Scullion and Starkey (2000) identify this as a relatively new and neglected area of study in IHRM.

3 International companies need to address national differences between their home and host-country operations, and there are studies exploring the management of people in international, multinational and transnational companies with particular reference to the home-country and host-country divide in their evaluations. These studies seek to explain and bridge the national differences in management of human resources, providing descriptive and prescriptive analysis and critical evaluation of the current trends.

GROUP ACTIVITY

Choose three companies, one which is nationally based, two with international operations, and discuss the relevance of IHRM issues to their business conduct.

PRESCRIPTIVE MODELS AND CRITICAL THEMES IN IHRM

Drawing on studies from the aforementioned three lines of inquiry, this section explores the models and emerging themes of IHRM. Since its inception in the 1980s, the theory and practice of IHRM has displayed various patterns and has experienced challenges. Seeking to offer academic solutions to the complex problems facing the IHRM practitioner, several authors have attempted to provide models of IHRM practice. Asdorian (1995), for example, identified three 'tricks' for a successful IHRM start-up:

1 Preventing the emergence of divisions and divisive perceptions between operations in different countries.
2 Working in each country using the terms of reference used in that country.
3 Avoiding the assumption that best practice can transcend national borders.

Asdorian's (1995) model emphasizes the significance of recognizing differences between countries and working to understand them in order to achieve business success for IHRM start-ups. Molnar and Loewe (1997) proposed seven keys to IHRM practice subsequent to the start-up stage:

1 Understanding the international and global context of business, including supply and demand dynamics of human resources in each country.
2 Providing guidelines on service policy for international operations of the company.

3 Considering the financial viability of human resource allocations internationally.
4 Documenting and outlining the personal and domestic arrangements of individual workers who are involved in international assignments, with a view to accommodating their requirements.
5 Providing clear guidelines on terms and conditions for international assignments to individual employees prior to allocation of their roles.
6 Arranging relocation of employees and their families.
7 Setting up a repatriation process which ensures smooth return and reintegration of the expatriates and their families.

Molnar and Loewe (1997) argue that even when companies choose to outsource their international human resources, they should continue to support international assignments with their policies and structures.

Torrington (1994) provides a simplified model for the management of human resources from the perspective of an international firm. He identifies seven 'C's which a firm will need to develop an understanding of in order to manage its diverse workforce effectively:

1 a *cosmopolitan* workforce, which draws its strength from diversity;
2 *culture* and its diversity across national borders;
3 *compensation* and its comparative meanings and value;
4 the value of *communication;*
5 the development of *competences;*
6 the use of *consultants*; and
7 *coordination* of international operations in a way which values diversity.

Based on a review of literature, Taylor *et al.* (1996) propose a model for strategic implementation of IHRM. Their model is underpinned by a resource-based theory of the firm, which elaborates that a company's business success is shaped by its success in using its key resources. In this model, it is explained that IHRM practice can draw on three resources for competitive advantage and business success:

1 The parent company's resources, in terms of a distinct range of economic, social and political conditions of the parent country;
2 the parent company's resources, which the company has developed as assets, competencies and capabilities; and
3 the host company's resources both at national and company levels that can provide competitive advantages and be sources of business success.

Taylor *et al.* (1996) specify three conditions which will enable the successful disposal of these resources:

1 The HRM competency of the parent firms plays a major role in this success.
2 Senior-level managerial commitment is pivotal.
3 Not only parent-company workers and expatriates, but also the host-country employees make a significant contribution to the success or failure of the business.

Steingruber (1997) criticized the strategic IHRM models' failure to distinguish between different kinds of international firms, arguing that differentiating international firms as 'multidomestic, global or hybrid' would enable a better understanding of differences between their respective strategies for management of human resources.

Although the emerging themes within IHRM were of a critical nature, the development of IHRM models followed a more prescriptive path. This difference was due to the academic nature of the former and the practical nature of the latter. Welch (1994) argues that although such prescriptive models should not be devalued, their contribution is somewhat limited to the scientific development of IHRM. Nevertheless, the main models of IHRM provide useful checklists for practitioners and students of IHRM. An examination of key themes emerging in the subject provides a series of critical issues that warrant academic and practitioner attention. The critical challenges facing practitioners and researchers of IHRM are explored in Chapter 10.

Case study 1

NISSERA UK – Making sense of Japanese work systems

Ayşe Saka

Background to the company

Nissera UK (a pseudonym) was established in the late 1980s on a greenfield site as part of a strategy to manufacture and sell car components to the European market. It is the UK subsidiary of a Japanese multinational company, Nissera (another pseudonym) that has been in operation for 60 years. The parent company's production output for Europe and the USA was 2 million instruments per year in 1999. Its market share was 10 per cent in each of the aforementioned markets in the same year. There was precision in the fabrication of products, which was reflected in Nissera's slogan: 'where our technical expertise meets the world'. In comparison to its UK subsidiary, Nissera had a much wider product range. These included control panels for printers, air conditioner remote controls (for office and home use), water heater/bath remote controls, hybrid integrated circuits and mushroom-seeding machine. Nissera employed 46 Japanese members overseas and 941 people in various sections, such as general affairs, international business, product engineering and so on at its headquarters.

Nissera UK adhered to operating along principles of quality, reliability and competitiveness. Manufacturing flexibility was one of the ways by which the company strived to maintain these

principles. Nissera UK aimed to deliver parts Just-in-Time, working closely in partnership with its customers to meet their current requirements and to develop the future technology needs of the market. It dedicated a design-interface team with its customers to liaise directly with their engineers to ensure that the product met exact specifications prior to manufacturing.

Restructuring the organization

Nissera UK had been taking steps to transmit a 'Japanese' approach to its British workforce from its inception, and expatriate managers were used extensively for this purpose, seconded to Britain for periods of generally a year. Production management and supervision were predominantly British and recruited locally. 'From the start the workforce was all local. The management structure was mostly Japanese. From day one it was planned that British managers would be selected to fill in the roles occupied by the Japanese over time', commented the production manager at Nissera UK. There were on the whole 12 Japanese managers based in the UK division.

Japanese managers trained supervisors and the workforce. Information was passed on in the form of job instructions rather than via formal off-the-job training. Job instructions were demonstrated and the operators were taken to the source of the problem when mistakes were made. As time progressed, Japanese expatriates delegated their training role to local British managers. However, as the human resource officer said, 'they [still did] show people how to do something when it [was] needed'. Japanese managers argued that one of the easiest ways to train British employees was through the British manager's acquisition of 'Nissera skills' in Japan. These managers were then expected to teach their employees what they had learnt in Japan. As production volume increased, less and less time was devoted to training British employees, which increased product defect rates and reduced quality levels.

Nissera's commitment and long-lasting efforts to create dedicated human capabilities decreased as Nissera UK failed to develop its own knowledge base and satisfactory results. The Japanese quality assurance manager at Nissera explained this as 'first time I was in the UK, we brought know-how with documentation and information [such as quality standards, instruction manuals, quality control process charts and drawings]. Japan did not send any know-how after that. Their manufacturing is old and manual, so we cannot transfer know-how'. Upon experiencing a continuous decline in profits from 1993 to 1997, Nissera UK decided to save costs by restructuring its organization. It shifted to a flatter structure in 1997. The pattern of authority relations changed from one based on superintendents, supervisors and hourly paid workers to one built around team leaders, team coaches and hourly paid workers arranged in a production cell layout rather than assembly lines. A Japanese production manager who had visited Nissera UK between 1993 and 1995 at the time of the quality problems and related financial loss had the opportunity to compare the work standards of the UK subsidiary with those of the parent company: 'If supervisor does not explain or check, the operator will just pass the equipment [even if quality is low]. There is a big difference in culture. Here, in Japan, the boss is followed. Nissera has its own standards and regulations. Employees do not have the chance to resist. We cannot transfer these regulations to the UK directly, so we had to take mid-point between these two systems. For example, at Nissera, all employees leave the office on time and return after the buzzer. In addition, every operator in Japan has to clean self-area [including the head-office staff]. In the UK, a separate company does the cleaning. I explain, but it is difficult for them [the British] to implement'.

Commitment to continuous improvement schemes

As was evident in the lack of interest in Kaizen activities, the level job satisfaction among the workforce at Nissera UK was quite low. The British production manager at Nissera UK argued that 'we have launched the suggestion scheme twice. People are just not motivated'. The young operators felt constrained by the strict factory rules. Employees were expected to value the details of work, stress quality rather than quantity, work in formalized work stages and exercise high levels of task-related discipline. However, it proved challenging to impart these principles to the workforce. According to the British production manager, 'we do not make perfection. We make something that is going to satisfy the customer's requirements. Standards of the customer may allow for some defect. Our company policy is "better in price, quick in delivery, better in quality". It is this married to those three . . . What is the point in someone manufacturing zero defect if they have problems supplying it?' There was a low sense of responsibility for quality-control processes as observed in the 'parts-testing' phase of the assembly process. Tests normally took seven minutes to complete, but operators found this too long and halted the process after two or three minutes.

HR policies at Nissera UK were different from those implemented in Japan. For instance, the company did not aim to bind its employees to long-term employment or lavish provisions in terms and conditions. However, there were concerns over the fact that instability in the employment base prevented the UK subsidiary from building upon its past experience. A Japanese quality-assurance manager at Nissera said that 'employees constantly change. Of 100 UK employees that were trained at the start of operations, only three remain at Nissera UK'.

Similarly, in the finance department, 'if the manager [at the subsidiary firm] leaves, there is a problem. The management system cannot succeed to the next manager. The new manager has to understand our intention ... A finance manager is responsible for managing daily operations, negotiating with the bank and getting in touch with Nissera. For example, in case of loans from the bank, if the manager changes, the bank may not provide finances. The finance manager needs to be trusted [not by Nissera alone, but by the external institutions as well].'

Although Nissera UK had an induction programme that outlined the espoused values of its management to newcomers, quality-improvement activities were difficult to implement due to differences in work attitudes between Japan and the UK. Operators' immediate concerns were different from the Japanese management's interest in issues that were perceived as important. The quality director at the parent company explained that '[T]he operator could not accept series development, Plan-Do-Check-Action (PDCA). In Japan, targets are set, methods of achieving those targets are identified and improvements are suggested. This is the responsibility of the top. They are then broken down to group leaders in the middle of the hierarchy.

Information is further cascaded down to the operator level. In the UK, you do not see PDCA at the operator level. The attitude is "ok, it is 16:30. I am going home". There is great loyalty at each level in Japan. Quality Circle (QC) education is not accepted here [in the UK]. QC is accepted as an individual employee activity. If there is no salary, there is no contribution.' It was easier for Nissera UK employees to follow Nissera practices where there was a clear job description. The electronic engineering manager at the Japanese headquarters commented, '[T]he document procedure is based on Nissera's procedures and written and settled at the technical centre. In order to make the technical centre's task clear, we need to provide in/out information as well as "control documents". The UK needs exact job description, but for Japan, this is not the case. In Japan, we do not need such clear job description. UK employees will not do it if it is not clear.'

Nissera UK invested considerable effort into implementing continuous improvement schemes by providing financial resources and employing high numbers of Japanese expatriates in the early years of operation. However, philosophies such as team spirit were more difficult for the UK workforce to accept than techniques such as team-based structures.

Case study discussion topics

1 What does the case demonstrate as regards the implementation of Japanese work systems?
2 What should the UK management do to reduce resistance by workers to continuous improvement schemes?
3 What is the role of IHRM in the implementation of foreign work systems?
4 Based on the case study above, discuss whether the mainstream HRM approaches would be adequate to respond to people management needs in Nissera and Nissera UK.

SUMMARY

This chapter has provided an introduction to international human resource management, exploring the development of HRM practice and theory in the international context. Reviewing the definitions and mainstream theoretical frameworks of HRM and IHRM, the chapter suggests that IHRM has established itself in a respected position between academic and practitioner communities. However, it has also been highlighted that IHRM currently experiences various challenges and dilemmas. These have been explored as contemporary models and themes in the subject. The next chapter explores in further detail whether HRM presents solutions to challenges facing practitioners of people management.

Chapter two

Aspects of International Human Resource Management

Mustafa Özbilgin

Case study by Peter Xu Lu

Learning outcomes

After reading this chapter, you should be able to:

- Understand an eight-dimensional framework of the aspects of international human resource management (IHRM).
- Discuss if IHRM presents a viable solution to the people-management problems faced in an international context.
- Evaluate a case study of an international merger.
- Apply the eight-dimensional framework to the case study.

INTRODUCTION

The previous chapter examined the dominant and mainstream models of HRM and highlighted their limitations in addressing the complexity and diversity of issues pertaining to the management of human resources in an international context. The chapter also set out the limitations of and opportunities for adopting a universal approach to human resource management.

This chapter provides a conceptual framework of aspects of IHRM that are central to both its study and practice. Based on this framework, the chapter goes on to question whether the identified aspects of IHRM offer a universal panacea. The framework also informs the structure of this book, as each aspect of IHRM in the framework is devoted a chapter. There is also a case study at the end of this chapter which examines the Chinese context of employment, calling for a reexamination of the dynamics of IHRM as different to dominant approaches to the management of human resources.

A FRAMEWORK OF KEY ASPECTS OF IHRM

Although there is lack of consensus on demarcations of the professional scope and academic study of IHRM, this book identifies and focuses on eight areas of research and practice as distinct and fundamental. These aspects are: the global workforce; the international context; the national context; strategic issues; operational aspects of IHRM; careers; professional competencies; and future issues.

These eight key aspects of IHRM are illustrated as an eight-point star in Figure 2.1. The significance of this visual representation is that these aspects are inextricably interlinked to form the main body of research and practice in this area, and therefore a true understanding of IHRM requires insights into all rather than some of these aspects.

This book also adopts this eightfold structure, each subsequent chapter exploring one of the aspects introduced in this chapter. Throughout the book the linkages between these different aspects are explored.

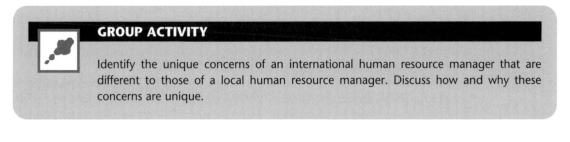

GROUP ACTIVITY

Identify the unique concerns of an international human resource manager that are different to those of a local human resource manager. Discuss how and why these concerns are unique.

Figure 2.1   *Eight-point star of IHRM: a framework of key aspects*

THE GLOBAL WORKFORCE

The global workforce refers to human capital available in the international arena and across national borders, and its study is important for understanding the supply and demand for labour. This knowledge is crucial when formulating people-management strategies both locally and internationally. Similarly, profiling the distributive attributes of the global workforce is essential in order to develop a comparative perspective on supply and demand for labour as well as conditions and terms of employment and work in an international context. Several sources of information such as the periodic reports from the United Nations, the International Labour Organization (ILO), the Organization of Economic Cooperation and Development (OECD) and other regional and international institutions provide global and aggregate figures on levels of employment, unemployment, education and training, costs and standards of life and work, cultural and social life.

This aspect of IHRM is also concerned with the attributes of the global workforce and trends in its employment experience in the context of globalization in the 2000s. As the impact of globalization is unevenly felt across regions of the world, management of human resources requires distinctly different approaches and competencies in different national contexts to match the demands of national and international labour markets (Mok *et al.* 2002; Rowley and Bae 2002; Warner 2002). Evaluating globalization as both a reality and a myth of IHRM, is therefore central to this aspect. For example, drawing on Bradley, Erickson, Stephenson and Williams (2002), it is important to ask why globalization may be considered both a myth and a reality at the same time, and what impact, if any, this has on our contemporary understanding of the intensification of international connectivity in business relations.

This aspect of the global workforce is also informed by contemporary issues of labour migration (Bhagat and London 1999) and institutions of labour mobility, regulation and management, such as social and economic alliances and blocs (for example the European Union and the North American Free Trade Association), international agencies of labour (such as the International Labour Organization), financial organizations (for example the World Bank and the International Monetary Fund) and multinational corporations as international employers of labour. This aspect of IHRM is explored further in Chapter 3.

> **?** In your opinion, what may be the characteristics of the global workforce? Using to the data sources identified in text, profile the global workforce.
>
> How may globalization affect management of human resources internationally?

THE INTERNATIONAL CONTEXT

The international context is concerned with global patterns of change, continuation, unification and diversification in the management of people. Mainstream texts have focused on industrialized countries and blocs such as the USA, the EU, Canada, Japan and Australia. However, there is a growing body of research on employment and management systems not only in industrialized countries, but also in developing and less-developed countries (Budhwar and Debrah 2001; Chow 2002; Grobler *et al.* 2002; Napier 1998). Drawing on this diverse literature, this aspect of IHRM requires an examination of international patterns of convergence and divergence in human resource management, to provide an understanding of how and why some attributes of HRM systems are becoming similar (converging), while others sustain their differences (divergence) across national borders.

The conceptual framework of convergence and divergence is often examined in the context of European HRM. However, there is a growing body of research that investigate convergence and divergence within a broader international scope. This aspect will be introduced in Chapter 4.

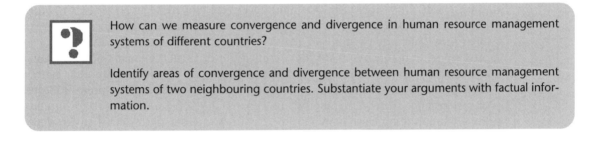

How can we measure convergence and divergence in human resource management systems of different countries?

Identify areas of convergence and divergence between human resource management systems of two neighbouring countries. Substantiate your arguments with factual information.

THE NATIONAL CONTEXT

This aspect of IHRM covers the common components of HRM at the national level, including employment law, employment systems, trade unions, employers' unions, society, culture and professionalization. Ferris *et al.* (1998) argue that there are linkages between HRM effectiveness and the social context, including aspects of culture, climate and the political environment of an organization. Similarly, structure, regulation and the functioning of the labour market at the national level have implications for international human resource managers. Furthermore, the professionalization of HRM at the national level will impact on the role of the international human resource manager.

Based on these components of the national context, this aspect partly accounts for why international firms need HRM approaches and strategies which are differentiated across national borders. This aspect is explored in Chapter 5.

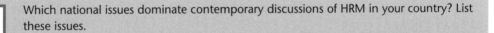

Which national issues dominate contemporary discussions of HRM in your country? List these issues.

Based on the components of national context identified in this section, describe the national context of HRM in your country.

STRATEGIC ISSUES

Strategic HRM is a well-documented and developed area of academic study (Schuler and Jackson 1999). Although McMahan, Bell and Virick (1998) offer a distinction between the formulations of strategic human resource management (SHRM) and strategic international human resource management (SIHRM), research on the latter is relatively sparse. Yet, this aspect of IHRM offers the broadest scope of study. The aspect broadly refers to the strategies for identifying the supply and demand of labour, the location, managing transfers, standardizing or differentiating management systems and managing international mergers and acquisitions, in a way which provides linkages between the previous three and the subsequent four aspects of IHRM.

Bird and Beechler (1995) identify two approaches to HRM strategies at the national level. They explain that the macro perspectives espouse either cost-leadership or differentiation strategies. While cost-leadership strategies lead companies to cut costs through a 'hard' HRM approach, the differentiation strategy seeks to achieve competitive advantage for the company through distinguishing its products and services, using a 'soft' HRM approach. The micro perspective of strategic HRM, on the other hand, offers linkages between organization-level strategy and policy, proposing to align firm policy to its strategic goals. However, the authors argue that these two predominant approaches in the literature fail to recognize the impact of the external environment on a firm's strategic choices and also fail to substantiate their central claim that a tighter fit between firm strategy and policy will result in improved levels of performance. Based on these two objections, they offer a framework for international human resource strategy informed by both internal and external environmental positioning of international firms.

Different configurations of location and host–home country relationships are explored and the strategic choices of international companies are identified as part of this aspect. Transfer of management systems and knowledge in international joint ventures (Iles and Yolles 2002) are also examined as strategic choices. Movements of the workforce – in terms of the use of expatriates, rotational systems and localized HRM strategies – as well as the highly topical issue of strategic aspects of managing human resources during international mergers and acquisitions, are included in this aspect. The strategic aspects of IHRM are examined in Chapter 6.

Why are strategic aspects of IHRM referred to as the broadest aspect in the framework of components of IHRM?

What do Bird and Beechler (1995) mean by internal and external environment?

OPERATIONAL ISSUES

Acceptable and formal methods of HRM display diversity across national borders. The operational aspects of IHRM include recruitment and selection, education and training, expatriation and repatriation, participation and involvement, pay and conditions, promotion, reward, career development, retirement, and downsizing of an international workforce.

Considering the diverse range of strategic choices available to organizations, and differences in configurations of national institutions, the operational aspects of managing international human resources are similarly detailed. Black and Mendenhall (1995) propose a theoretical framework for such operational or practical aspects of IHRM. The diversity of these operational aspects is addressed in Chapter 7.

What are the key contemporary themes in each component (from the list above) of operational aspects of IHRM in your country?

What are the differences between the strategic and operational aspects of IHRM?

IHRM AS A CAREER

There are some distinctive attributes of a career in IHRM. Research data from international human resource recruitment agencies and employers of international human resource managers set the context for identifying the nature of the labour market and availability of career opportunities in this field. This aspect is also concerned with the education, training and development of international human resource managers (Griffin and Pustay 1998), their career development and patterns of employment (Carrell *et al.* 2000). This aspect offers an analytical look at various models, frameworks and theories of an IHRM career, identifying key concerns in management of such a career from individual as well as organizational perspectives. This career aspect of IHRM is examined in Chapter 8.

What are the similarities and differences between national and international contexts for careers in HRM?

What would impact the career success of a human resource manager from a neighbouring country if he or she relocates as a manager in your country?

PROFESSIONAL COMPETENCIES

This aspect focuses on the international human resource manager as a professional, identifying his or her competencies. International human resource managers interact in more diverse and dynamic environments than their counterparts who are responsible from single-country operations. Using surveys on international management development, this aspect relates to the competencies expected of an international human resource manager, including learning and knowledge skills to transferable, affective and people-management skills (Mead 1998). As an international human resource manager is required to possess varied skills and competencies depending on the region, sector and nature of the workforce, this aspect also refers to cross-national and sectoral distinctions within such competencies. The aspect is explored further in Chapter 9.

If you are to become an international human resource manager, what professional competencies would you need in order to lead a successful career?

When answering the above question, what information sources can you use to support and substantiate your argument?

THE FUTURE

The future aspect of IHRM involves the contemporary challenges that face those operating in this field. The complexities brought forth by globalization, managing values and diversity, are explored here. Thus, this aspect focuses on the qualitative, value-based and ethical dimensions (Grossman and Schoenfeldt 2001) of IHRM, highlighting the significance and long-term relevance of value-based decision-making in IHRM practice.

This aspect is examined in the final chapter of this text and offers the reader a critical evaluation of the IHRM discourse and practice. The previous aspects are summarized and contextualized from a broader, unifying perspective, in order to highlight the trends, dilemmas and challenges facing IHRM in the 2000s.

> **?**
>
> Why are 'globalization' and 'ethical considerations' highlighted as relevant for the future of IHRM?
>
> What do you consider to be the level of public interest in the future of IHRM?

DOES IHRM OFFER A UNIVERSAL PANACEA?

The question of whether a subject presents viable solutions to management problems is often posed for newly emerging areas of business studies. Posing the same question for the very subject of IHRM may prove useful. However, we need to be mindful of our expectations from an answer to this question, as the study of IHRM performs two functions. It defines both context-specific and idiosyncratic variations in the practice of HRM from a cross-national perspective, and it also provides us with conceptual and theoretical frameworks through which we can define, examine, make decisions and prescribe solutions to the problems of people-management facing us in international settings. While the former use of the study presents country-specific patterns, themes and facts, the latter guides us in the ways we process such information.

This text offers both cross-national comparative insights and, more importantly, a broad framework for use in exploring issues of HRM in an international context. Subsequent chapters will further elaborate on each of these aspects and introduce subject-specific approaches, perspectives and frameworks.

Responding to our original question, we can say that although the framework proposed in this book does not claim to offer solutions to all problems, it nevertheless highlights the key aspects of IHRM so that these may be considered when seeking solutions and reaching decisions. There has been exclusive specialization in each of these aspects and very little connectivity has been evident in their study. There is an inherent need for more integrated approaches to the study and practice of IHRM. By presenting these aspects as part of a conceptual framework, this book seeks to offer such connectivity.

The framework of the aspects of IHRM are presented using a funnelling approach, starting with macro issues such as the global workforce and the international context. The national considerations are followed by organizational aspects and the individual considerations such as careers and competencies are presented at the micro level.

Therefore the considerations for macro and micro structures and individual issues are examined in the context of IHRM.

It should be noted that the study and practice of IHRM are relatively demarcated to industrialized and developing countries with its major contributions originating from the English-speaking world. Therefore, even if IHRM may fail to offer a universal panacea for managing people across borders, cultures and structures, it provides both useful insights and frameworks for decision-making where local knowledge of employment systems is inadequate.

 Does HRM offer a universal panacea? Discuss.

Case study 2

TIAN BAO GARMENT FACTORY: HRM in Chinese Private Enterprises

Peter Xu Lu

With the rapid development of private business, China is undergoing two major transitional phases: from a command economy to a market-based one, and from a rural, agricultural society to an urban industrialized one. Accordingly, China is experiencing significant changes in its economic-social-political environment, which this old oriental country has never experienced in its history of over 5,000 years. Chinese private enterprises are, obviously, the first to be affected by the impact of these economic and social changes.

All these unprecedented transitions in China are creating a great demand for knowledge on this new emerging economic force – Chinese private enterprises. However, due to an apparent lack of empirical insights, our current understanding on the management of Chinese private enterprises has failed to catch up with dramatic developments in China's private sector as well as its economy and society.

Nowadays, more and more Western investors are coming to China to seek investment opportunities. Due to the complexity of the business environment in China, joint-venture investment has become one of the most efficient ways to enter the Chinese market. No doubt, dynamic Chinese private enterprises are the most ideal cooperative partners to be sought after by Western investors. However, the management of Chinese private enterprises remains mysterious and, in many respects, confusing to Westerners (Blackman 1997; Pye 1982; Tung 1996, 1997). These problems have been sharpened by the fact that, until recently, there has been scant academic attention to the management of contemporary Chinese private enterprises. It is within this framework that the author has conducted an empirical research on the management of such companies, focusing on their unique HRM systems.

Characteristics of people management in Chinese private enterprises

Hofstede and Bond (1988) added a fifth cultural dimension, 'Confucian Dynamism', to Hofstede's four original cultural dimensions (1980). They believed that the success of Eastern Asian countries is driven, to a large extent, by the Confucian cultural values – persistence, diligence, thrift and family-orientation – as the key supporting factors for economic development in those countries.

Chinese private enterprises, based on related theories, are in a very vulnerable social, economic and political position in China. By overcoming their disadvantageous weaknesses, Chinese private entrepreneurs have developed their own unique strategies to adapt themselves in this hostile business environment, adopting quite different ways of management from their counterparts in other countries in order to achieve their success. Chinese traditional cultural values, which are regarded as barriers by Kirby and Fan (1995), could be the strengths of Chinese private enterprises.

Chen (1995) indicated that, comparing with the rational and open process of the Western way of the management, the management of traditional Chinese business is characterized by an informal and personalized relationship between the private entrepreneur and their employees. As Tang and Ward (2003) indicate, many Chinese entrepreneurs actively seek to cast themselves in the role of benevolent father or concerned elder bother in their relationships with their employees. Chen (1995) summarized the following characteristics of people management in traditional Chinese family businesses:

- *Benevolent relationships.* Chinese management control is the art of weaving and balancing networks inside the enterprise (Chen 1995, p. 90). In Chinese family business the entrepreneur often pays special attention to the degree of 'manager or employee loyalty', always trying to maintain good relationships with those 'loyal' managers or employees who, the boss believes, are competent and capable of special skills.

There are tangible and intangible ways of building good relationships and 'trust' between the employer and employees in a Chinese family business. Tangibly, the boss may give substantial personal rewards in the form of bonuses to loyal employees. Intangibly, Chinese entrepreneurs make an investment in a shared sentiment in their relationships with employees. If a boss treats his employees as insiders of the clan, the employees normally express loyalty to the boss. This is a benevolent relationship. Thus, the Chinese way of management control is a hybrid process of materialized reward, motivation and an exchange of sentiment and trust.

The cultural roots of benevolent relationships in Chinese family business originate from the Confucian teaching of '*Ren Yi*', which emphasizes the kind and gentle nature of the superior. The Confucian humanism of the relationships between superiors and subordinates is further cemented by a practical concern for the superior to exchange favours for indebtedness, personal loyalty and obedience from subordinates (Farh and Cheng 2000). The relationship within Chinese family business is, in fact, the repetition of independent, reciprocal and ubiquitous relationships (*Guanxi*) within traditional Chinese societies (Yang 1994; Tsui and Farh 1997).

- *Cultivating a family atmosphere.* Because Chinese entrepreneurs seek to take on the role of benevolent fathers or elder brothers, they try to create a harmonious family atmosphere in their enterprises. 'This may take the form of celebrating festivals together, or displaying concern for an employee's personal affairs' (Tang and Ward 2003, p. 112). Chinese entrepreneurs believe that cultivating a family atmosphere is good for their business and enhances the good relationships with their employees; employees' loyalty will be increased and internal friction will be diminished. From the employees' point of view, they feel they have been given 'face', and their loyalty rewarded. In return, their sense of gratitude and obligation will be cultivated as well.

- *Subjective assessment.* Chen (1995) indicated that employee assessment in Chinese family businesses is quite different from Western managerial techniques in the area of HRM. Western human resource methods such as the principle of management by objectives, which emphasizes individual competitiveness, self-actualization, personal achievement and open confrontation, cannot be transferred to the context of the Chinese family business. This is because of the bosses' personal management control in such businesses. Given the family ownership, the boss holds ultimate control over decisions relating to pay increases, bonuses and even the social behaviour of employees, and this results in a lack of open and fair assessment mechanisms within the organization. However, harmonious relationships and the bosses' power domination may have been strengthened in the organization.

Chinese bosses' methods of people management include an unwillingness to delegate, top-down communication, information secrecy and imposing tight control. Subordinate compliance and obedience are manifest in behaviours such as showing public support for the leader, suppressing dissenting views, avoiding open confrontations, unconditionally accepting the leaders' directives and displaying loyalty to and trust in the leader.

People management in the Tian Bao Garment Factory

Consistent with the above themes, this case study focuses on the exploration of the HRM system in the Tian Bao Garment Factory, based on the study of employee management within the enterprise such as recruitment, promotion, motivation and the relationships between employer and employees.

The level of a Chinese private enterprise's 'family-ism' may be evaluated on the basis of the number of family members working in the enterprise and the entrepreneur's personal attitude towards family-ism. A number of techniques suggested by McCall and Simmons (1969) were adopted in the case study, and the research on Tian Bao is based on interviews conducted by the author with Mr Wang, the boss of the factory; Ms Xin, vice-manager of production; Mr Liu Gang, the sales manager; Mr Liu Chuan (Mr Liu Gang's

brother), the production supervisor and three worker supervisors, Ms Li, Ms Guo and Ms Xin. The study was also based on two days of field observation and secondary data collection, by the author, including a review of Mr Wang's meeting reports and the factory manual of regulations.

Founded in 1980 by Mr Wang, Tian Bao is one of the most profitable private garment factories in Shenyang, the provincial capital of Liaoning. Tian Bao Garment Factory has 450 staff with fixed assets of 3,700,000 yuan. The whole factory covers an area of 20,000 square metres and has 350 sets of various imported industrial sewing machines and accessories producing various kinds of garments and knitted underwear. Tian Bao's products are not only sold locally, but also domestically and internationally. Compared with some large state-owned factories, Tian Bao may only be classified as a medium-sized garment factory. However, in terms of its speed of development and profitability, it has already surpassed most of the large state-owned garment factories in Shenyang.

Flexible and localized approach to worker recruitment

Mr Wang's workers are all recruited from remote villages; in fact, most of his workers are from two poor counties in Liaoning: Chang Tu and Kai Yuan. Two methods are employed to recruit them. The first is Mr Wang's visit to villages in these two counties before the busiest seasons of production every year. The recruitment strategy is very simple; he promises to provide free accommodation and meals, which means that workers are able to save all of their salaries, and in addition he also offers free return transportation from the factory to workers' home villages before and after the Spring Festival.

The recruitment package is very attractive because most of the workers who come to work in such factories are girls. It is a local tradition that girls have to save some money for their dowry before their marriage, so those girls whose families cannot afford a dowry are very happy to work in the garment factories in big cities. They typically worked in Mr Wang's factory for two years before returning home, having saved sufficient money for their dowries.

The other way of recruiting workers is to pay commission to previous or present workers who introduce their relatives or other village folk to the factory. This is a very efficient way to recruit staff because people tend to believe those whom they know. In addition, for many young girls from the countryside it is the first time they have worked in a city and they are very concerned about safety; they feel safer sharing accommodation with those who come from the same village.

From Mr Wang's point of view, there are two main reasons that he likes to recruit workers from the countryside. Firstly, cost. Mr Wang has to maintain low product prices to compete with his rivals, especially with large state-owned factories which have competitive advantages in technology above and beyond what he has in his own factory. It would be more costly and problematic to recruit workers from the city because most of them would have worked in either the collective or state-owned factories. As Wang explained, 'they always require more, but work less'. In terms of the salary standard, Tian Bao's pay is less competitive compared with other factories. Also, according to Mr Wang's experience, many workers who used to work in state-owned factories always feel that they lose 'face' if they switch to work in a private enterprise. Most state-owned workers still retain work attitudes formed in their previous state-owned factories.

The second reason to recruit workers from the countryside is that they are easily managed. They can be divided into several production units according to the village and region they come from, and in Mr Wang's opinion workers from the countryside are sincere and honest. As he said: 'I am a hard-working man. Of course, I like hard-working workers.'

The management system
Mr Wang's management system can be identified in terms of two key practices, Tian Bao's free boarding policy and the worker supervising system.

Free board: 'Mr Wang's People's Commune'
Hearing that Mr Wang provided free meals for his workers, the author was very curious to see this in practice as it sounded very much like a People's Commune in Mao's era. Mr Wang normally had his lunch with his workers, so when lunch started the author went to the factory's catering room with Mr Wang. This room is very big, able to contain more than one hundred people. It is also the factory's meeting room. Mr Wang and the author stood in the queue moving towards the service area. The author noticed that the workers, in front of and behind them, kept a discreet distance from Mr Wang and himself; and each worker passing by nodded to Mr Wang with the greeting 'Ni hao [Hello] Uncle Wang.'

Lunch was quite simple, two pieces of steamed bread and a bowl of Chinese cabbage soup. But it was totally adequate for a person to refuel his or her energy after four and a half hours hard work (7:30 am to 12 am). Maybe influenced by workers who were all engorging around him, the author found the lunch very delicious. In fact, he was surprised that his stomach could take in two big pieces of bread with a pot-sized bowl of soup.

Mr Wang was in a very good mood (perhaps noticing that I ate all of the food provided). He said that normally three meals were provided each day so that his workers didn't need to go outside or cook for themselves. In fact, it was quite difficult for workers to eat outside or buy food because the location of the factory was quite remote. 'We normally improve the food significantly during the Chinese Spring New Year and other important festivals', said Mr Wang and continued:

The reason that I provide the free meals is because it is very easy for me to organize production. During the busiest seasons of production, workers are normally divided into three groups of working shifts. Each group has their own fixed time for meals. Another reason is that I try to create a 'familial' working environment. Workers themselves manage the catering. Five workers are selected each week to cook. They are given a fixed sum of money each week to buy rice, meat and vegetables. The food is simple, but it tastes not too bad, doesn't it? As long as I am in the factory, I come to join my workers for dinner.

Mr Wang's People's Commune catering style works very well, and is one of his advantages in recruiing workers compared with his competitors. According to Mr Wang, because of costs he could hardly afford to buy health and social insurance for his workers, and free accommodation and meals are probably the most efficient ways to motivate his workers.

The workers come from several villages in the two poorest counties, Kaiyuan and Changtu, of Liaoning province. According to local tradition, women should stay at home to do the housework and field work when they get married, so unmarried girls always like to work in the cities for a few years to save some money for their dowries. For these reasons, the girls working in Tian Bao rarely change their jobs; since they don't need to pay for their accommodation or meals, they are able to save a substantial sum of money for their trousseau.

Worker supervision

The author also discovered to his interest that in Tian Bao, except for Mr Wang, other managers did not have formal titles or positions. There are four main functional departments in Tian Bao – production, sales, material purchase, and accounting – of which, as shown in Figure 2.2, Mr Wang is General Manager. One of Mr Wang's daughters is Vice-Manager in charge of production and sales, and Mr Wang's brother is Vice-Manager in charge of materials purchase and machinery maintenance. In fact, according to Mr Wang, there is no formal contract between himself and his daughter and brother; he has to call them 'vice-managers' only because of the requirements of government taxation.

There are two types of workers in the factory, permanent and temporary. Permanent workers have been working in Tian Bao for many years and have won Mr Wang's trust to supervise the temporary workers. Most are men and they are in charge of main departments and working units of the factory including sales, production and materials purchase. Worker supervisors are appointed to lead the workers who come from the same village, their leadership being accepted more

Figure 2.2   Management structure of Tian Bao

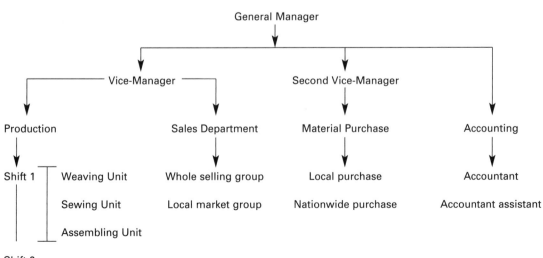

readily because of their common background. Often they know each other very well; some are even relatives. Furthermore, because they are same-village folk, the worker supervisors can't abuse their power; they would be concerned about their reputation and 'face' in the village. In Mr Wang's words, this is a 'self-surveillance' strategy.

The disadvantage of this system is that the worker supervisor and his village folk could work together to slow down production. To overcome this weakness, Mr Wang always asked two different groups of workers to work together on the same shift or working unit so that the two groups, from different villages, could 'supervise' and 'compete' with each other.

The worker supervisors are selected carefully, according to a standard before promotion to be a supervisor. First of all, according to Mr Wang, he should know that worker very well, through practice and training: 'when I find someone who is clever and trustworthy, I will send them to do some challenging jobs. Based on the way they tackle the problem, I can understand the kind of personality, ability and virtue they possess.'

Little He is Mr Wang's car driver; he and his brother have been working for Mr Wang for many years. Little He's duties include helping Mr Wang deal with all kinds of external business, including welcoming clients at the airport, negotiating prices with dealers, delivery of goods and purchasing of materials. Little He came to work for Mr Wang when the factory was first established. After passing Mr Wang's 'training' and 'evaluation' tests, he was sent to learn driving skills and gained a license. He is also studying a part-time management course in a local college, his tuition fees and full salary paid by Mr Wang.

Little He's elder brother also works as a production supervisor in the factory, and, according to Mr Wang, the two brothers have become his 'left and right arms'. Before every Chinese New Year, Mr Wang invites Little He's mother to his home and gives Little He's and his brother's 'red bags' (their annual bonus) to their mother in person.

The second condition for a worker to be promoted to be a supervisor is that he or she should have the virtue of honesty and a mind of reciprocity. 'It is more and more difficult to find someone who you can trust these days', said Mr Wang, 'people want to earn quick money, as much as they can. I am not opposing this trend. However, if the fortune is based on the price of social morality, that's a backward step. It is never too late for people to learn something if they lack skills or techniques. But people's good nature or virtues may hardly be regained if they are lost.'

Little Yu was a worker supervisor in charge of product sales in a local market. She came from a small and poor village in Taiyuan county, Liaoning, and her hard work, persistence and honesty had won Mr Wang's appreciation, leading to her promotion to be in charge of local market sales. The market is a wholesale business located in Shenyang city, and is not an easy task because every deal is made in cash. Every morning, Little Yu goes to the market with goods and returns at noon with thousands of yuan in her pocket.

When Little Yu got married, she and her husband decided to move to Shenyang, but they couldn't afford to buy an apartment. Mr Wang lent them a sum of money without interest that and they could pay him back monthly. He also helped them sort out city residency through his friend who was working in the government department. This was a great help for the couple because it is normally very hard for peasants to change their resident status in China. However, Mr Wang said: 'My help to her and her family is nothing compared with her contribution to the factory. This is a "heart to heart" exchange.'

Conclusion

Tian Bao Garment Factory is a typical example of HRM in a Chinese private enterprise. Generally, the main characteristics of HRM in Tian Bao can be summarized as:

1 *Harmonious relationships*. The relationship between employer and employees in Tian Bao

is informal and reciprocal. Mr Wang is fully aware of the needs and conditions of his workers, which enables him to design his unique way of management with initiatives such as his worker recruitment strategy, his 'people's commune' style of catering and accommodation, and the worker supervisor system. His positive relationship with the government also enables him to obtain the maximum convenience in relations with the local government.

2   The second characteristic is the *paternal and effective management system*. Mr Wang is the central pole of Tian Bao; not only the founder of the factory, but also the hope of the factory. Because of his deep understanding of every aspect of his business, he has designed a very feasible HRM system for his factory.

His worker supervisor system, for example, is a very practical approach that fits the real situation in his factory. If he recruited managers rather than promoting supervisors directly from his workers, there could well have been severe conflict between urban 'modern' managers and 'clan' or 'village'-oriented workers. If he didn't provide workers with free meals and accommodation, the location of his factory might be less competitive compared with factories located near to the cities, because city life might be more attractive to young workers who had just left their families from the countryside.

It can be concluded that this entrepreneur in Tian Bao captured the benefits of retaining good relationships with his senior staff. The Chinese traditional cultural value, '*renqing*', is the key to maintaining such relationships. *Renqing* is a unique Chinese expression, difficult to translate into English. Chen (1995, p. 55) translated it as 'humanized obligation', which implies that 'for a continued exchange of favours a sentimental touch is needed'. Several characteristics of *renqing* have been reflected in this case study:

■   Firstly, 'renqing' covers not only sentiment, but also its social expressions such as the offering of congratulations or condolences and the making of gifts on appropriate occasions (Yao 1987; Yang 1994). In this case study, Mr Wang expressed his *renqing* to his worker supervisors by providing more self-developed opportunities and helping them to settle down in cities. He is concerned about improving their living standards and the technical skills of his worker supervisors. This is because directly materialized benefits and career prospects are very important for these workers from the countryside.

■   Secondly, since *renqing* involves social exchanges, there is an inherent obligation for people to keep equity in mind. *Renqing* is one of the commonly accepted social norms regulating Chinese interpersonal relationships, based on the Confucian concept of reciprocity (Yao 1987).

Western investors and managers should be responsive to the unique system of employee management in Chinese private enterprises when they set up joint ventures with their Chinese counterparts. They should notice that there are rules which may remain invisible to outsiders for management of people in such enterprises, such as reciprocally beneficial relationships. Without fully understanding the specific characteristics of HRM in Chinese enterprises, a joint-venture cooperation is likely to end in failure.

Case study discussion topics

1   Based on the eight-point framework explained earlier in this chapter,

   (a)   evaluate the key concerns for the HR director of a US company hoping to set up a joint venture with Tian Bao;

      (b)   identify what you would like to know further in order to assess the difficulties that a joint-venture company might experience managing people in the process of a joint venture?

2   Could you suggest improvements to the HRM system of Tian Bao? Discuss

3   How far do you agree with the conclusions of the case study? Discuss

SUMMARY

This chapter has examined eight aspects of IHRM in a conceptual framework, and discussed the relevance of these aspects to the study and practice of people management globally. The chapter has also explored whether IHRM presents an overarching solution to the problems experienced in managing human resources in an international context.

The case study in this chapter offers insights into HRM practices in a Chinese company. The case study questions are designed to explore whether the eight-point framework elaborated in this chapter may prove useful in analysing specific situations of people management in a global context. The next chapter will explore the first of the aspects of IHRM, namely the global workforce.

Chapter three

The Global Workforce

Mine Karataş-Özkan

Learning outcomes

After reading this chapter, you should be able to:

- Evaluate the attributes of the global workforce.
- Identify institutions of interest for employment issues in a global context.
- Explain globalization and its impact on employment practices.
- Appraise the impact of globalization on employment practices.
- Problematise the uneven impact of globalization and international employment practices.

INTRODUCTION

Globalization combined with domestic restructuring has dramatically changed the workforce of many companies in recent years (Zakaria 2000). Emerging technologies have enabled employees to be located free from geographic constraints and this has resulted in workforces becoming much more mobile (San Martin and Flinn 2003). This chapter examines the attributes and trends of the global workforce in the context of globalization in the 2000s. The significance of contemporary issues and institutions of mobility, regulation and management of labour across national borders, such as social and economic alliances and blocs (for example the European Union and North American Free Trade Association), international agencies of labour (such as the International Labour Organization), financial organizations (for example the World Bank and the International Monetary Fund) and the multinational corporations as international employers of labour, will be examined.

This chapter will demonstrate an understanding of the complex impact of globalization on international employment patterns and it will identify the forces of change from a macro international perspective. There will be exercises to discuss the implications of these wider issues on management of human resources (HR) from a comparative perspective.

The chapter concludes that despite increased volumes of international trade, the impact of globalization is unevenly felt in each country. Thus, management of human resources requires distinctly different approaches across national borders in order to address the demands of their national and global labour markets. HR managers' roles are to understand the human capital available in a country, its profile, skills, levels of education, requirements of pay and conditions and those of training.

WHAT ARE THE ATTRIBUTES OF THE GLOBAL WORKFORCE?

As introduced in the previous chapter, the global workforce refers to human capital available in the international arena and across national borders. Therefore, it is by definition quite diverse and its effective management could result not only in the enhancement of organizational performance, but also the provision of social justice and equality. Current trends such as the internationalization of business and the proliferation of intergovernmental and non-governmental organizations make the need for studying the global workforce more important than ever before. Equally important is the recognition of the differing characteristics of the global workforce in developing a comparative perspective on supply and demand for labour in an international context.

The remainder of this section provides a detailed examination of the attributes of the global workforce using the recent periodical reports of the International Labour Organization (ILO), the United Nations (UN) *Human Development Reports* and those of the Organization for Economic Cooperation and Development (OECD). Based on these main data sources, it is attempted to profile the global workforce to help develop a foundation for understanding the complex nature of the international labour market as well as conditions of employment in an international arena.

The most recent edition of the ILO's *Key Indicators of the Labour Market* (KILM) 2001–02 report compiles labour market information for over 200 economies. Labour productivity is defined as output per unit of labour input. The labour productivity combined with the growth rate as a key measure of economic performance is worth noting here in order to show the trends affecting the global workforce and employment. Table 3.1 illustrates that, on average, labour productivity in the majority of European countries grew somewhat faster than in the United States between 1980 and 2000. In the Unites States, labour productivity rates increased from less than 1 per cent in the early part of the decade to more than 2.5 per cent by the year 2000. In most European countries, labour productivity also rose throughout the 1990s although growth rates slowed in later years. In Germany the annual growth rate between 1995 and 2000 was 1.6 per cent compared to a rate of 2.4 per cent for the first half of the decade. Japan also showed lower growth in the later 1990s, less than 1 per cent annually between 1995 and 2000. In order to develop a global view, the situation in developing countries needs to be examined, and Figure 3.1 depicts the levels of labour productivity in the developing countries relative to the United States, illustrating that the developing countries have lower levels of labour productivity in comparison.

Relevant to the performance of economies, Table 3.2 outlines the levels of unemployment in the OECD countries in 2000. It illustrates that there is great variation in unemployment rates, ranging between 1.4 per cent in Iceland to 18.8 per cent in Slovakia. Unemployment is an important social, economic and political agenda item for nation states as well as international agencies that seek to eradicate poverty or improve social inclusion.

The labour force participation rate is defined by the ILO as a measure of the extent of an economy's working-age population that is economically active; it provides an

Table 3.1   *Labour productivity and unit labour cost growth, total economy, 1980–99/2000*

Country	Value added per person employed, 1980–2000 growth rate (%)	Value added per hour worked, 1980–99 growth rate (%)	Labour compensation per unit of output, 1980–99 growth rate (%)
Major Europe (and transition economies)			
Austria	1.2	1.9	2.6
Belgium	1.7	2.1	1.3
Czech Republic	0.3[5]	0.1[5]	. . .
Denmark	1.9	2.1	2.0
Finland	2.6	3.0	1.6
France	1.6	2.1	1.3
Germany, Federal Republic of (Western)	1.8[3]	2.5	1.9[3]
Germany	2.1[5]	2.5[5]	0.5[6]
Greece	1.0	1.4	2.8
Hungary	1.8	2.1[4]	. . .
Ireland	3.7	3.7	0.7
Italy	1.6	1.9	2.3
Netherlands	0.3	1.2	1.0
Norway	2.0	2.4	1.6
Poland	2.6	3.8[4]	. . .
Portugal	1.5	1.9	3.7[2]
Spain	1.6	2.0	1.5
Sweden	1.9	1.4	1.1
Switzerland	0.4	1.2[2]	1.2[6]
Turkey	2.7	3.7[2]	4.0[7]
United Kingdom	1.7	2.1	2.9
Weighted average	1.7[8]	1.8[9]	1.6[9]
Major non-Europe			
Australia	1.7	1.6	0.8[2]
Canada	1.2	1.3	1.9
Japan	1.8	2.3	4.8[2]
New Zealand	0.5	0.7[5]	1.5[2]
United States	1.4	1.2	3.3
Weighted average	1.4	1.7[12]	3.3
Asia and the Pacific			
China	5.0[3]	. . .	. . .
India	3.4[1]	. . .	. . .
Indonesia	1.6[1]	. . .	. . .
Hong Kong, China	3.1[1]	3.3	. . .
Korea, Republic of	5.6	5.5[2]	0.6[2]
Malaysia	3.0[1]	. . .	. . .
Pakistan	3.3[1]	. . .	. . .
Philippines	−0.9[1]	. . .	. . .
Singapore	4.3[1]	4.4[2]	. . .
Sri Lanka	5.5[3]	. . .	. . .
Taiwan, China	5.1[1]	5.7	. . .
Thailand	4.1[1]	. . .	. . .
Weighted average	3.9[1]	. . .	. . .
Latin America			
Argentina	0.3[1]	0.8[2]	. . .
Brazil	−0.2[1]	0.2[2]	5.0[2/11]
Chile	2.0[1]	1.8[2]	0.6[4/11]
Colombia	0.9[1]	1.4[2]	1.6[2/11]
Mexico	0.0	−0.3	0.1[2/11]
Peru	−1.4[2]	. . .	0.0[5/11]
Venezuela	−1.5[1]	0.9[2]	−1.0[2/11]
Weighted average	−0.1[1]	0.1[2/10]	2.3[2/10/11]

Notes: [1] 1980–99; [2] 1980–98; [3] 1980–97; [4] 1989–99; [5] 1990–98; [6] 1990–97; [7] 1988–98; [8] excluding Czech Republic and East German states; [9] excluding Czech Republic, East German states, Poland, Hungary, Switzerland and Turkey; [10] excluding Argentina and Peru; [11] only employee compensation per unit of output; [12] excluding New Zealand.
Source: KILM (2001–02).

Figure 3.1 Labour productivity (value added per person employed), total economy, selected developing countries as a percentage of the United States level, 1980 and 1999

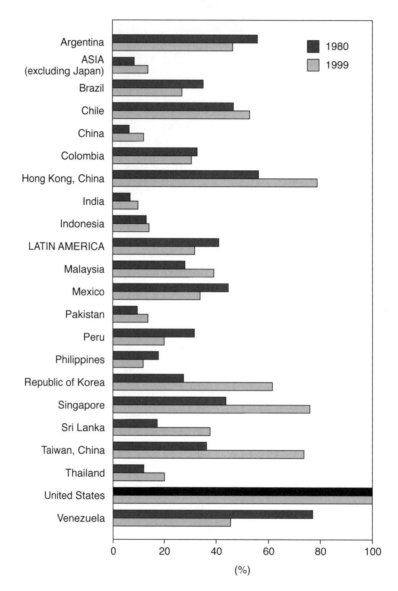

Notes: Data for Republic of Korea and Mexico are for 2000; data for China and Peru are for 1998. Converted to US dollar basis at purchasing power parity (PPP) for 1990.
Source: KILM (2001–02).

indication of the relative size of the supply of labour available for the production of goods and services. The breakdown of the labour force by sex and age group gives a profile of the distribution of the economically active population within a country. Given the employment and unemployment rates, it is significant to look at labour force participation rates and the relevant aspects of employment which characterize the global workforce. The analysis of the labour force participation rates gives a profile of human capital available in the international context, focusing, worldwide, on the

Table 3.2 Unemployment rates in OECD countries, 2000

Country	Unemployment rate %
Iceland	1.4
Switzerland	2.0
Mexico	2.2
Netherlands	2.6
Luxembourg	2.6
Norway	3.4
United States	4.0
Portugal	4.0
Korea, Republic of	4.1
Ireland	4.3
Denmark	4.7
Sweden	4.7
Austria	4.7
Japan	4.7
United Kingdom	5.5
New Zealand	6.0
Australia	6.3
Turkey	6.4
Hungary	6.5
Canada	6.8
Belgium	7.0
Germany	7.5
Czech Republic	8.9
France	9.5
Finland	9.8
Italy	10.7
Greece	11.4
Spain	14.1
Poland	16.1
Slovakia	18.8

Sources: OECD (2001); *Economic Outlook*, 2 (70), Paris.

relationship between the labour force participation rate and the level of development of an economy as measured by its per capita gross domestic product (GDP), evaluated at purchasing power parity (PPP) in 1990 prices (KILM 2002). Analysis in the 1999 KILM confirmed that the labour force participation rate is generally higher at the early stages of economic development, but drops quickly as GDP increases. It then moves slowly along a mild downward path before climbing upwards at the highest levels of development. This pattern was found to be more or less the same for men and women, although it was more accentuated for women and the gradual increase in the labour force participation rate occurred earlier for women than for men (KILM 2002).

According to the most recent KILM report of the ILO (KILM 2002), the most important determinant of the labour force participation rate is age, followed by sex. The analysis by sex shows that in every economy for which information is available, women are less likely than men to participate in the labour force. This reflects the reality that for women, more so than men, demographic, social, legal and cultural trends and norms determine whether their activities are regarded as economic. In this sense, women have to overcome more hurdles to enter the labour market than do men. In addition to the structural constraints, that is the educational, institutional and cultural barriers that many women face, most women must also deal with the competing demands of household work.

GROUP ACTIVITY

Based on a review of the national and international literature, explore the characteristics of the female labour workforce in your country. Discuss the problems they encounter in relation to the information provided in this section about working women in other parts of the world.

Comparing the results with those presented in the previous edition, KILM (1999), the 2002 report shows similar patterns in the analysis of the labour force participation rates by sex. The economies in the Middle East and North Africa continue to exhibit the lowest female labour force participation rates, while the highest female rates continue to be among the sub-Saharan African economies, and economies in Asia and the Pacific, as well as Iceland, Norway and Sweden amongst the industrialized countries. In the case of men, the position of sub-Saharan Africa is firmly maintained as the region with the highest male labour force participation rates, whereas the lowest can be found among the transition and developed economies (KILM 2002). However, again caution should be applied to methods of data collection, particularly in terms of what is recorded as active labour in each country.

The KILM report (2002) also reveals that although female labour force participation rates continue to increase in most parts of the world, women's wages are almost invariably lower than men's, with women predominating in part-time and often low-paid jobs. As commented in the ILO magazine *World of Work* (2001), manufacturing wage indices show that nominal wages rose faster for women than for men in many economies, and that where real wages have been falling the declines have been smaller for women than for men (p. 11). Therefore, it is possible to speculate that although the gender wage gap is decreasing, the pace of change is slow.

Another important aspect of work in the globalized era is the rise in part-time employment. In the 1990s, the share of part-time employment within total employment rose in most of the developed economies. As much as one-half to two-thirds of all part-time workers are women and part-time work is especially common for women in the industrialized economies of Europe (*World of Work* 2001, p. 12). It can be argued that what is commonly called atypical work is no longer atypical, and that indeed it is becoming a common form of work internationally.

Discuss the implications of the rise of part-time employment – particularly of women – on the HRM policies of organizations.

What kind of evidence can you give for the changing HRM practices in your country in relation to the changing trends in the global workforce?

Finally, another major trend worth mentioning is the growth of the service sector and the consequent increase in employment opportunities in that sector internationally. Referring to KILM (2002), employment opportunities in the service sector of industrialized economies continue to be more than those in the manufacturing sector, and the agricultural sector accounts for only a tiny fraction (less than 5 per cent) of overall employment. Among the largest industrialized economies, the percentage of employment in the service sector exceeds 70 per cent in Canada, France, the USA and the UK. In Germany, Italy and Japan, services account for almost 65 per cent of total employment (*World of Work* 2001, p. 12).

GROUP ACTIVITY

Using the data provided in this section, summarize the major characteristics of the global workforce.

WHAT ARE THE INTERNATIONAL INSTITUTIONS OF INTEREST?

Regional trade blocs, international organizations and multinational companies play an increasingly significant role in setting the context for IHRM decisions and practices. They intervene directly in international human resource management (IHRM) matters using their influence over nation states through processes such as international employment regulations which set benefits and compensation standards, safety legislations, minimum wage levels, and so on (Mabey *et al.* 2002). This section will examine some of these international institutions as well as social and economic alliances and blocs that play a pivotal role in regulation of employment relations at an international level.

The International Labour Organization (ILO)

Founded in 1919 following the Treaty of Versailles which brought about the League of Nations, the ILO is the specialized agency of the UN which seeks to promote social justice through establishing and safeguarding internationally recognized human and labour rights. It brings together governments, employers and workers of its 176 member states in common action to improve social protection and conditions of life and work throughout the world. The International Labour Office, in Geneva, is the permanent Secretariat of the Organization.

The underpinning idea of its creation was the recognition by the member states that international peace was linked to the creation and maintenance of social justice both within individual member states and internationally, and that social unrest caused by unfair treatment of workers and other disadvantaged groups might constitute a threat to world peace. Besides these social and ethical considerations, there were some economic motivations such as the realization that social justice would have a positive impact on the labour market, production costs and international competitiveness.

The main characteristic of the ILO is that it is tripartite; that is, it brings together representatives of employees, employers and governments. Each group has a say in the formulation of its policies and in decision-making and implementation. This tripartism and the search for consensus are the underlying features of the ILO. The International Labour Conference is organized annually in order to discuss pertinent issues, and the ILO also issues conventions and offers policy recommendations and oversees compliance by member states. The ILO therefore sets international standards by issuing conventions or recommendations in a number of areas of work and employment. Examples include social security, the abolition of forced labour, equal opportunities, human resource development via training, conditions of work including hours, minimum age of entry into the labour market and maternity protection. It does this by formulating international labour standards which set out the minimum standards of labour rights: 'freedom of association, the right to organize, collective bargaining, abolition of forced labour, equality of opportunity and treatment, and other standards regulating conditions across the entire spectrum of work related issues' (ILO, 2003).

Conventions become effective once they have been ratified by the member states, who are required to report to the ILO on a regular basis. If they do not comply with conventions they have ratified, they will be given recommendations on how compliance can or should be achieved. If they still do not comply, the issue may be referred to the International Court of Justice (see the official website of the ILO for further information: www.ilo.org).

To sum up, covering a broad range of activities and initiatives encompassing technical assistance and cooperation, employment generation and development, industrial and labour relations, health and safety and equality issues, the ILO remains a significant international organization setting and monitoring labour standards in order to provide social justice by pursuing consensus and cooperation between the main actors in the international labour market (Hollinshead and Leat 1995).

GROUP ACTIVITY

Select two countries and discuss the implications of their membership or non-membership of the ILO in terms of conditions, terms and patterns of employment in their labour markets.

The International Monetary Fund (IMF)

The IMF is an international organization of 184 member countries. It was established to promote international monetary cooperation, exchange stability and orderly exchange arrangements to foster economic growth and high levels of employment, and to provide temporary financial assistance to help ease balance of payments adjustments in countries which experience financial difficulty. Since the IMF was established, its purposes have remained the same. However, the IMF has developed certain policies and practices to meet the changing needs of its member countries in an evolving world economy.

The first article of the IMF's Articles of Agreement mandates the Fund to facilitate the expansion and balanced growth of international trade and to contribute thereby to promotion and maintenance of high levels of employment and real income. As will be explored in the following section, the movement to lower trade barriers and open world trade has increased world growth in goods and services; it has increased incomes and raised standards of living globally, in aggregate numbers. However, this does not equate to an improvement in standards of living in each region or for each individual. Therefore, international institutions such as the IMF have crucial roles in ensuring that globalization is for the benefit of all.

Expressions of public protest against the skewed impact of globalization in recent years, have been pushing the agenda for social responsibility. In cooperation with the ILO and the World Bank (WB), the IMF is actively involved in a number of projects which have significant impacts on work and employment conditions in the world. One recent example is the ILO–WB and IMF initiative on poverty reduction. As an important area of concern for the ILO, poverty reduction has been the subject of major international attention. Through concessional financing by the WB and the IMF, this particular initiative aims to ensure that employment and decent work issues are addressed as an integral part of the economic and social analyses and policies (ILO 2003).

As pointed out by Camdessus (1996), one of the greatest fears of the IMF is that a global labour market allows extremely low-paid workers in developing countries to undercut the wages of less-skilled workers in developed countries. In the last 20 years, there has been a marked increase in unemployment of the low-skilled populations in most developed countries. The impact of international institutions on global labour and employment issues are therefore by their nature complex, dynamic and diverse. Within the broader international arena, they might not fully achieve the aims set out in their foundation, and in some cases they may even serve to sustain and create imbalances and unfair practices in the international labour markets. In recounting the role of these agencies in regulating employment relationships, it is important not to lose sight of the complex and emergent nature of their involvement in international politics.

GROUP ACTIVITY

Based on a review of the recent national and international press as well as academic literature, identify an example of a situation where the IMF was involved as an international institution and its involvement had an impact on employment issues. Discuss the impact and influence of the IMF on that particular country or region from different perspectives.

The World Bank (WB)

Established in 1944, the WB is one of the specialized agencies of the United Nations and is made up of 184 member countries. These countries are jointly responsible for how the institution is financed and how its money is spent. The 'World Bank' is the name that has come to be used for the International Bank for Reconstruction and Development and the International Development Association. Together, these organizations provide low-interest loans, interest-free credit and grants to developing countries.

As noted in Caufield's (2001) study, the WB was created to make long-term loans for productive projects to ensure that countries could borrow the foreign capital required to build modern infrastructures and enter international trade, whereas the role of the IMF as its sister organization was to make short-term general loans to help countries through balance of payment crises.

Similar to the IMF, the WB supports social programmes on employment in developing countries and works in collaboration with the other international organizations.

GROUP ACTIVITY

Provide examples of IMF–WB collaboration in projects pertaining to employment conditions in developing countries.

The World Trade Organization (WTO)

As stated on their official website, the WTO is the only global international organization dealing with the rules of trade between nations. At its heart are the WTO agreements, negotiated and signed by the bulk of the world's trading nations and ratified in their parliaments. The goal is to help producers of goods and services, as well as exporters and importers, conduct their business.

The WTO currently has 144 member countries (see the WTO website www.wto.org). The WTO is recognized as a member-driven organization, which nearly works on a consensus basis, serving as a forum for trade negotiations (DTI 2003). Promoting opportunities for international trade, one of its functions is to act as a vehicle to encourage higher standards of employment in developed and developing countries. Departing from the idea that trade is an increasingly powerful engine of growth and can contribute to sustainable development in world economies, it has recently been recognized that major reforms need to be undertaken in WTO agreements to fulfil its objectives. In 1999, the EU proposed to establish an ILO–WTO forum to establish links between trade liberalization and labour standards, and it was argued that all WTO member states should commit themselves to respecting the core labour standards (Gallin, 1999). In 2001 at the Doha WTO conference, this need was reinforced by stating that the linkage between trade and labour rights must be recognized and institutionalized within the WTO system. The arguments focus on the joint forum with the ILO in order to employ strict measures to protect labour rights in international trade and investment relations.

The North American Free Trade Agreement (NAFTA)

NAFTA is the regional economic bloc between the USA, Canada and Mexico. The United States and Mexico first indicated their intent to enter into a comprehensive free trade agreement during 1990, and Canada's involvement with US trade as outlined in the US–Canada Free Trade Agreement of 1988 resulted in Canada becoming the third party to the NAFTA negotiations in 1991. The negotiations resulted in forming NAFTA in 1994.

NAFTA adds a new institutional layer to other international mechanisms like the General Agreement on Tariffs and Trade (GATT) alongside domestic rules and regulations affecting trade (Rugman et al., 1999). With its labour counterpart, the North American Agreement on Labour Cooperation (NAALC), NAFTA has influenced labour market conditions in the member countries.

Since it took effect in 1994, the most obvious impact has been on trade volumes between the three countries (Gooley, 1998); increasing trade volumes have created more employment and affected the workplace rules and practices. One example could be the rising numbers of 'the maquiladoras', which are foreign-owned assembly plants over the Mexican border (Sunoo 2000). As stated in Sunoo's (2000) study, maquiladoras were first established in 1965, and since NAFTA the tax breaks enjoyed by the industry have expanded throughout Mexico. Most are clustered near border towns are operated predominately by US companies eager to benefit from Mexico's proximity, cheap labour and tax breaks. Sunoo (2000) maintains that establishing a stable maquiladora requires business savvy, cultural sensitivity and social responsibility. The maquiladoras also seem to constitute an attractive home for international HR professionals who deal with many issues varying from recruiting and retention, to workers' health and safety. To sum up, it is useful to highlight that all these HRM activities are taking place within a broader set of relationships created by the international arrangements such as NAFTA and domestic regulations of the countries involved.

The European Union (EU)

Briefly looking at its history, in 1957 six European countries, Belgium, France, Italy, Luxembourg, the Netherlands and West Germany, came together in formulating the Treaty of Rome which created the European Economic Community (EEC), the forerunner of the current EU. Broadly, the major objectives were to create a Europe that was economically more interdependent, thereby rendering war between European countries less likely, and to create a large economic bloc in order to trade more effectively to compete internationally. In 1967, the EEC merged with the Coal and Steel and Atomic Energy Communities to create the European Community (EC).

The Treaty on European Union, which was agreed at Maastricht in 1991, paved the way for the Community to gain a social dimension and to become the European Union. After several enlargement drives, the EU currently has 15 members including Belgium, Germany, France, Italy, Luxembourg and the Netherlands being the founding members; Denmark, Ireland and the United Kingdom which joined in 1973, Greece in 1981, Spain and Portugal in 1986, Austria, Finland and Sweden in 1995. In 2004 the biggest ever enlargement will take place with 10 new countries joining. The newcomers are Cyprus, the Czech Republic, Estonia, Hungary, Latvia, Lithuania, Malta, Poland, Slovakia and Slovenia. Further applicant countries are Bulgaria, Romania and Turkey.

There are five EU institutions, each playing a specific role:

- The European Parliament (elected by the people of the member states).
- The Council of the European Union (representing the governments of the member states).
- The European Commission (the driving force and executive body).
- The Court of Justice (ensuring compliance with the law).
- The Court of Auditors (controlling sound and lawful management of the EU budget).

Pertaining to IHRM, it is worth noting the Social Chapter. Among the issues covered by the Social Chapter of the Maastricht Treaty are improved labour mobility, working conditions, equal opportunities and union representation, access to information, employee participation and health and safety provisions. The free movement of labour is therefore a significant aspect of the EU. From the very beginning it has been envisaged that labour as well as goods, services and capital should trade freely within the Union for an effective single market. However, there are some problems associated with the free movement of labour. Hollinshead and Leat (1995) draw attention to the process known as social dumping as a consequence of which capital investments relocate to developing regions in pursuit of cheap labour, pushing down labour costs and engendering social and employment dislocation within and between the member states. Therefore, the demographic front and social dimensions of the mobility of labour should be considered in evaluating the impact of the EU on international labour markets. The supply of labour and the composition of the EU workforce have dramatically changed and will continue to change in member states (EC 1995).

Therefore, EU legislations and regulations do influence the management of the workforce, particularly in the areas of employee participation in decision-making processes as well as health, safety and equality. HR managers should be aware of the pertinent legislations and principles and therefore establish effective communication systems (McKenna and Beech 2002).

In a broader sense, the international organizations and regional alliances outlined above are the various agents that determine global labour and employment strategies and they form a set of powerful bodies. As Banerjee (2003) notes, there is a nexus between the policies of these organizations and business organizations, especially multinational companies. Multinational companies are key actors within this complex set of relationships, and they play a significant role in shaping and reshaping policies regarding managing the global workforce. HR managers of contemporary organizations still rely on the domestic context and associated rules, regulations, social and cultural factors; however, there is an increasing awareness of the new international mechanisms. As a result, an in-depth evaluation and exploitation of such vehicles has become more crucial in policy-making processes of HR managers.

WHAT IS GLOBALIZATION?

Globalization describes the way that world trade, culture and technologies have become rapidly integrated over the last 20 years. It is both a process and a new multicultural way of living. New technologies have increased the ease of global communication and also international bodies such as the WTO, the WB, the IMF and regional blocs such as the EU and NAFTA have been created to help reduce barriers to trade and investment. Therefore, globalization is marked by:

■ the liberalization of economic policies – the opening of trade which allows goods and services to travel across the world more freely, the opening of capital markets which have increased the flow of money across the world;
■ an increase in foreign investment – companies investing overseas by building subsidiaries, by forming joint ventures or buying stock in foreign countries;
■ the emergence of new international business blocs;
■ the increased mobility of labour across national borders; and
■ increased competition in the international context.

GROUP ACTIVITY

Analyse the impacts of globalization on the labour market conditions in your country, comparing it with two other countries and discuss how these conditions affect HRM policies and practices in your chosen countries.

Globalization has brought about a number of interrelated concerns with respect to its social repercussions. These include its impact on employment, the distribution of income, and the role of labour standards (Lee 1997). Although regional blocs such as the EU and NAFTA were designed to remove barriers to trade, investment and movement of labour, they created new barriers to trade for non-member countries in reality. Therefore, it is crucial to evaluate globalization as both a reality and a myth of IHRM, taking into accout its social dimensions when considering its impact on workforce management. Sharing the same concern, the 90th International Labour Conference on globalization in 2002 adopted a series of measures designed to promote a more rigorous approach to tackling the challenges of globalization, to create an 'anchor' for personal security through poverty reduction, job-creation and improved workplace health and safety, and to reinforce the ILO's tripartite structure (*World of Work* 2002a). The following words of the ILO Director-General, Juan Somavia, explain the deepening consensus on tackling the emerging problems of employment and work in a globalized era: 'Until we see a globalization that prioritises the creation of employment and the reduction of poverty, the whole concept is going to remain dogged by controversy' (*World of Work* 2002b, p. 22). In June 2002, the World Commission on the Social Dimension of Globalization was launched by the ILO. Its objectives include:

■ to help to move the debate on globalization from confrontation to dialogue;
■ to articulate a realizable vision for a fair and sustainable model of globalization to meet the needs of people around which consensus can be built (*World of Work* 2002c, p. 29).

Embarking on an overall aim of looking at globalization through the eyes of people, at the time of writing, the Commission is working on an authoritative report which will include an in-depth analysis of the social dimension of globalization and the implications of this analysis on decent work, poverty reduction and development. The Commission is expected to conduct its work in cooperation with other international organizations such as the IMF and the WTO through a number of meetings. If the Commission is able to identify policies, processes and institutional changes necessary to realize the objectives outlined above, a whole range of organizations including MNCs will benefit from the report when formulating people-management strategies in an international context.

Linked with these social and ethical considerations, another aspect of globalization relevant for the future of IHRM is 'international migration'. An ILO study shows that globalization has increased migration pressures which are set to accelerate even further in the years ahead (*World of Work* 2000). The argument is that flows of goods and capital between rich and poor countries will not be large enough to offset the needs for employment in poorer countries. Instead, social disruption caused by economic restructuring is likely to uproot more people from their communities and encourage them to look abroad for work (*ibid.*, p. 4). Due to the increased speed of communication and falling prices of transportation, it is noted that the character of international migration has changed and migration flows have become more complex and diverse. Three trends which increase the complexity of migration patterns as identified in the ILO study can be summarized as follows: social and political pressures because of host governments and communities becoming more resistant to new arrivals; the emergence of a commercial migration industry helping migrants for a fee to secure visas, transportation and employment; and the growth of illegal trafficking (*World of Work* 2000). Therefore, governments, companies as employers, and international agencies of employment are increasingly concerned about international migration and need to consider the particularities of each situation to formulate strategies by developing a fuller understanding of the issue.

GROUP ACTIVITY

Reflect on the various aspects of globalization which impact on the management of human resources internationally.

Given this discussion on globalization with a particular focus on its impact on the management of human resources, it is worth noting that the UN identifies 53,000 companies as multinationals, that collectively have 450,000 affiliates worldwide. The top 100 global companies employ more than 6 million foreign nationals. These numbers are hard to ignore and almost every aspect of business is in some way affected by globalization. Managing a global workforce, which is the main focus of this book, is a challenging job that requires special skills. Marks (2001) argues that this is pertinent for companies of all sizes, whether the task is telling employees about internal developments or conveying a corporate strategy, training sales people about product updates, or just ensuring that employees feel connected to the organization. The following section will examine some of the principles of HRM in this age of globalization.

GROUP ACTIVITY

Identify some examples of multinational companies whose HRM policies are significantly affected by the globalization.

WHAT ARE THE PRINCIPLES OF HRM IN AN AGE OF GLOBALIZATION?

There exist some ways in which organizations can successfully respond to the challenges of globalization. At the outset, there should be a clear recognition of the notion that globalization does not lead to a homogenous labour market. Although some international mechanisms are in place to impose certain regulations and policies on national governments and firms as discussed above, there are national and cultural differences in their perception and implementation. Guillen (2001) challenges the conventional wisdom that globalization compels countries, industries and firms to converge towards unification. He contends that globalization requires countries to be unique, in his terms 'to use their unique economic, political and social advantages as leverage in the global marketplace' (p. 3). While recognizing the roles played by supra-national organizations such as the WTO, the IMF and the WB as powerful agencies in advancing discourses of globalization, sustainable economic development and improved conditions of labour, it is significant not to lose sight of the importance of the individual cultural forces that structure work and employment conditions.

Acknowledging diversity as the distinguishing attribute of the global workforce, and managing that diversity should be at the top of the agenda in organizations. At the corporate level, approaches should be developed to help HR managers understand different cultural, racial and ethnic backgrounds. Schell and Solomon (1997) draw attention to the significance of individual understanding of the values, norms, perceptions and beliefs which are shaped by the culture we are born into. Then, managers can appreciate how people from different cultures approach the ideas or activities in organizations. Managing diversity is a well-studied area of HRM, and there are a variety of approaches (Liff 1996) which fall beyond the scope of this chapter. As Liff (1996) argues, the core idea, though, is to recognize individual differences.

Many differences exist between people and these constitute important issues that should be captured and addressed by HR policies and programmes. Rather than reaf-firming stereotypes and developing uniform policies for particular social groups such as women, the divergent needs and desires of individuals should be recognized and addressed.

As emphasized by Caudron (1994), diversity issues go beyond social group differences to include differences in communication styles, problem-solving, professional experience, functional expertise, management level issues, training and education and work ethics. People's social backgrounds might also impact on their work outcomes. If cross-national differences are brought into the picture, managing diversity emerges as an even more essential tool for effective management of a global workforce. At the level of implementation, diversity-management policies should attempt to identify individual needs and desires and seek to accommodate these through individually tailored career management or training schemes.

Case study 3

RHINELAND CHEMICAL

The MNC under study is one of the world's largest chemical manufacturers, founded in Germany in the late 1850s. It is named as Rhineland Chemical for the purposes of this case study. The company's operations include process-ing and marketing of oil and gas, chemicals, agri-cultural products, plastics and fibres, finishing products, and consumer products. The company employs more than 100,000 people located in almost 40 countries, producing more than 8,000 different products, and holds a 50 per cent share in more than 80 other companies in its supply chain. Acquisitions into related businesses have figured prominently in its global expansion and diversification. The company became a leading plastics and synthetic-fibre manufacturer by moving away from coal-based products into petrochemicals. In the late 1950s, Rhineland Chemical began joint ventures abroad, particu-larly with companies in the USA, and conse-quently its market share increased considerably in a short span of time in the USA. It continued to grow through acquisitions of some European companies and to expand in related industries around the world. In addition to its strategic acquisitions strategy, Rhineland Chemical owes much of its success to innovation and managing its global workforce. The President of the company explains this in the following words:

> Our challenge is to overcome the cultural and communication differences that divide us, and ensure that each and every one of our employees knows how he or she can participate in the growth and prosperity of the corporation. To facilitate this, we have attempted to develop a corporate culture that accommodates the wide range of national cultures where we operate.

The rapid pace of globalization and internationalization of the company has led to a more strategic role for HRM in Rhineland Chemical. As argued by company officials, the company has always aimed to find the best fit between its business strategy, structure and HRM approach. Rhineland Chemical claims that it has always avoided the stereotypical role of the German corporation imposing its corporate policies and procedures upon its offshore operations, and has attempted to acquire a far deeper understanding of local needs to allow it to provide superior products and service to its customers.

The company recruits almost all employees at both middle-management and more operative levels locally. University-educated and highly skilled people with technical and managerial expertise are selected for employment across the board. However, parent-country nationals and in recent years EU nationals due to the increased mobility of labour are favoured for senior and top-management posts. Senior managers are recruited through an assessment of their professional managerial skills and technical competence, as well as their contextual adaptiveness.

Rhineland Chemical has a large, well-resourced corporate human resources department based in the parent country which exercises centralized control over the careers and mobility of senior management positions worldwide, including expatriate transfers which have reflected the need for a high degree of coordination and control. They have very recently applied a sophisticated database management system for the HR department at its headquarters in Germany. With the increasing need of coordination and control, this project is targeted to replace paper files and to support its current paper-intensive system of cataloguing personnel files. In addition to providing faster access to current employee files, this new process will make it possible for staff at multiple locations to access the same data simultaneously.

The company puts a strong emphasis on training and development of employees, regarding it as important to upgrade worker skills and also managerial and professional skills. Foreign assignments are used to allow employees to gain corporate-wide, international management competencies and skills. However, there appear contradictions within the overall HR strategy. On the one hand, there is the commitment to human resource development, but at the same time the company permanently reserves senior management positions in their own subsidiaries for expatriate staff, and tends to train them more, effectively ignoring the developmental needs of local managers. The strategy, therefore, is not trouble-free. A policy such as this limits the understanding of local managers to their knowledge of the local market, hindering their professional development which lacks broader global insights.

The company is recently implementing a new HRM system that provides managers and employees with self-service personnel information on compensation, benefits, as well as other personnel processes and outcomes. This enhancement will allow HR to sharpen its focus on strategic issues and partnering with line management to add value to Rhineland's current HR operations. At the same time, their HR professionals are embracing new and innovative web-based solutions to design workflow processes that are becoming the industry standard.

These recent developments indicate an awareness of understanding the strategic importance of HRM for the company in the future. However,

HR managers at Rhineland prepare themselves for the challenges of managing a global workforce that is set to become more even demanding as the competition, particularly for skilled labour, intensifies in the international business environment.

Case study discussion topics

1   To what extent is the HR approach of Rhineland Chemical compatible with the contemporary development in IHRM and the critical themes pertaining to the global workforce as identified in this chapter?
2   How far do the policies and practices outlined in the case support the President's view that 'Our challenge is to overcome the cultural and communication differences that divide us, and ensure that everyone of our employees knows how he or she can participate in the growth and prosperity of the corporation?
3   Based on this case study, is it realistic to expect that 'a centralized and unified' way of managing people can be an effective prescription for IHRM?

SUMMARY

This chapter has examined the attributes and trends of the global workforce in the context of globalization in the 2000s. The global workforce has been defined as human capital available in the international arena and across national borders. Reviewing the current trends influencing the global workforce and the international institutions of interest, it has been suggested that the impact of globalization on patterns of international employment is complex and requires an in-depth examination. Although the volumes of international trade have increased significantly and international organizations play an increasing role in regulating and supervising employment conditions, the impact of globalization is unevenly felt in each country. Therefore, management of human resources requires distinctly different approaches across national borders in order to address the demands of national and global labour markets. The following chapter will explore the divergence and convergence of HRM systems from a comparative perspective.

Chapter four

Human Resource Management in an International Context

K. Zeynep Girgin

Learning outcomes

After reading this chapter, you should be able to:

■ Identify different approaches to international human resource management (IHRM).
■ Evaluate the reasons for the growth of IHRM.
■ Examine the convergence and divergence debate in IHRM.
■ Understand the multinational company as a particular domain in IHRM.

INTRODUCTION

Business has become more international since the Second World War, with increased foreign direct investment (FDI) especially by US companies in many countries. Research on internationalization of business has also gained momentum. How businesses have managed their people in different countries for increased economic performance and the implications of this on managerial behaviour and work organization have emerged as key concerns. Within this environment, academic and practitioner interest in the management of human resources internationally has also increased. However, there is still a lack of consensus about what international human resource management (IHRM) entails (Scullion, 2001). This chapter discusses the specific reasons for the rapid growth of interest in IHRM and examines various approaches to the management of international human resources. The chapter explains the significance of multinational companies as a particular domain of study and practice. This is followed by a discussion of the convergence and divergence debates in IHRM, and the chapter concludes by questioning whether we can identify 'an' IHRM. The case study presented at the end of this chapter provides insights into convergence and divergence of HR practices, drawing on evidence from multinational companies operating in a developing country.

REASONS FOR THE GROWTH OF INTEREST IN IHRM

IHRM is a rapidly developing field of study. Although Laurent (1986) described it as 'a field in the infancy state of development' less than two decades ago, it is argued that considerable progress has been attained recently and only a few scholars would claim that it is still in the infancy stage (Scullion 2001). IHRM gained increased interest from both academic and practitioner communities after the 1970s, with the rapid increase in international business, especially in the form of foreign direct investment (FDI) (UNCTAD 1999). Since the mid-1980s, but particularly during the 1990s, business has become even more international as a result of such developments as the opening of previously closed market economies in Eastern Europe, former Russian republics and China, to international trade supported by extensive deregulation and regional integration, for example through the EU, NAFTA, ASEAN. These changes, together with improvements in communication technologies, have helped to develop a 'globalized' world. Among other reasons cited for the growing interest in IHRM are the growing awareness that the success of international business depends primarily on the quality and effective management of human resources (Scullion 2001).

What kind of evidence can you find for increased interest in IHRM among academic and practitioner communities?

GROUP ACTIVITY

Browse through copies of the *Journal of International Human Resource Management* (JIHRM) in the last 10 years. How has a journal based solely on IHRM issues been justified? Discuss.

Can you identify any significant themes in the JIHRM in the last five years?

Different approaches to IHRM

Looking at various books with the title of 'international' HRM or related chapters on international and comparative issues in mainstream HRM books will reveal that they consider the subject from a number of different perspectives. Dowling, Welch and Schuler (1999, p. 2), for example, identify three broad approaches in the field of IHRM:

1 earlier studies examining human behaviour in organizations with an international perspective, which emphasized a cross-cultural approach;
2 studies that seek to describe, compare and analyse HRM in different countries; and
3 studies that concentrate on aspects of HRM in multinational companies (MNCs).

In fact, as Sorge (1995, p. vii) argues, '[events and developments in] international management and organization, international human resources, international industrial relations and the international enterprise cannot be seen as separate from each other'. However, it is difficult to find a unifying approach in the literature where the above are represented together. Moreover, many of the earlier studies that focused on aspects of HRM in MNCs have in fact merely dealt with the management of high-level expatriate managers (home-country nationals) instead of a systematic study of broader issues concerning HRM in MNCs in different countries.

Recruitment and selection, training and development, performance appraisal and compensation of expatriates have been widely studied in recent years. Management of expatriates, especially, dominated IHRM books: see for example the various editions of *International Human Resource Management* by Dowling *et al.* (1990, 1994, 1999). Although in the third edition two comparative sections have been added, the majority of the chapters are still concerned with the HRM issues pertaining to home-country nationals. Briscoe (1995) also deals with expatriate issues in half of his book, which he argues to be 'the first comprehensive book on IHRM'. The edited volume by Harzing and Ruysseveldt (1995) offers a unifying approach, bringing together the organizational, management, HR and Industrial Relations (IR) issues emanating from the internationalization of business, which is quite different from the expatriate orientations of most of the IHRM books.

In addition to IHRM books, there is a growing body of literature which deals with expatriate issues. The research on the human and financial costs of poor performance or failure of expatriates on international assignments suggests that there is a strong business case for IHRM (Tung 1981; Mendenhall and Oddou 1985; Ronen 1989; Black and Mendenhall 1990; Scullion 1995; Dowling *et al.* 1999). Furthermore, some authors have attempted to explain the benefits and methods of cross-cultural training of expatriates (Gudykunst, Hammer and Wiseman 1977; Earley 1987; Mendenhall, Dunbar and Oddou 1987; Black and Mendenhall 1989; Bhawuk 1990; Bhagat and Prien 1996; Blake, Heslin and Curtis 1996; Gudykunst, Guzley and Hammer 1996).

Despite this strong emphasis on expatriate HR management, particularly in the early literature, there were also comparative studies of HRM and IR at the national (USA, Japan, European countries) or regional levels (EU, Australasia, Latin America). One of the most extensive comparative surveys is the Price Waterhouse Cranfield survey (Cranet-E), which started by comparing HRM practices in five European countries and has recently been extended to cover over 16 countries with the inclusion of Eastern European states and Turkey. Brewster and colleagues have reported widely on these surveys and developed a 'European model' of HRM based on the extensive research databank (see for example Brewster and Bournois 1991; Brewster and Larsen 1992; Brewster 1995). Despite some methodological problems, endemic in comparative studies, some common trends were observed across the participating countries, such as increased variable pay, merit and performance-related pay, flexible working patterns, and a higher importance placed on communication in management of human resources.

Other significant examples of comparative employment studies, such as the ones by Bean (1999), Ferner and Hyman (1992, 1998) and Hyman and Ferner (1994), are centrally concerned with examining and comparing industrial relations in various countries. However, Holden (2001) argues that HRM is not their central concern. A more recent research project is the Best International Human Resource Management Practices Project, which covers 40 countries with an international research team using common research questions, design, and methodology. A first in-depth discussion of the findings from a subset of these countries can be found in the special issue of the journal Human Resource Management (Spring 2002). Members of the research team, led by Von Glinow (2002), present the comparative analyses of 10 countries in terms of selection, compensation, training and development, and the role of HRM.

Some recent HRM books devote chapter(s) or sections to IHRM, such as in Mondy, Noe and Premeaux (1999), Dessler (2000) and Gomez-Mejia, Balkin and Cardy (2001). In these examples, IHRM is considered in a single chapter and largely from the common 'expatriate management' perspective. Two significant examples of HRM books that deal with IHRM as a separate issue in a comprehensive way are the edited volumes by Beardwell and Holden (2001) and Storey (1995, 2001). Storey's edited volume (1995, 2001) has a very similar approach and includes three chapters on international and comparative HRM, such as the European dimension by Brewster (2001, 1995) and the American dimension by Kochan and Dyer (1995, 2001).

What are some of the possible reasons for the emphasis on expatriate management issues within the IHRM literature?

What kind of insight can regional surveys like the Cranet-E provide?

GROUP ACTIVITY

Find the Best International Human Resource Management Practices Project in the special issue of the *Human Resource Management* journal mentioned above. What are some of the methodological problems involved in such large-scale regional surveys?

International HRM is a complicated field of study to define. Early research and publications in the field has been anecdotal, descriptive and lacking in analytical rigour (Brewster and Scullion 1997). There have been attempts at defining IHRM through models and examples, but it has been difficult to find a commonly agreed definition. Scullion (1995), for example, suggested the following as a definition of IHRM:

> The HRM issues and problems arising from the internationalization of business, and the HRM strategies, policies and practices which firms pursue in response to the internationalization process. (p. 352)

Although he argues that this definition covers a much broader area than only the management of expatriates, and includes management of people worldwide, it is obviously concerned with HRM in MNCs. He also claims that such a definition emphasizes that IHRM is a separate field from comparative employment relations, therefore arguing implicitly that a distinction between international and comparative HRM should be made and that they should be treated separately.

Dowling *et al.* (1999) take a similar approach and define international HRM in terms of HRM practices in MNCs with a model adapted from Morgan (1986; cited in Dowling *et al.* 1999). According to this model, they argue that IHRM involves broadly the same activities as domestic HRM; however, it is the 'complexities of operating in different countries and employing different national categories of workers' (p. 4) that differentiates IHRM from domestic HRM. They claim that, otherwise, the major HRM activities performed by MNCs in various countries would be the same as their domestic activities but on a larger scale. Although Dowling *et al.* (1999) argue for the divergence debate, which will be discussed later in this chapter, their definition implies a *universal* HRM where the activities would be the same but how they are performed might be different. However, evidence for this claim is still lacking in that, reportedly, mainstream HRM approaches and activities do not easily translate or transfer across national borders.

Brewster (2001) argues that HRM is universal in the sense that 'every organization has to utilize and, hence, in some way, to manage human resources' (p. 255). While questioning the 'universality' of HRM practices in the world, he takes a comparative approach. As already discussed above, based on the data sets gathered by the Price Waterhouse-Cranfield survey, Brewster explores the extent of differences in HRM practices in various countries and regions, questioning if HRM models are converging towards a universal one. In this comparative approach the differences between HRM practices at the national and regional levels are discussed, while a trend towards 'a distinctive and converging European' pattern of HRM is identified. It is important to note that Brewster's (2001) analysis at the country level is based on the divergence approach, which he names as the 'contextual paradigm'. He recognizes that the level of examination can vary from workplace to national settings, and there might be differences such as size, ownership structure and sector among organizations in the same country.

Holden (2001) proposes that drawing a distinction between international and comparative HRM is useful in order to understand and decipher the various approaches and debates in the IHRM field as a whole. He defines international HRM as 'the creation and implementation of HRM strategy and policies and issues of international organizations', and comparative HRM as 'dealing with HRM concerns in national and regional contexts' (p. 647). Bean (1999) argues for a similar conceptual distinction within industrial relations, which can be used in the area of international HRM, furthering Holden's (2001) proposal:

1 'international' or 'transnational' studies deal with 'institutions and phenomena that cross national boundaries, such as the IR aspects of MNCs';
2 'foreign' studies describe IR in other countries to one's own;
3 'comparative' studies offer systematic and analytic investigation of IR in two or more countries (p.4).

GROUP ACTIVITY

Find earlier definitions of IHRM from a variety of sources. Have there been any significant changes in the definitions through the years? What kind of characteristics can you observe?

In the light of the above discussion, MNCs take a special place at the intersection of comparative and international HRM. The important questions are: if the level of analysis taken is the country (national) level, where do the MNCs belong? Are they considered as domestic companies in the respective country? In the Price Waterhouse-Cranfield survey, for example, subsidiaries of MNCs in the participating countries

Figure 4.1   *Influences on HRM behaviour of MNCs*

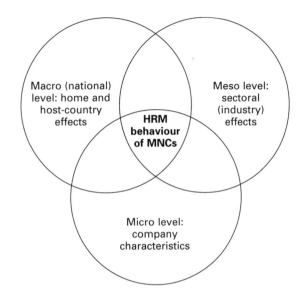

were included, but in the analysis they were not treated differently from the domestic companies. In many ways MNCs probably cannot be regarded simply in the same category as domestic companies because of home-country and host-country effects on their HR behaviour.

In fact, the HR behaviour of MNCs is affected by three groups of factors at three levels (Figure 4.1). At the macro level is the national business systems, in terms of home-country and host-country effects; it is argued that MNCs are 'embedded' in their home countries' national business systems and when they go to other countries they are faced with different national business systems (Ferner 2000; Holden 2001). Industry-sector effects represent the mezzo level, and the company characteristics are at the micro level. The HR policies and practices of a MNC in any host country therefore need to be analysed at the intersection of these fields, using both international *and* comparative HRM. Within this theoretical framework, the comparative HRM studies at the macro level, dealing with HRM at the national level, have used various perspectives based on theories of different disciplines. In the next section we will discuss the convergence and divergence debates and the significant approaches within them.

APPROACHES TO HRM IN MNCS: THE CONVERGENCE AND DIVERGENCE DEBATES

The acceleration of international business in the 1950s brought about a search for management practices, especially in the form of a 'one best way' approach to managing people in an effective way across national borders. One of the dominant strands in international management research, the convergence approach, which Brewster (2001) called the 'universalist paradigm', propagated this perspective (p. 256). It has been the dominant approach in the USA. It is argued that the convergence perspective and its enduring influences on management and organization emanated from the seminal text by Kerr *et al.* (1960), *Industrialism and the Industrial Man.* Kerr *et al.* firmly supported the argument that business practices around the world would converge towards the most efficient, namely the US model, as technology imposes similar structures and work organization (Holden 2001). As a 'monothetic' social science approach (Brewster 2001, p. 256) the convergence approach looks for similarities in business, and for our purposes, in HRM, applications in different countries. The convergence perspective has three main assumptions: firstly, improving performance through high-performance work systems is the ultimate objective in all organizations and cases (Brewster 2001). Secondly, this universal aim can be achieved by using sound and effective management principles that hold true regardless of differences between national environments. Finally, it argues that if local practices are different from these principles, they are expected to be replaced with the 'one best way', converging mainly on the American model as the leading industrial economy (Dowling *et al.* 1999).

The studies by Drucker (1950), Galbraith (1967) and especially Kerr *et al.* (1960) are regarded as the origins of the more recent globalization debate. The forces of globalization, such as the opening of world markets, deregulation, regional integration and improvements in communication technologies have been encouraging notions of convergence around one-best-way practices. Taking its roots from convergence theory, the proponents of the more recent globalization theory claim a 'borderless world' where 'transnational' or 'global' companies operate in many countries like 'insiders', detached from their original nationalities (Ohmae 1990; Reich 1990). The main proposition of the globalization argument is that nationality factors in the operation of economic systems and of companies are no longer influential or important, as international companies become 'transnationals' which converge to a new 'best model' (Bartlett and Ghoshal 1989).

The convergence hypothesis has gained much support in the context of globalization, and has become influential in the management and international HRM literature. However, there is a growing body of empirical support for the continuing influences of national and regional variations on the distinctiveness of management and organizational behaviour. The challenge to the globalization thesis gained ground in the 1970s especially when Japan, with its distinctive work organization and managerial practices, started to emerge as an industrial power in the world economy: there was much less convergence found than expected in Japanese organizations towards Western (American) employment policies and practices. Even Kerr *et al.* (1971; cited in Bean 1999) in a later postscript modified their views, stating that they had been too simplistic in theorizing how technology would uniformly influence organization and management. They proposed that the convergence of industrial countries would be towards a range of alternatives, rather than to one specific model.

GROUP ACTIVITY

Japanese management systems have subsequently been at the core of a similar convergence debate, especially in the automobile production industry. Find some of the sources on this issue, starting with Womack *et al.*'s *The Machine that Changed the World* (1990), to compare and contrast the arguments between the two theses, that is convergence towards American and Japanese management systems.

Despite a growing body of evidence refuting the convergence hypothesis, it has been argued that it 'became an established paradigm which many researchers found difficult to give up' (Dowling *et al.* 1999, p. 13). The arguments and evidence challenging globalization and convergence are provided mainly by two strands of literature, namely the culturalist and institutionalist perspectives. We will discuss two of these approaches in the next section, which in fact both reject the convergence/globalization thesis on the basis of the influence of national and regional specificities on the business environment and behaviour of companies, but with considerably different theoretical frameworks.

The divergence approach or 'contextual paradigm' in Brewster's terminology (2001, p. 258) does not set out to search for evidence to support the claims that management is becoming more alike around the world. Instead it searches to find the 'contextually unique' (Brewster 2001, p. 258) practices and approaches. For our purposes in IHRM, this research paradigm focuses on the variation of policies and applications across different national and regional contexts and tries to understand the particularities of the context with a view to decipher why and how such differences have emerged in these settings. There are two main strands of literature in the divergence paradigm:

The culturalist approach

The culturalist approach explains the differences in managerial behaviour as mainly stemming from variations in national culture (Hofstede 1980; Laurent 1983; Adler 1991). It argues that globalization as a unifying influence as such can never be realized because of the deep and multi-layered influence of national culture on the organization and behaviour of companies (Adler 1991). The culturalist perspective attempts to explain variances in work organization, managerial behaviour and HR/personnel practices by the national 'cultural distinctiveness in terms of values, ideas and beliefs shared by people in a society' (Olie 1996, p. 127). This approach found widespread acceptance in the IHRM literature and many studies, based mostly on Hofstede's concepts of national culture and value-based behavioural dimensions, have attempted to account for the influence of culture upon MNCs' behaviour (see for example Kogut and Singh 1988; Wong and Birnbaum-More 1994).

Although this approach offers a counter-argument for the sweeping claims of globalization and the prevalent acceptance and usage with which globalization is treated in the literature, there are some key problems with the culturalist approach. Firstly, the literature, which draws on the culturalist approach, suffers from methodological inadequacies and weak conceptualizations of culture where culture is used simply as a synonym for nation without any further theoretical grounding (Olie 1996). Moreover, this approach views national values and norms as fixed and static constants of national societies. The behavioural indices developed by Hofstede (1980) present such artificial constructs of such national values and norms. Finally, even when the dimensions of Hofstede's (1980) or Laurent's (1983) theories are used to explain the effects of these behavioural indices on the variations of work organization and managerial behaviour in different countries, they are still of very limited use in explaining the underlying reasons for such differences (Ferner 2000). While many researchers acknowledge the significance of culture and the influence of underlying cultural differences on the HRM behaviour, methodological problems in defining culture so as to capture meaningful insights should be acknowledged (Holden 2001).

GROUP ACTIVITY

Perform a literature search on 'cultural' IHRM. Identify one of the papers that uses Hofstede's well-known behavioural indices, and discuss the reasons for their use as a theoretical framework for IHRM research.

The institutionalist perspective

The institutionalist perspective presents itself as a more comprehensive framework for the comparative study of different national systems. This approach is variously characterized by Maurice *et al.* (1980) as the 'societal effect' approach, by Lane (1989, 1992) and Whitley (1992) as the 'national business systems' perspective, and Hollingsworth and Boyer (1997) as the 'social system of production' approach. The variances among these perspectives are in fact small and they all argue that organizational behaviour is determined by the social-institutional environment of nation states or at sub- or supra-national levels.

Hollingsworth and Boyer (1997) define the social system of production as consisting of:

> institutions or structures of a country or a region . . . integrated into a social configuration: the industrial relations system; the system of training of workers and managers; the internal structure of corporate firms, the structured relationship among firms in the same industry on the one hand, and on the other firms' relations with the suppliers and customers; the financial markets of a society; the conceptions of fairness and justice held by capital and labour; the structure of the state and its policies; and a society's idiosyncratic customs and traditions as well as norms, moral principles, rules, laws, and recipes for action. (p. 2)

Business systems, as the sum of intertwined structures and institutions, thus shape the internal organization of firms and the nature of markets and competition. They reportedly have evolved over time, and the different national development paths followed by countries have meant different national forms of business organization. Lane (1992) argues that national systems gain their distinctive character at an initial stage of industrialization but they continue to evolve as they face social, economic, political and technological challenges, and thus are not rigid and unchanging. The interrelated nature of the institutional components, however, means that change in one will lead to change in the others. In addition to the historical, path-dependent evolutionary nature of business systems, Lane (p. 64) also argues that there is a two-way relationship between social institutions and businesses, that is a 'reciprocal conditioning of business organizations and institutional complexities'.

As such, the institutionalist approach presents a framework useful for the comparative study of different national systems. Arguing that business organizations are 'embedded' in their own national systems, such a framework also allows the comparison of the organizational behaviour of companies from different national environments. By using this framework, the case of MNCs – which are in effect embedded in two distinct institutional environments, that of the parent country and the host country or countries – can be analysed, offering insights into how MNCs behave in host countries in which the institutions that shape market and internal structures are particularly different from those of their countries of origin.

Compare and contrast advantages and disadvantages of adopting culturalist or instrumentalist approaches for studying IHRM?

INTERNATIONAL AND COMPARATIVE HRM IN MNCS: MICRO, MESO AND MACRO EFFECTS

As identified in Figure 4.1, there are three main levels of influence over the behaviour of MNCs. Host-country national business systems present themselves as macro level effects. The meso level effects come from the industry sector, as different industries may predict different HRM approaches. Finally at the micro level is the company (institution), which is characterized by such variables as age, size, ownership structure, employee relations, management style and organizational culture. The HRM behaviour of MNCs is shaped at the intersection of these three different levels of variables. In addition to the divergence debate discussed above, sectoral effects as the meso variable and the company characteristics as the micro level will also be discussed shortly, to be able to give a framework for investigating the HRM behaviour of MNCs.

MNCs are not the only actors in the international business arena any more. It is argued that the rapid internationalization of business now includes small and medium-sized enterprises (SMEs) as well as public-sector organizations (Dowling *et al.* 1999; Brewster 2001). Despite the growing international role of SMEs and public-sector organizations, MNCs, as the established players of the international arena, still have the major share, representing a significant domain of research and practice in IHRM.

As the discussion on divergence above reflects, the HRM behaviour of MNCs is shaped by their own national business environments in which they are deeply 'embedded'. MNCs from different national origins display variances in their HRM behaviour, which reflect the differences inherent in their market conditions as well as the resources available to them. Large MNCs overwhelmingly originate from the most economically developed countries, and have HRM policies and applications that are shaped in response to the specific conditions of their home-countries' national business systems. As the national business systems of even the developed countries, let alone those of the less-developed/developing countries, are not fast-becoming similar to each other, or to the American model, it can be argued that the MNCs in different host countries have to adapt their HRM behaviour to the specific conditions and circumstances of the host countries.

The middle-level element of the framework is the sectoral effects, the industry to which the companies belong can be of vital importance for a number of reasons. Firstly, the structure and operation of the industry shape many aspects of individual firm behaviour and performance. Secondly, the sector is the intermediate level where the effects of a national business system meet the individual firm. Such effects might be varied in defining firms' behaviours in different industries. That is, although the elements of a national business system affect an individual firm's behaviour, it is not possible to find the same features in all industries within the same national system. In the case of MNCs, the sectoral effect can be even more important as the industry can act as the mediator in international business. Marginson and Sisson (1994), for example, claim that the nature of particular business sectors has even more effect on the HRM practices of MNCs than home- or host-country effects.

In a similar vein, Ferner (1997) hypothesizes that the transmission of home-country influences will be more significant in more 'globalized', highly internationalized sectors as opposed to domestically oriented industries. It is argued that in highly integrated production or service sectors, such as automobile production, chemicals, electronics or investment banking, multinationals tend to have a centralized approach towards their HRM/IR applications where operating units are more integrated into the international corporate strategy of the parent company (Ferner 1997). This facilitates the transfer of home-country employment policies and practices to foreign subsidiaries. On the other hand, diversified conglomerates or companies which operate in more 'polycentric' or 'multi-domestic' sectors serving national markets, such as food and drinks, textiles, clothing and retail banking, are likely to call for a decentralized approach with greater local management autonomy and lower international integration. In such industries transmission of country-of-origin policies and practices to host countries might be expected to be much less, with greater adaptation to host-country practices. Therefore sectoral effects need to be taken into consideration as a crucial element for the understanding of a MNCs' HRM behaviour, together with the notions of national business systems and company characteristics.

A further component of the conceptual framework is the impact of the company's features, such as its age, size, ownership structure, employee relations, management style and organizational culture on HRM in MNCs. The age, time and length of internationalization of the company can predict some aspects of its HRM behaviour. For instance, a younger and newly internationalizing company might not have firmly established international HRM policies and practices. Size of the company, in terms of the number of its employees, can also predict establishment of HRM applications: smaller companies might not need an established, systematic HRM approach. If the MNC is large internationally but small in size in that particular host country, it can handle its HRM by, for example, an ethnocentric approach (Perlmutter 1969; Dowling et al. 1999), that is by transferring its home-country applications directly to the subsidiary, or by a polycentric approach which involves adopting the host-country applications.

The ownership structure of the MNC is also argued to be an important variable in shaping the HRM behaviour. Many MNCs engage in FDI, particularly in developing countries, through international joint ventures (IJVs) rather than wholly-owned subsidiaries (WOS). Such ventures are increasing in number at a growing pace, especially where American companies are involved (Beamish 1988; Hladik 1985; Shenkar and Zeira 1987). IJVs are generally defined as subsidiaries of MNCs where the equity ownership is shared between a local and a foreign partner, with percentage ownership of partners defined for individual studies, ranging from 5–20 per cent minimum to 80–95 per cent maximum (Beamish 1988; Martinez and Ricks 1989; Demirbağ et al. 1995; Tatoğlu and Glaister 2000).

Research findings suggest that there are certain implications of shared ownership for the transfer or the choice of home-country HR/IR policies and host-country applications adopted. The parent on which the subsidiary is more resource-dependent, for example, is found to be more influential on the HR decisions of US companies in Mexico (Martinez and Ricks 1989). While the ability of the local partner to use its expertise and knowledge to access raw materials and local markets is a source of influence, control of product and process technologies is the main source of power in decision-making (Shenkar and Zeira 1987). The effects of the ownership structure can therefore be considered as a possible source of impact on the transfer of parent-country HR policies and applications to subsidiaries.

What are the issues that make IHRM in MNCs a complicated field both for academics and practitioners? How do these issues interact with each other?

By investigating MNCs from different home-countries operating in various host-countries, research in IHRM works to understand the interrelation between parent- and host-country effects and how these shape the transfer of international HR policies and practices of MNCs. The mezzo-level, that is the industry sector, effects and the company characteristics as the micro-level effects, need to be taken into consideration as well. Research with such a framework can provide especially interesting results if the MNC is from a developed country and their subsidiaries are located in the distinctive business environments of less-developed or developing countries. In the case that follows, summary findings from such a study are presented for discussion.

Case study 4

US MNCS IN TURKEY

Research on international and comparative HRM is still dominated by those done in and about developed countries, especially the Triad, that is the USA, EU countries and Japan. Although recent years have seen increases in the number of similar research in the developing or 'emerging' markets such as China, India, and Eastern European countries, these do not yet represent a significant share. In fact, studies on HRM in multinational companies in such different environments may shed light on our understanding of comparative and international HRM, and especially the role of MNCs in the convergence or divergence of HR management. The following case study draws on some findings from a qualitative research done on the transfer of HR policy and practices by American MNCs their subsidiaries in Turkey.

Insight into the Turkish business environment

Turkey is not an entirely unfamiliar country to those in Europe, especially through its long-standing efforts to become a member state of the European Union. It is generally classified among the developing countries by international organizations such as OECD. It has indeed got many of the characteristics of developing countries, in terms of its market size (large and growing), labour market (young and abundant workforce, which is cheap but unskilled, with a high unemployment rate), political and economic environment (instability and widespread corruption). However it has also some features that are argued to make its business system a 'distinctive' one, which does not simply fit into developing/emerging markets category.

Two of these factors are about the role of the state in the business and some related features of the Turkish private sector within this environment. Although interventionist and in many instances suppressive, the state has been in support of the development of a well-functioning private sector. Therefore legislation created a business environment favouring the employers, rather than workers. There has been a tradition of private sector since the 1950s, even though the state-owned enterprises (SEEs) in many sectors, from banking to textiles to food, have been dominant. The economy has been liberalized and an export-oriented approach has been brought in since the 1980s, which had aimed at the growth of the private sector by providing some of the necessary conditions. So the business environment is now argued to be quite permissive for the management of human resources, especially in terms of collective employment relations, hiring and firing, compensation, etc. The labour and union laws are argued to be loose and more in favour of employers than of employees. Unionization and unions are weak, especially since after the 1980s because of the changes in law, which were arguably introduced in order to provide a more accommodating environment for the employers to flourish in international markets.

Turkey has long been among the most liberal environments for foreign direct investment. In many of the emerging economies certain restrictions have been imposed on FDI, in terms of establishment of compulsory joint ventures, employment of home-country nationals, use of expatriates, etc., whereas in Turkey no such restrictions existed for a long time. Restrictions on the type of industries that foreign capital can invest have also been largely lifted, except partial limitations in some sensitive industries, such as defence.

Within this environment, one of the distinctive characteristics of the Turkish private sector has been large holding companies that

(a) operate in many (significant) sectors, including banking and finance

(b) have been in operation for decades, which started as family businesses, and very much respected and trusted by consumers and employees;

(c) are also quite powerful in their individual company relationship with the state/government due to the same respect, and have always been supported by the state;

(d) have powerful strong collective relationships with the state through their various associations.

These holding companies engaged in IJVs with foreign partners, more so after the liberalization of economy in the post-1980 period. Establishing partnerships with foreign firms was among the ways of competing in the domestic market after the reduced or altogether abolished tariffs and taxes. They were also very eager to learn from their foreign partners about production and management. These large holding companies act upon their power on, and knowledge of, the market and in their relationship with the state/government. They also have a long-standing experience of manufacturing and management (by licensing arrangements, contract manufacturing, etc., especially in some sectors such as pharmaceuticals, car production, household electronics), and available financial resources. These large holding companies in Turkey hence use their 'resources', namely (i) market power and knowledge, (ii) previous long-standing experience in manufacturing, (iii) good reputation, (iv) links to the state, and (v) access to financial resources, in the IJVs. Therefore they were/are not in a weak position when it comes to forming IJVs, especially in comparison with their counterparts in the above mentioned emerging markets (Child and Faulkner, 1998) which are at more disadvantaged positions due to their lack of the similar resources. As such, Turkish, especially holding, companies can be in a rather strong position in negotiating with their joint venture partners. This argument is discussed below in relation to their roles in the management of companies, especially HRM.

Three cases

In the research, from which partial findings are cited here, one of the major issues studies is how the Turkish business environment influences the transfer of American MNC's HR policies to their subsidiaries operating in Turkey. Selection, training and development, performance management and industrial relations are among the substantive areas of HRM studied for two reasons: first, these are the most likely areas that American companies want to transfer their corporate policies; second, they are also the ones that might be most affected by the particular business system. Case companies in the research project are selected to represent both IJVs and WOS in various sectors, although only three IJVs are discussed here.

IJV1

The Turkish parent of IJV1 is one of the most reputable large holding companies in the country and is active in a number of sectors, including pharmaceuticals, bathroom suites, personal care and cosmetics, finance, and IT. It started as a family company in the 1960s and developed into a conglomerate holding company. Although still owned by the family in majority, some of its affiliates' shares are partly publicly traded. It has extensive experience in and knowledge of the Turkish market in the various industries it operates. Its owners have very good relations with the state and are powerful business people.

The Turkish parent company started the production and sales of the American parent's product under a license agreement in the early 1960s. It had since then gained experience in manufacturing, and acquired the majority share in this sector through its marketing and sales activities. In the early 1990s, IJV1, in which Turkish and American parents shared 50–50 equity ownership, was established. IJV1 is the only joint venture that the American parent has been involved in its international operations, whereas the Turkish parent does not accept a minority share in any of its IJVs with various foreign parents. In the IJV agreement, management and functional areas were shared between the two parents, where sales and marketing together with HRM were left to the Turkish parent, while production (and related functions such as quality assurance) and finance were given to the American parent. Production is the core area where the American parent has extensive investment in R&D, hence the know how, and international experience. Sales and distribution of their products require the Turkish parent's broad knowledge of and experience in this sector in the Turkish business environment as a majority of

sales are made to the national services which can only be realized through the large-scale bidding regularly invited by the state institutions. HR/IR can also be argued to be a similar function in terms of the experience and knowledge needed, although less so as American parent's HR policies can in fact be transferred and applied through experienced and knowledgeable managers in the Turkish business system.

The HR function, managed by Turkish nationals, has very close connections with the Turkish holding's HR coordination unit. Selection, performance evaluation and compensation policies are set and applications are closely controlled by the holding HR coordination. However, some of the policies and applications in these areas closely resemble American HR policies in general. There are also some training methods taken from the American parent and used in the Turkish subsidiary.

Although there are no formal reporting lines in the HR function between the Turkish subsidiary IJV1 and the American parent's corporate head office, regular reports summarizing significant issues are sent. The American parent is argued to have a more of a consultation and supporting role in HRM: 'they are very much willing to share their knowledge and experience about the issues that we ask help for'. The HR management team in the Turkish subsidiary is invited into international HR conferences and meetings held by the American parent where information on the current and future policies as well as 'best practices' from subsidiaries are shared. IJV1 is also provided with information on changes and development of policies and given extensive help in incorporating these into its HR system if it decides to do so. The American parent is argued to be very much willing to take more control in HRM where and if it can, although it had from the beginning been agreed that HR is within the Turkish parent's responsibility.

Unionization is quite strong in the sector and IJV1 used to be unionized before the IJV was established. However, through the use of a subcontracted workforce in manufacturing, the company went through a de-unionization process. Currently there are neither collective employment procedures nor a recognized union. The Turkish parent's other company in the same industry (and companies in some other industries) continues to be unionized. The American parent, although unionized in some countries, such as in the UK, is strongly inclined to avoid unions when and where it can.

IJV2

In IJV2 a very similar situation to that of IJV1 is observed: the Turkish parent is another one of the oldest and largest holdings in Turkey. It is active in many industries, e.g. banking, car production, household equipment manufacturing, food, and retailing to name but a few. It has been in many of these sectors since the 1960s and 1970s, and developed a very trusted and respected name in the country. Some of its companies' shares are publicly traded, although the holding and the affiliates still largely belong to the family members. The owners' relationship with the state has always been very positive and active business members are among the most powerful businesspeople in the country. Although it is involved in many IJVs in various industries with parents from different countries, like IJV1, it never accepts a minority ownership. In all of the IJVs it is involved it has therefore at least 50 per cent, or equal share with the foreign parents.

The Turkish parent established its first relationship with the American parent very early, in the late 1920s, when it had began distributing the latter's products in Turkey. In the late 1950s, a licensing agreement was signed between the Turkish and American parents for the licensed manufacturing of the products. The Turkish parent established the company, which later was the basis for IJV2, and started manufacturing in a new plant, which was then a very important achievement for the Turkish industry. The American parent took a minority equity stake in that company in the early 1980s. As part of the American parent's move to enlarge its 'traditional'

markets into 'emerging' markets, a new JV agreement was reached in the late 1990s, where the equity shares of the two parents were equalized (both less than 50 per cent), and the board and management responsibilities were shared equally. Company structure and functions are agreed in detail in the JV contract, where the general manager is from the Turkish parent and deputy general manager is from the American parent. Finance, and sales and marketing are within the American parent's responsibility, whereas production and HR/IR functions are left to the Turkish parent.

The American parent had made a large investment for a new production site in one of the most industrialized areas of Turkey, providing thousands of new jobs. The land was acquired and permission for the site was taken from the government. Although the company continues to serve the domestic market, its production is now geared towards supplying the European markets of the American parent. The American parent's production system, which involves work group organization, has been brought and applied into the new plant.

IJV2's relations in HRM with the Turkish parent are organic, although there are no formal reporting lines in place. As in IJV1 described above, selection, performance management and compensation systems are developed by and transferred from the Turkish parent's holding HR coordination unit. There are no formal or informal lines of reporting and communication between IJV2's HR/IR function and American parent's regional or corporate head office HR/IR. However, the new production system transferred from the American parent requires certain HR/IR policies and practices to be applied, especially in selection, training and health and safety areas.

New employees hired need to have a certain level of formal education and skills, which will allow for further development through company training. In the new work group organization, each employee has to be in command of a minimum number of different tasks and able to replace each other. Therefore continuous and rigorous training and development of blue-collar workers have become a very important task for the HR/IR function. Although there are no formal reporting lines with the American parent specifically in HR/IR, through the reporting procedure of the production system used (although in varying degrees) globally, certain HR/IR issues are reported. The annual audit done by the American parent has sections on employee training and development, and health and safety.

As in IJV1's industry, unionization is also strong in this sector, nationally and internationally. IJV2, since its initial establishment as a Turkish company producing under license, has long been unionized. There have been no changes in the relations with the unions since the new IJV arrangements in the late 1990s. In fact, both management and the union agree that employment relations continue smoothly, where both parties support each other, being aware of the face that 'we are on this boat together'. Unions have been in a very supportive role during the economic crisis in 2001, and in the establishment of the new production site and the new work group organization. The American company, perhaps as a feature of its sector, is unionized in many countries and is not known to be specifically against unions.

IJV3

The Turkish parent in IJV3 can be described in almost the same way, with the Turkish parents in IJV1 and IJV2, in terms of its history, the industries it is active in, reputation in the market, and relations with the state. IJV3 however was first established in the early 1990s where the Turkish and American parents share the equity ownership 25:75. The American and Turkish parents had no previous business relationship and this initial business venture has been realized after the liberalization of the Turkish business environment.

The Turkish parent is not involved in the management of IJV3 at all. It is represented in the quarterly board meetings but the company is managed entirely by the American parent, although the management almost completely consists of Turkish nationals, except the finance director's position, recently filled by a Turkish manager. The absence of the Turkish parent in the management is reflected in HRM, where the managers define their company as 'an entirely American company'.

The HR policies are developed at the American parent's corporate headquarters, disseminated to the subsidiaries through regional head offices. Some policies might be adapted to the legal and market environment, such as when ethnic diversity is not an issue for the specific country, but gender diversity is closely followed in the application of the diversity policy where they aspire for 30 per cent female managers. Selection criteria and methods are centrally designed and closely followed. As for compensation, 'you cannot argue that you want to be in the 4th quartile in Turkey when the company policy is to be in the 3rd quartile of the market in the respective country'. International reporting lines are formally set, annual plans and budget are agreed, and applications are closely monitored through regular and rigorous reports by the regional head office of the American parent.

Although not involved in the management of the IJV3, the Turkish parent has a very significant role in the relations and communication because of its strong and powerful connections with the state. The company operates in a very 'sensitive' sector and communication and negotiations with the government have always been very important. The Turkish parent must have been especially indispensable at the start-up phase, as the sector used to be a state monopoly by law and was then opened to private businesses for the first time.

IJV3 was never unionized. A union has tried to be organized at the plant but was not successful 'because our employees did not want a union'. Management claims that employees would want a union only to be able to get better terms and conditions but the company already provides them with excellent conditions in compensation (pay and benefits), promotion, communication, and working environment. However, they also claim that they would in any way not oppose it should their employees want a union, as their (American parent's) corporate policy is not to conflict with employees' rights and wants. The American parent is unionized in the USA and the union has a powerful stance, especially in its main plants.

Case study discussion topics

1 What are the similarities and differences in the three cases described?
2 What might be the reasons for American parents to engage in IJVs with their Turkish partners?
3 How do these differences influence the relationship between the American parent and the Turkish subsidiary in terms of HRM?
4 What might be the possible (international and domestic) outcomes of these arrangements on the transfer and application of HR policies of American parents to their Turkish subsidiaries?
5 Discuss some possible learning points for American parents from their experiences in Turkey that might be transferred to their subsidiaries in other developing countries.

SUMMARY

This chapter has examined the reasons for the growth of IHRM as a field of study, and has identified the various approaches within IHRM, such as international and comparative studies. The chapter also reviewed the convergence and divergence debates that prevail in the IHRM literature. Finally the chapter examined MNC as a particular domain within the IHRM field, and has concluded with a case study on HRM policies and practices of various US MNCs in a developing country, Turkey, in an attempt to understand the significant factors that impact on the transfer and application of their HRM policies to their subsidiaries.

Chapter five

National Context of International Human Resource Management

Moira Calveley
Case study by Geraldine Healy

Learning outcomes

After reading this chapter, you should be able to:

- Consider the role of government in the management of people.
- Explain the role of employers' associations and associations for HRM professionals.
- Discuss the nature of employee voice through the different mechanisms of trade unions and works councils.

INTRODUCTION

Throughout the world, organizations are 'managed' by people. Salamon (2000, p. 227) suggests that: 'the characteristic which delineates management, as a group, from other roles in the organization is that, through the formal authority structure of the organization, they represent, make decisions and act on behalf of the organization as an entity'.

However, as discussed in other chapters (for example Chapters 4 and 9), organizations do not exist in a vacuum. The organization, and hence the role of the manager, is influenced by external factors whether they be economic, political, legislative or social. Governments and employee representative bodies (see below) have an impact on how organizations and their managers, both from a general business-specific management perspective and from a human resource management (HRM) perspective, operate. In order to ensure some 'voice' in how their businesses are influenced by external factors, and to protect their business interests, employers frequently belong to organizations which represent their industry. Likewise, at the operating level, HR managers are likely to belong to professional bodies which provide support and information with regard to managing people and also ethical guidelines as to how this should be done. The following sections will consider the role of national governments in influencing the way people are managed; how employers organize into employers' associations in order to influence government policies and practices; professional associations for HR managers; and finally how employees themselves are able to have a 'voice' in the employment relationship through the collective channel of independent trade unions or the more institutionalized forum of works councils.

THE ROLE OF GOVERNMENT

National governments influence the relationship between organizations and their workers in a number of different ways. They may, for example, introduce legislation which regulates the employment relationship by providing statutory rights for workers. Such rights may well include legislation regarding the promotion of equal opportunities in the workplace so that men and women, workers from minority ethnic groups and workers with disabilities are treated in an equal and fair manner; in short, that workers from diverse backgrounds are not discriminated against in the workplace.

Governments may also introduce legislation relating to economic policies. For example, many countries (such as Australia, Canada, France, Japan, United Kingdom) have a national minimum wage (NMW) set by the government. This policy is an attempt by governments to ensure that workers earn a basic standard of living with a view to minimizing or reducing the effects of poverty within the nation.

Such legislation clearly has an impact in the workplace as organizations are legally bound to follow government policy. The extent of intervention does, however, vary between countries and some governments are seen to take an interventionist approach where they are heavily involved in regulating the labour market (as is the case in France), or a voluntarist approach whereby the parties involved in the regulation of employment (employers and trade unions) 'determine the nature and content of their relationship and to regulate it without governmental or legal integration' (Salamon 2000, p. 63).

Another aspect of how national governments influence employment relations in the workplace is their approach to trade unions. In some instances, for example Germany, trade unions are seen as part of the national framework and a corporatist approach to employment relations is employed by the government. In such cases, a tripartite approach to decision-making is taken with governments attempting to integrate their own interests in maintaining a globally competitive economy with the interests of capital (the employers) and labour (the workforce as represented by trade unions – see below).

It is evident that governments play a role in employment relations within the country they are governing; however, the role they play not only differs by country but can also differ across the political spectrum *within* a country. To this end, the extent to which a government takes a voluntarist or interventionist approach to employment relations may vary according to the political party elected; government initiatives and policies evolve and change over time. The following sections will consider how employers and trade unions attempt to influence the policies instigated at national, and sometimes international, levels.

EMPLOYERS' ASSOCIATIONS

Although the focus of this book is human resource management, it is important to recognize the significance of employers' associations as decisions are often taken at national, industry level which affect people at the local workplace level. Indeed, Salamon states that 'the main focus of an employers' association is the regulation, directly or indirectly, of employment relations' (2000, p. 268); interestingly, despite this many books with HRM in the title omit any reference to employers' associations. In most countries, these associations were established in response to the growing popularity of trade unions, as employers felt the need to have a representative body to negotiate with trade unions at the national level. The main functions of employers' associations are likely to be:

■ to lobby the government and represent employers when national decisions are being made which may impact on the industry/employer;
■ to represent members in discussions with trade unions at industry level;
■ to provide advice and guidelines to employers on employment-relations issues and how to avoid/deal with industrial unrest;
■ to represent employers at employment tribunals; and
■ to provide guidelines on 'best practice' in employment relations.

Although the functions of the associations tend to be similar across countries, their main objectives may vary slightly. In Italy, for example, the Confindustria, the main employers' association, has two main objectives; the first fits with the functions as identified above, whilst the other concerns the 'broader economic, technical and political needs of members' (Pellegrini 1998, p. 153).

Further to these functions, employers' associations in some industries may also represent the commercial interests of that industry; for example, in the USA there are powerful 'producer cartels' (Farnham 2000, p. 42) where organizations combine to control prices and production.

GROUP ACTIVITY

Identify the main employers' associations in your country and specify their current concerns.

Make a list of issues on which you think employers' associations might advise their members.

In order to undertake these functions, employers' associations employ specialists in the relevant areas, such as employment law. Advice provided by the associations is of particular importance to smaller organizations who may not have the resources to employ their own specialists.

In their representative role, the associations may reach agreements with governments and/or trade unions which impact on the organizations within that industry. For example, the employers' association may be involved in discussions with the government and trade unions' representative body (see below) on economic issues such as setting a national minimum wage (NMW). It is the task of the HR manager to act upon advice given, or implement the decisions made, by the association.

Employers' associations themselves are usually represented in their own countries by a central organization; for example, the Confederation of British Industry (CBI) in the UK, the Confederation of Australian Industry (CAI) in Australia (Davis *et al.* 1998) and the Japan Federation of Employers' Associations, Nikkeiren, in Japan (Kuwahara 1998). Additionally, employers are represented at the international level by organizations such as the Union of Industrial and Employers' Confederations of Europe (UNICE).

Further to this, the national associations are represented on a regional basis, for example the Federation of European Employers, and on an international basis, for example the International Organization of Employers.

PROFESSIONAL ASSOCIATIONS FOR HUMAN RESOURCE MANAGERS

As can be seen from the discussion above, the role of HR managers is influenced by employers' associations. Their decisions with regard to people management are also affected by issues outside the immediate organization, sometimes at industry level, but also as a result of issues in the wider political and economic spectrum. It is necessary, therefore, for the HR manager to have the support and advice they need to carry out their role; they too seek a 'voice' – in their case with regard to people-management issues. As a result, throughout the world people responsible for managing human resources join associations in order to promote and protect their professionalism and to seek help and advice when necessary. Such organizations include: the Associação Brasileira de Recursos Humanos (ABRH) in Brazil; the Association Nationale des Directeurs et Cadres de la Fonction Personnel (ANDCP) in France; the Hong Kong Institute of Human Resource Management (HKIHRM); the Chartered Institute of Personnel and Development (CIPD) in the UK; and the Society for Human Resource Management (SHRM) in the USA.

GROUP ACTIVITY

In groups, discuss what you think the role of these professional bodies might be.

Find out about the professional body for HRM in your country and identify their main aims.

Like the employers' organizations, organizations representing HR professionals also have specific functions. In most cases these are to regulate the professionalization of human resources, offering advice, networking possibilities, support, education and training to their members and other national and industrial agencies about management of people.

Importantly, and of particular relevance to our discussion here, is the acknowledgement that people management is a global issue. To support HR professionals on a worldwide basis, the World Federation of Personnel Management Associations (WFPMA) was established in 1976. The main aim of the Federation is to 'aid the development and improve the effectiveness of professional people management all over the world' (WFPMA 2003). The Federation is able to claim more than 50 national person-nel associations as members, constituting some 300,000 people management profes-sionals (*ibid.*). In order to maintain their objective, representatives from the member organizations have regular meetings, commission research projects and have a bien-nial international congress.

EMPLOYEE VOICE

Having considered the extent to which employers and HR professionals 'combine' or 'collectivize' in order to attempt to influence issues regarding the business and people management of organizations, this section will consider how employees are also able to have a 'voice' within the employment relationship.

The extent to which employees are able to have a voice in the way their workplace is operated can be seen as employee participation. This can take various forms; however, this section will consider firstly employee collectivism through the channels of trade union representation, and then move on to consider employee participation through works councils.

Trade unions

Trade unions are the mechanism which provides a collective voice for employees. A trade union is: 'any organization, whose membership consists of employees, which seeks to organize and represent their interests both in the workplace and society and, in particular, seeks to regulate their employment relationship through the direct process of collective bargaining with management' (Salamon 1992, p. 78).

We can see by this definition that trade unions consist of, and act on behalf of, workers – their members. It is also clear from the above that the role of trade unions is wider than representing their members at the local workplace level, and includes representing them at a societal level. This is important as it can be argued that a single worker may not have their voice heard either in the workplace or in the wider context in which organizations operate, but by 'combining' with their colleagues they have a collective voice to which management and governments are more likely to listen. Indeed, Hollinshead and Leat argue that 'collective bargaining is one of the most frequently used and common mechanisms or processes through which employees and their representatives influence and participate in decision making within human resource systems' (1995, p. 143). Nevertheless, despite collectivism being the fundamental *raison d'être* of trade unions across the world, they are complex organizations which vary in size, function, political allegiance and ability, and/or willingness to take industrial action. By its very nature, this section provides only a limited and very general overview of the nature of trade unions on a global basis.

Trade union density (the number of employees who are members of trade unions as a percentage of all employees) varies widely both internationally and regionally. Figures quoted by Carley show that union membership is 'clearly an altogether more common phenomenon in Europe than the minority pursuit it is in Japan and the USA' (2001, p. 4). Drawing upon figures for 1998 and 1999, Carley states the European Union average as being 30.4 per cent whilst that of Japan is 21.5 per cent and the USA 13.5 per cent (*ibid.*). However, within the European state, the density varies signifi-cantly from around 70 per cent for countries such as Belgium and Denmark, to as little as 9.1 per cent in France (*ibid.*). In Australia, union density in 1998 was approximately 28.1 per cent (ACTU 2003).

Workers affiliate to trade unions primarily to protect their terms and conditions of employment, and this is known as instrumental collectivism. However, they also unionize because they believe in the role of trade unions as the collective voice of labour, referred to as solidaristic collectivism. In some cases, workers join unions for political reasons, and indeed in a country such as France unionism is characterized by political and ideological beliefs (Bean 1994; Hollinshead and Leat 1995).

The influence of the trade union varies within and across international boundaries, depending on the attitude of employers and governments. These attitudes are not static but are of a dynamic nature, changing over time and according to the predominant political ideology at both the micro (organization) and macro (governmental) levels. Employers in some organizations will fully accept trade unions as the collective voice of their employees; indeed they will welcome this as an appropriate way to communicate, consult and negotiate with the workforce. Although all these processes are important it is the negotiation role of the trade union which is of most significance for the workforce; this allows for fruitful discussion with employers (usually represented by HR managers) on the implementation of issues such as pay and working conditions. Management and trade union negotiation is a channel whereby the representations of workers are voiced.

GROUP ACTIVITY

Draw up a list of people-management issues which you think fall into the different categories of communication, consultation and negotiation. Give reasons for your categorization.

In organizations which recognize the value of trade union organization, it is often the case that employees enjoy better and more secure working conditions. Trade unions negotiate with employers on issues wider than that of pay, such as training and development, equal opportunities policies and practices, health and safety matters, to name but a few. Where unions are accepted by management as an official form of employee representation, they will be integrated into the system of people management in that organization and will be consulted on the implementation of policies and practices. For example, trade unions will have input into the designing of discipline and grievance procedures and will then play a role in ensuring that such procedures are adhered to by employers and employees alike.

The ultimate sanction of workers who collectivize through trade unions is their ability to take 'industrial action' if they are in dispute with practices implemented by management. Such action can be a complete withdrawal of labour by workers, that is to take strike action, or alternatively it can be action short of a strike which normally involves 'working to rule'. The latter action would cause a general disruption to the operation of an organization as workers closely follow bureaucratic rules. Clearly, if such actions can be taken collectively by trade-union members, then the role of the HR practitioner is important as he or she becomes involved in negotiating with the trade-union representatives to avoid any conflict developing.

Nevertheless, it is not always the case that organizations recognize trade unions as the voice of their workers. In some cases employers will instigate other forms of consultation and communication with their employees (such as works councils as discussed below), however, this usually falls short of negotiation.

As discussed above, trade unions are also institutions for the representation of workers within society. To this end, trade unions attempt to influence government policy on employment issues as it is in the interests of their members to do so. Some governments take a positive attitude towards this role of trade unions and will implement legislation encouraging their recognition in the workplace. For example in Germany, the government maintain close links with trade unions as practices are put in place in order to 'discuss IR [industrial relations] issues in an effort to combine competitiveness, increased productivity and the creation of jobs' (Klikauer 2002, p. 301).

In countries where the government seeks a close involvement of both trade unions and employer organizations in centralized decision-making on fiscal and policy decisions which relate to employment matters, this is known as a 'corporatist' or 'tripartite' approach to employment relations. This is seen to lead to the understanding that trade unions and employer organizations are 'social partners' and are working together for the greater good of the country and those working in it.

GROUP ACTIVITY

Make a list of areas of national significance which you think could be discussed and influenced by the 'social partners'.

At a national and international level, trade unions will voice their concerns to governments and attempt to influence organizations who engage in the process of what has become termed 'social dumping' (Leat 1998, p. 55). This process is one in which an organization will locate their business in, or relocate it to, a country where the costs of production (in particular, labour costs) and standards of employment are low. This course of action is one sometimes followed by large multinational organizations who have the systems in place to relocate in order to reduce costs. The promise of inward investment and new jobs or the threat of job losses and divestment due to relocation can put pressure on national governments to support these organizations. Although according to Price (1997, quoted in Eaton 2000), trade unions were initially slow to take action against social dumping, they are clearly taking this issue very seriously now. In 2004 the European Trade Union College organized a course for trade union representatives on how to combat social dumping.

As with employers, trade unions associate at national, regional and international levels. Within the UK the representative body of trade unions at the national level is the Trades Union Congress (TUC), in Australia it is the Australian Council of Trade Unions (ACTU) and in the USA the American Federation of Labor and Congress of Industrial Organizations (AFL-CIO). At the European level the European Trade Union Confederation (ETUC) represents 77 national trade union confederations across the continent (ETUC 2003). As the national unions enter into dialogue with the national employers associations, ETUC enters into dialogue of European relevance with UNICE.

At an international level, the International Confederation of Free Trade Unions (ICFTU) was established in 1949, has 231 affiliated organizations in 150 countries across the world, and represents some 158 million workers (ICFTU 2003). The organization campaigns for workers' rights at a global level, listing amongst its activities the eradication of forced and child labour and the promotion of equal rights for women (ICFTU 2003).

As stated earlier, trade unions are also involved in the fight for social justice both within their own countries and on a worldwide basis. An example of this is the global International Human Rights day organized by ICFTU, and AIDS awareness campaigns organized by trade unions across the world, usually under the umbrella of ICFTU.

This section has discussed worker voice through the collective channel of trade-union representation. In some cases, however, management may attempt to promote joint consultation between employers and employees through the creation of a works council, as will be discussed in the following section.

Works councils

It would appear that on the whole, works councils (WCs) are mainly a European phenomenon where they are supported by legislation at both national and European level, although there is much variation at the national level (Slomp 1995). They were introduced throughout Europe 'as an integral statutory part of the postwar industrial relations system to aid co-operative efforts for economic recovery' (Salamon 2000, p. 400). Despite this, in the UK there is no national legislation requiring worker participation through works councils. However, European legislation requires the formation of European Works Councils (EWCs) in companies with at least 1,000 employees and more than 150 employees in two or more member states (Blyton and Turnbull 1998). The view at European level is that employees have a right to be informed and consulted over issues which affect their working lives; EWCs are viewed as a way of supplementing the national structures 'to secure information and consultation rights for employee representatives with regard to transnational business and employment issues' (Blyton and Turnbull 1998, p. 240).

Works councils are formed by the election of members from the local workforce. Elections take place at a regular interval (usually between two and four years) and turnout for the elections tends to be at least 70 per cent (Slomp 1995). In many cases it is trade union members and activists who also become council members (Slomp 1995), and in Germany over 80 per cent of works councillors are members of the DGB unions (Eaton 2000).

GROUP ACTIVITY

In groups, draw up a list of issues which you think should fall under the jurisdiction of works councils and a list of issues which you think should be left to management. Give reasons for you choices.

As can be seen from above, the functions of works councils is to encourage worker involvement in decision-making by informing and consulting representatives on issues of business concern. The council is seen as a forum whereby employees are able to give 'voice' to their views and concerns. The councils have certain rights which vary between countries, but, they all have the main right to receive information about the general condition of the company and its future prospects (Slomp 1995). In some cases the works councils have the right to veto management decisions; for example in Germany the councillors are able to give consent to decisions regarding working time or dismissal of workers (Hollinshead and Leat 1995). Works councils differ from trade unions in that they are not an independent body to the organization; whereas trade unions can utilize their membership's power in order to withdraw labour, this is not a function of the works councils who generally only have rights to consultation and information.

This type of employee involvement can be seen as management, albeit whilst complying with government-imposed regulation, accepting the right of workers to be able to influence the decision-making processes which impact on their working lives. Nonetheless, Slomp (1995) has identified that even where works councils have been historic features of the national system, there is not a full uptake by companies. In Germany, for example, there are WCs in only 80 per cent of workplaces with over 100 workers, and in 60 per cent of those with 50–100 employees; and the rate falls to a mere 10 per cent in small workplaces of between 5 and 10 employees (Slomp 1995), thus demonstrating that a belief in the value of such councils is not widespread amongst management.

Case study 5

MAKING INTERNATIONAL COMPARISONS

Geraldine Healy

What follows is a UK National Statistics feature drawn from *Labour Market Trends 2003* on international comparisons of labour disputes. This has been used as an exercise to enable readers to confront the difficulties of making international comparisons. Whilst the statistics are on strike data, the questions that they raise will have general applicability. An engagement with this article will provide readers with a range of skills that will encourage such data to be treated in a questioning way. A critical approach will expose the way that data are gathered, the political uses of the data, and the way that the same data may be used to make opposing arguments. Indeed such an approach may lead to a fundamental questioning of the value of making international comparisons.

As an exercise, the article should be given to the students in advance. During the session, the participants should explore a number of questions in groups of four to six.

Based on the following article and the data presented therein, address the following questions:

1 What can you learn by making international comparisons of labour disputes?
2 What are the limitations of making international comparisons?
3 Accepting that there are limitations in making international comparisons, how important is it that we collect such data?
4 How might different actors use international labour dispute data and how might they use it in different ways:

    i   the state
    ii   employers' associations
    iii trade unions
    iv   employers

5 What other international employment data are the above actors likely to seek when operating in a globalized context?

International comparisons of labour disputes in 2001

By **Joanne Monger**, Employment, Earnings and Productivity Division, Office for National Statistics

This article compares trends in strike activity in the UK, EU and OECD countries over the ten-year period from 1992 to 2001.

Key points

● In 2001 the UK had the eleventh lowest strike rate (defined as the number of working days lost due to labour disputes per thousand employees) of the 23 countries that supplied data in the OECD – the same ranking as in 2000.

● Of the 23 OECD countries where data are presented ten saw a fall in their strike rates between 2000 and 2001, 11 saw a rise and two countries, including the UK, stayed the same.

● The OECD average strike rate of 29 days in 2001 is the lowest in this series and the lowest since 1983. The fall between 2000 and 2001 was heavily influenced by the USA where one large dispute distorted the 2000 average.

● The UK strike rate has been below both the EU and the OECD averages since 1992, with the exception of 1996.

● The average UK strike rate for the five years 1997 to 2001 was 52 per cent lower than the previous five-year period (1992-1996). The equivalent falls for the EU and the OECD were 45 per cent and 23 per cent respectively.

● The UK strike rate for the production and construction industries has remained fairly constant since 1996. The 1997 to 2001 five-year average was 15 per cent lower than the average for the previous five years. This compares with falls of 27 per cent in the EU and 10 per cent in the OECD.

● The UK five-year average strike rate for the service sector fell by 56 per cent over the five years 1997 to 2001, while there was a 40 per cent fall in the EU and a 15 per cent rise in the OECD.

Introduction

THIS ARTICLE continues a regular series of international labour dispute features, and presents data on labour disputes in member countries of the Organisation for Economic Co-operation and Development (OECD) between 1992 and 2001. Data for international comparisons are always a little behind those available for the UK alone. More recent figures for the UK are presented in Tables H.11 and H.12 (see ppS84-85). For a detailed analysis of labour disputes in the UK in 2001 see pp589-603, *Labour Market Trends*, November 2002.

The statistics presented in this article are useful for showing relative levels of working days lost through disputes in each country and how they have changed over time. However, an exact comparison between countries is not possible because there are important differences in the methods used for compiling statistics on labour disputes in the individual countries. These differences in coverage are shown in the technical note and are discussed in the second half of the article.

It should also be noted that, although these articles appear annually and cover ten-year periods, there are often revisions to previous years' data in the current article. Generally these revisions will only affect recent years and will have arisen because the data on either working days lost or employment have been revised by the individual countries during the year. In some cases

Table	Labour disputes: working days not worked per 1,000 employees[a] in all industries and services; 1992-2001										Average[b]			Percentage change 1992-96 to 1997-01
	1992	1993	1994	1995	1996	1997	1998	1999	2000	2001	1992-96	1997-01	1992-01	
United Kingdom	24	30	13	18	55	10	11	10	20	20	29	14	21	-52
[UK ranking]	[8]	[13]	[7]	[5]	[16]	[9]	[9]	[10]	[11]	[11]	[6]	[8]	[7]	
Austria	8	4	0	0	0	6	0	0	1	0	2	1	2	-50
Belgium	65	18	24	33	48	13	28	8	8	47	38	21	29	-45
Denmark	27	50	33	85	32	42	1,317	38	51	24	46	292	172	535
Finland	41	10	307	493	11	56	70	10	126	30	170	58	112	-66
France	37	48	39	300	57	42	51	70	114	83	97	73	84	-25
Germany	47	18	7	8	3	2	1	2	0	1	17	1	9	-94
Ireland	217	68	27	132	110	69	32	168	72	82	110	86	96	-22
Italy	180	236	238	65	137	84	40	62	59	66	172	62	116	-64
Luxembourg	0	0	0	60	2	0	0	0	5	0	13	1	6	-92
Netherlands	15	8	8	115	1	2	5	11	1	6	30	5	17	-83
Portugal	57	25	30	20	17	25	28	19	11	12	30	19	24	-37
Spain	676	238	698	157	165	182	121	132	296	152	385	178	271	-54
Sweden	7	54	15	177	17	7	0	22	0	3	54	6	30	-89
EU average[c]	103	69	98	96	53	37	53	37	60	43	84	46	64	-45
Iceland	3	1	864	1,887	0	292	557	0	368	1,571	556	571	564	3
Norway	207	19	54	27	286	4	141	3	239	0	121	78	98	-36
Switzerland	0	0	4	0	2	0	7	1	1	6	1	3	2	200
Turkey	152	75	30	580	31	20	30	24	36	29	175	28	95	-84
Australia	148	100	76	79	131	77	72	88	61	50	107	69	87	-36
Canada	184	132	137	133	280	296	196	190	125	164	174	192	183	10
Japan	5	2	2	1	1	2	2	2	1	1	2	1	2	-50
New Zealand	98	20	31	41	51	18	9	12	8	37	48	17	31	-65
United States	37	36	45	51	42	38	42	16	163	9	42	54	48	29
OECD average	69	48	61R	77	51	41	46	30	90	29	61	47	54	-23

Sources for working days not worked: ILO; Eurostat; national statistical offices
Sources for employees: OECD; except UK, Office for National Statistics

a Some employee figures have been estimated.
b Annual averages for those years within each period for which data are available, weighted for employment.
c Greece no longer collects data on labour disputes; the European Union average therefore excludes Greece.
R revised

the revisions can be quite large and users should take particular care when making comparisons between articles.

Overall comparisons

Table 1 shows the number of working days lost through labour disputes per thousand employees over the ten-year period 1992 to 2001 for each of the OECD countries where data are presented. This shows that in 2001 the UK's strike rate was ranked eleventh lowest out of 23, the same as in 2000. Over the OECD as a whole, ten countries saw a fall in their rate over the

year, 11 saw a rise and two showed no change. The OECD average strike rate of 29 days in 2001 shows a sharp drop from 90 in 2000, and is the lowest rate in this series. However, it should be noted that the USA's increase in strike rate from 16 in 1999 to 163 in 2000 (due to the large dispute in the recreational, cultural and sporting activities sector) did distort the OECD average.

Figure 1 shows the strike rates in 2001 for each of the 14 EU[1] countries that supplied data, with the UK having the seventh lowest rate. *Figure 2* displays the UK rate against the EU average for each year from 1992 to

2001. The UK rate has been significantly below the EU average since 1992, with the exception of 1996. Within the EU, Spain has experienced consistently high rates over this ten-year period, while Austria, Germany and Luxembourg have generally shown very low rates. In 2001 Belgium saw the largest annual increase in its strike rate (from 8 to 47).

In most countries there has been considerable variation in the rates from year to year, and some years have been dominated by a small number of very large strikes. In the UK, 60 per cent of the working days lost in 1996 were as a

Figure 1 Working days not worked per thousand employees (strike rate); EU; 2001

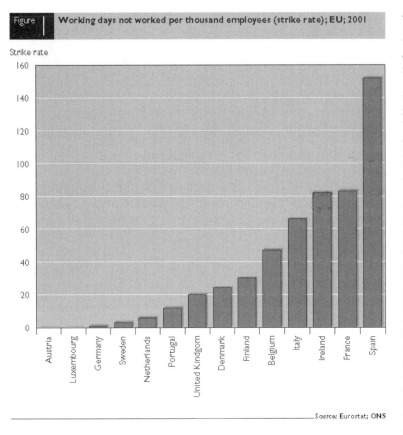

Strike rate

Source: Eurostat; ONS

and 2001, with Belgium showing the largest increase. In order to lessen the weight of a single year's data, comparisons can be made over a number of years.

Figure 3 shows average strike rates in the UK, the EU and the OECD over rolling five-year periods from 1992. This shows the overall decline in strike activity over the decade, with the UK rate consistently below both the EU and OECD averages. The average rates for the periods 1992 to 1996 and 1997 to 2001 are also shown in *Table 1*. Over this period, the average rate fell in the EU by 45 per cent and in the OECD by 23 per cent. The countries seeing an increase in their rates were Denmark, Iceland, Switzerland, Canada and the USA. Of these, Denmark had a particularly high strike rate in 1998, and Iceland is unusual in having very high figures for 1994, 1995, 1997, 1998, 2000 and 2001, and either very low or negligible figures for 1992, 1993, 1996 and 1999. The five-year on five-year comparisons need to be interpreted carefully, as most of the rises were not trends but dominated by one-year high values, for example Denmark in 1998 and the USA in 2000. Also, percentage change comparisons for countries with very low strike rates (anything under 5) should be treated with caution. Between 1997 and 2001 the average number of working days lost per thousand

result of one stoppage in the transport, storage and communication group. Other examples include the public sector strike in France in 1995, the large private sector strike in Denmark in

1998, the health sector strike in Ireland in 1999 and the transport, storage and communication group strike in Finland in 2000. Seven countries in the EU saw a rise in their strike rate between 2000

Figure 2 Average strike rates; United Kingdom and EU averages; 1992-2001

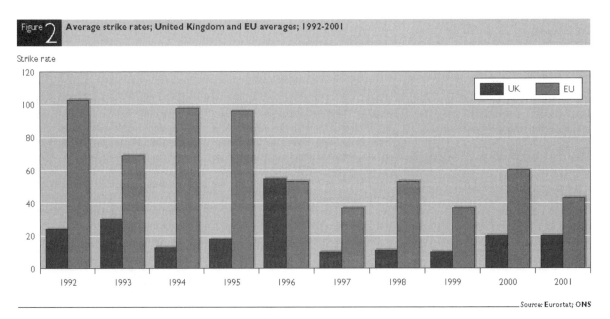

Strike rate

Source: Eurostat; ONS

	1992	1993	1994	1995	1996	1997	1998	1999	2000	2001	Average[b] 1992-96	1997-01	1992-01	Percentage change 1992-96 to 1997-01
Table 2 — Labour disputes: working days not worked per 1,000 employees[a] in the production and construction industries; 1992-2001														
United Kingdom	25	27	13	15	20	19	9	20	20	15	20	17	18	-15
Austria	1	0	0	0	0	0	0	0	0	0	0	0	0	0
Belgium	155	60	80	115	135	48	25	20	28	156	109	55	83	-50
Denmark	79	159	101	197	101	98	3,200	94	112	70	128	724	430	466
Finland	112	28	1,041	28	20	47	37	20	275	15	237	80	154	-66
France	46	63	75	112	58	52	43	79	84	31	71	58	64	-18
Germany	30	41	12	19	7	3	1	6	0	2	22	2	13	-91
Ireland	43	43	29	60	116	45	29	81	43	41	59	48	53	-19
Italy	281	356	278	92	308	164	63	116	62	126	264	106	186	-60
Luxembourg	..	..	..	..	..	..	..	..	..	..	..	..	..	..
Netherlands	24	10	8	443	4	7	2	14	2	6	97	6	51	-94
Portugal	62	44	54	43	32	55	39	20	12	15	47	27	37	-43
Spain	497	412	323	286	320	349	253	135	534	363	371	331	349	-11
Sweden	0	190	29	13	0	2	2	2	0	9	45	3	24	-93
EU average[c]	(108)	(117)	(99)	(84)	(89)	(69)	(97)	(48)	(84)	(69)	(100)	(73)	(87)	-27
Iceland	..	..	..	..	..	..	..	..	..	..	..	..	..	..
Norway	52	12	29	1	1,106	13	12	8	842	0	249	173	210	-31
Switzerland	..	..	..	..	..	..	..	..	..	..	..	..	..	..
Turkey	124	160	54	1,053	59	40	32	55	56	42	294	45	159	-85
Australia	314	243	217	263	383	237	236	247	183	217	284	224	254	-21
Canada	464	244	260	323	380	349	364	293	194	217	333	280	306	-16
Japan	2	2	2	1	1	1	1	1	1	0	1	1	1	0
New Zealand	338	11	41	72	53	42	7	7	27	70	97	31	63	-68
United States	74	111	109	188	116	78	137	62	55	14	120	70	94	-42
OECD average	(91)	(98)	(87)	(145)	(96)	(67)	(97)	(54)	(67)	(46)	(84)	(76)	(80)	-10

Sources for working days not worked: ILO; Eurostat; national statistical offices
Sources for employees: OECD; except UK, Office for National Statistics

See footnotes to Table 1.
( ) Brackets indicate averages based on incomplete data.
.. Not available.

Figure 3 — Five-year average strike rates; UK, EU and OECD; 1992-2001

Strike rate

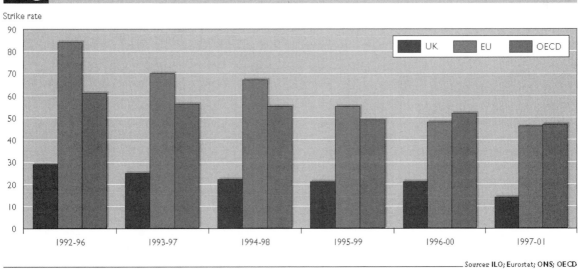

Sources: ILO; Eurostat; ONS; OECD

Table 3

Table 3 Labour disputes: working days not worked per 1,000 employees[a] in the service industries; 1992-2001

	1992	1993	1994	1995	1996	1997	1998	1999	2000	2001	Average[b] 1992-96	Average[b] 1997-01	Average[b] 1992-01	Percentage change 1992-96 to 1997-01
United Kingdom	24	32	13	20	66	7	13	7	20	22	32	14	22	-56
Austria	12	7	0	0	0	9	0	0	1	0	4	2	3	-50
Belgium	26	0	0	0	15	0	30	4	1	5	8	8	8	0
Denmark	2	7	5	9	3	20	494	5	14	5	5	106	57	2,020
Finland	12	3	12	718	8	62	75	5	52	36	150	46	95	-69
France	23	41	22	279	58	35	54	69	130	104	86	79	82	-8
Germany	61	3	4	1	1	1	0	1	0	0	14	1	7	-93
Ireland	315	83	26	173	111	85	34	214	87	102	139	106	120	-24
Italy	112	149	208	44	32	33	22	33	59R	35	109	37	72	-66
Luxembourg	..	..	..	..	..	..	..	..	..	..	..	..	..	..
Netherlands	12	7	9	12	0	1	6	11	1	7	8	5	7	-38
Portugal	56	15	17	7	8	8	21	10	11	10	21	12	16	-43
Spain	404	121	62	74	99	116	39	61	197	37	150	90	117	-40
Sweden	10	6	10	241	24	9	0	29	0	1	58	8	32	-86
EU average[c]	(69)	(41)	(36)	(84)	(37)	(22)	(30)	(26)	(51)	(32)	(53)	(32)	(42)	-40
Iceland	..	..	..	..	..	..	..	..	..	..	..	..	..	..
Norway	263	22	64	37	30	0	185	2	67	0	82	51	65	-38
Switzerland	..	..	..	..	..	..	..	..	..	..	..	..	..	..
Turkey	5	9	7	143	11	4	31	2	25	17	36	16	25	-56
Australia	99	55	34	26	61	32	28	47	28	8	54	28	40	-48
Canada	97	99	100	69	259	309	127	163	103	161	124	171	148	38
Japan	6	2	2	2	1	3	3	2	1	1	3	2	2	-33
New Zealand	26	11	28	31	49	9	9	13	2	33	30	13	21	-57
United States	25	12	24	6	19	25	1	2	200	8	17	48	33	182
OECD average	(44)	(26)	(28)	(40)	(33)	(31)	(19)	(18)	(102)	(22)	(34)	(39)	(37)	15

Sources for working days not worked: ILO; Eurostat; national statistical offices
Sources for employees: OECD; except UK, Office for National Statistics

See footnotes to *Table 1*.
( ) Brackets indicate averages based on incomplete data.
.. Not available.

employees in the UK was 14, a fall of 52 per cent over the previous five-year period. As shown in *Table 1*, nine other countries saw sharper falls over the same period.

Comparisons by industry

One particular characteristic of labour disputes is the variation between industries in the incidence of strikes: some industries such as manufacturing and transport have consistently high strike rates while others like agriculture have very low ones. Since the industrial composition of employment can vary quite significantly between countries this can sometimes explain why one country has a particularly high or low ranking compared with another. In addition, the different industrial classifications and groupings used by the separate countries when compiling statistics on labour disputes means that it is only possible to compare strike rates by industry at a broad level.

Table 2 shows working days lost per thousand employees for the production and construction[2] industries for each OECD country where data are available for 1992 to 2001. Ten countries saw falls in their strike rates for the production and construction industries between 2000 and 2001, and nine countries saw a rise.[3] *Table 3* shows the equivalent for the service industries. Within the service industry group, 11 countries (notably Spain and the USA) saw falls in their strike rates between 2000 and 2001, and seven countries

(notably Canada and New Zealand) saw a rise. In the UK, the strike rate in the production and construction industries fell from 20 working days lost per thousand employees to 15 between 2000 and 2001, while the rate in the service sector saw a slight rise from 20 to 22 working days lost per thousand employees.

Over the average ten-year period from 1992 to 2001 the strike rate in both the OECD and EU production and construction industries was more than double the rate in the service sector. Over the same period, the production and construction sector rate in the UK was 18 per cent lower than the service sector rate. Between 1992 and 2001, 14 of the 20 OECD countries where data are available had a higher average rate

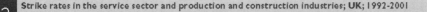

Figure 4a   Strike rates in the service sector and production and construction industries; **UK; 1992-2001**

Strike rate

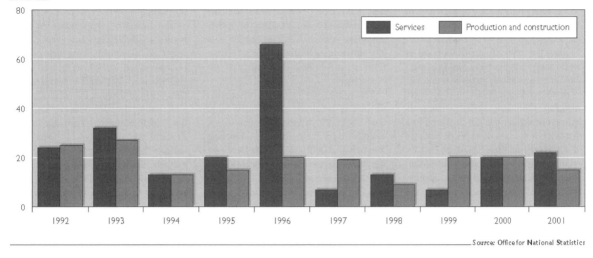

Services   Production and construction

Source: Office for National Statistics

Figure 4b   Strike rates in the service sector and production and construction industries; **OECD** average; 1992-2001

Strike rate

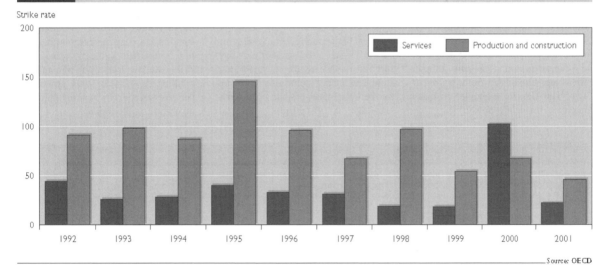

Services   Production and construction

Source: OECD

in the production and construction industries than in the service industries.

Figure 4a shows the UK strike rates in the two industry groups for each year from 1992 to 2001, and *Figure 4b* shows the equivalent figures for the OECD. In the UK the strike rates in both industry groups have been fairly consistent, with 1996 being the exception. In the production and construction sector the UK rate has been substantially below the OECD average since 1992. However, in the OECD the strike rate in this sector has been higher

than that for the service sector since 1992, with 2000 being the exception.

Tables 2 and *3* also show average rates by industry for the five-year periods 1992 to 1996 and 1997 to 2001. Between these periods, the OECD saw a 10 per cent fall in the production sector rate and a 15 per cent rise for the service sector rate. The equivalent figures for the EU were falls of 27 per cent and 40 per cent respectively. Over the same period the UK saw a fall of 15 per cent for the production and construction industries, and a fall of 56 per cent in the

service sector. Only one OECD country (Denmark) saw a rise in its production and construction industry rate over the period. Similarly, only three countries saw a rise in their service sector rates (Denmark, Canada and the USA).

Coverage and comparability

Because of the differences in definitions and coverage, international comparisons of labour dispute statistics

77

need to be made with care: in particular, differences in the rates in *Tables 1* to *3* may not be significant when coverage is taken into account. Most countries rely on voluntary notification of disputes to a national or local government department, backed up by media reports.

None of the 23 OECD countries mentioned in this article aim to record the full effects of stoppages of work. For example, most countries do not measure working time lost at establishments whose employees are not involved in a dispute but are unable to work because of shortages of materials supplied by establishments that are on strike. Similarly, other forms of labour dispute, such as go-slows, work-to-rules and overtime bans, are not generally reported.

There are significant differences between countries in the criteria that exist to determine whether a particular stoppage will be entered in the official records. Most countries exclude small stoppages from the statistics, the threshold being defined in terms of the number of workers involved, the length of the dispute, the number of days lost, or a combination of all or some of these. These are summarised in the *technical note*. The UK, for example, excludes disputes involving fewer than ten

workers or lasting less than one day, unless the aggregate number of days lost exceeds 100. Germany adopts the same criteria but has other exclusions that make direct comparisons with the UK difficult. A number of other countries' thresholds are similar, but any differences in thresholds affect the number of working days lost that are recorded.

There are two countries where the thresholds used are particularly high: the USA and Denmark. The USA includes only those disputes involving more than 1,000 workers. In Denmark the threshold used is 100 working days lost. Hence, the strike rates for the USA and Denmark are clearly not directly comparable with those for the UK, Germany and other countries with similar thresholds.

There are a number of other important differences that may be significant when making international comparisons. Some countries exclude the effects of disputes in certain industrial sectors. For example, Portugal omits public sector strikes and general strikes, and Japan excludes days lost in unofficial disputes. Political stoppages are not included in the figures for the UK, Turkey and the USA. In the UK this is insignificant; the last

identified political strike in the UK was in 1986 (resulting from a visit by an MP to the coal industry), and the total number of working days lost amounted to less than 1,000.

The inclusion or omission of those workers indirectly involved in a stoppage (those who are unable to work because others at their workplace are on strike) varies between countries. Half the countries listed in the *technical note* – including the UK, France, Belgium, the Netherlands, Australia, New Zealand and the USA – attempt to include them. Among the countries that exclude them are Germany, Canada, Italy and Japan. This leads these countries to record a lower number of working days lost than countries that include indirectly affected workers in their statistics. Consequently, even though Germany, for example, has a similar threshold for inclusion of disputes to that used in the UK, comparisons between the two countries' records should be made with care. It is worth noting, however, that evidence from the UK suggests that working days lost by workers indirectly affected by strikes are few: from the total number of working days lost in 2001 just over 1 per cent were lost by workers indirectly involved in strike action.

Notes

1 Greece no longer collects data on labour disputes; the European Union average therefore excludes Greece.
2 Production and construction industries include mining and quarrying, energy and water supply, manufacturing and construction.
3 Service industries include retail sales, wholesale, hotels and catering, transport, storage and communication, finance, business services, public administration, education, health and social services.

Labour disputes; comparisons of coverage and methodology

	Minimum criteria for inclusion in statistics	Are political stoppages included?	Are indirectly affected workers included?	Sources and notes
United Kingdom	Ten workers involved and of one day duration unless 100 workdays not worked.	No	Yes	Office for National Statistics collects information initially from press reports, and then contacts employers and trade unions directly.
Australia	Ten workdays not worked.	Yes	Yes	Information gathered from Industrial Relations Department, employers, unions and press.
Austria	No restrictions on size.	Yes	No	Trade unions provide information.
Belgium	No restrictions on size. Excluding public sector stoppages.	Yes	No	Questionnaires to employers following police or media coverage.
Canada	Half a day duration plus 10 workdays not worked.	Yes	No	Reports from Canada Manpower Centres, provincial Labour Departments conciliation services and press.
Denmark	100 workdays not worked.	Yes	Yes	Voluntary reports submitted annually by employers' organisations.
Finland	One hour duration.	Yes	Yes	Principally, returns from employers (+90 per cent) some reports from employees and press.
France	One workday not worked. Excluding agriculture.	Yes	Yes	Labour inspectors' reports.
Germany	Ten workers involved and of one day duration unless 100 workdays not worked. Excluding public administration. From 1993 data cover the entire FRG; earlier data represented West Germany only.	Yes	No	Compulsory notification by employers to local employment offices.
Iceland	Restrictions on size.	Not known	No	No information.
Ireland	Ten workdays not worked or one day duration.	Yes	Yes	Reports from Department of Enterprise and Employment, Department of Social Welfare and press.
Italy	No restrictions on size.	Yes	No	No information.

Technical note

Labour disputes; comparisons of coverage and methodology

	Minimum criteria for inclusion in statistics	Are political stoppages included?	Are indirectly affected workers included?	Sources and notes
Japan	Half a day duration. Excluding unofficial disputes.	Yes	No	Legal requirement to report to Labour Relations Commission.
Luxembourg	No information.	Not known	Not known	No information.
Netherlands	No restrictions on size.	Yes	Yes	Questionnaires to employers following a strike. National Dutch Press Bureau collects relevant news items on a contractual basis for Statistics Netherlands.
New Zealand	Ten workdays not worked. Before 1988 excluding public sector stoppages.	Yes	Yes	Information initially from press reports, employee and employer organisations, and labour inspectors, and subsequently from employer report forms.
Norway	One day duration.	Yes	No	Employers' reports to the Ministry of Labour and Government Administration, and press.
Portugal	Strikes only. No restriction on size. Excluding general strikes at the national level; excluding public administration.	Yes	No	Legal obligation on trade unions to notify Ministry of Labour and Social Security.
Spain	Strikes only before 1990. One hour duration. Before 1989, excluding the civil service.	Yes	No	Legal obligation on party instigating strike to notify competent labour authority.
Sweden	Eight hours not worked.	Yes	No	Information gathered following press reports.
Switzerland	One day duration.	Yes	Yes	Federal Office for Industry, Crafts, Occupations and Employment requests returns from employers and unions following press reports.
Turkey	No restriction on size. Excluding energy services and most public services; excluding general strikes.	No	Yes	Legal obligation on the part of trade unions to notify Regional Directorates of Labour.
United States	One day or one shift duration and one thousand workers involved.	No	Yes	Reports from press, employers, unions and agencies.

Source: ILO sources and methods: Labour Statistics, Vol 7. Strikes and lockouts (Geneva, 1993); and ILO's statistical website: http://laborsta.ilo.org

SUMMARY

This chapter has examined the role of government in regulating people-management activities. It has explained that trade unions, employers' associations and the government have a key role in establishing the rules, processes and outcomes of employment. The chapter also introduced the issue of employee voice through both collective and individual mechanisms. The case study encourages debate on comparative strike data in terms of how these data were aggregated and how they can be interpreted.

Chapter six

Strategic Aspects of International Human Resource Management

Ahu Tatlı

Learning outcomes

After reading this chapter, you should be able to:

- Understand the concept of 'strategic fit' and the main theoretical approaches to strategic HRM.
- Define strategic IHRM.
- Discuss the differences between domestic strategic HRM and international strategic HRM.
- Evaluate the challenges of multiple national frameworks for HRM strategies.
- Analyse different strategic options for MNCs regarding the issues of identifying location, managing cultural diversity and international transfers, and mergers and acquisitions.
- Apply the premises of strategic IHRM to the case study.

INTRODUCTION

The term strategy, which is more or less associated with military operations in the common sense understanding, is defined in the Oxford Dictionary as 'a plan designed for a particular purpose'. In a sense, strategy associates available resources with future objectives. With the conceptual shift from 'personnel management' (PM) to 'human resource management' (HRM), the strategic approach has become prominent. This shift means 'reorientation to an integrative, proactive and strategic way of looking at personnel in the firm' (Staehle 1990, p. 27). In this regard, human resource strategy basically concerns how human resources may be utilized in order to achieve the objectives of a firm. So, the link between corporate strategy and management of human resources has started to be considered as one of the main parameters of business success. In the mid-1980s the concept of strategic HRM entered management terminology to further emphasize the importance of HRM strategies regarding the overall corporate strategy.

In a parallel vein with this paradigm shift from PM to HRM, studies in the area of HRM strategies have formed a growing literature in the last two decades. However, works on strategic aspects of IHRM are still scarce, despite the fact that issues of strategic HRM becomes even more diverse and complicated for firms operating in a global context. It is now commonly argued that strategy for human resources and the corporate strategy should be interlinked for achieving organizational success, for responding to rapidly changing business circumstances in a flexible manner so as to gain a competitive edge in the international environment.

Throughout this chapter it is attempted to define strategic IHRM and operationalize its premises regarding the areas in which management of human resources is a vital strategic issue for the successful operation of MNCs. To this aim, the chapter starts by defining the strategic aspects of IHRM. Within this context, firstly, the importance of the concept strategy in the HRM literature is explored and different approaches to strategic HRM are summarized in order to link corporate strategy and HRM. Then, on this theoretical basis, the framework of strategic IHRM is drawn. At the end of the chapter, three strategic HRM areas for MNCs – identifying location, managing cultural diversity and transfers, and managing mergers and acquisitions – are explored. These three areas are worth considering because they reveal the problems and issues of strategic HRM faced by companies operating internationally; that is, they clarify the differences with regard to the scope and agenda of national and international HRM.

The case study, titled 'Koshita Manufacturing Technologies', at the end of the chapter examines the failure of an internationalization attempt by a hypothetical Japanese company. It urges for the consideration of strategic IHRM issues as one of the most crucial and challenging aspects of international operations of MNCs.

DEFINITION OF STRATEGIC IHRM

As pointed out above, strategic HRM owes its prominence to the shift from PM to HRM. Foot and Hook (1996) argue that in contrast to the tactical and rather short-term focus of PM, HRM is strategic and long-term. Armstrong (1992, p. 47) argues that 'strategic orientation is a vital ingredient in human resource management. It provides the framework within which a coherent approach can be developed to the creation and installation of HRM policies, systems and practices'. Furthermore, HRM, different from PM, places emphasis upon involvement, teamwork, flexibility and change (Foot and Hook 1996). In a similar vein, while indicating the main differences between PM and HRM, Mckenna and Beech (1995, p. 9) direct attention to the emphasis put in the HRM literature on creation of a 'strong culture' to embrace 'congruency between individual and organizational goals'. They define strong culture as 'one in which there are clear organizational values and approaches which are held by all members of the organization' (*ibid.*). The strong culture is expected to enhance employee commitment:

> There is a concern for core workers who are essential to the operation of the organization since high commitment is required from these workers. They are expected to be flexible about the hours they work above and beyond their job descriptions. (*Ibid.*, p. 4)

The increasing interest in business and academic circles on corporate culture, commitment and teamwork, and the rising need for flexibility and change, are among the most crucial issues that build the symbiotic relationship between corporate strategy and HRM strategy. Moreover, the very same concern with the issue of creating a strong corporate culture which will, in turn, enable high levels of commitment and flexibility, is one of the most complicated issues in strategic international HRM, as will be explained later.

THE CALL FOR 'STRATEGIC FIT': CORPORATE STRATEGY AND HRM STRATEGY

Human resources is one of the strategic dimensions in the portfolio of a firm and needs to be allocated effectively for fostering success and competitive advantage. As put forward by Boxall and Purcell (2003, p. 35) 'choices about competitive strategy (which markets to enter and how to compete in them), financial strategy (how to fund the business over time), operational strategy (what supplies, technology and methods to use in producing the goods and services), and human resource strategy (how to recruit, organize and motivate the people needed now and over time)' have to be effectively configured for business success. This means, simply, that decisions regarding the selection, recruitment, development, deployment and training of human resources are strategic in nature, and need to be harmonized with the corporate strategy. Armstrong explains the purpose of this strategic fit (1992, p. 47):

> The aim of strategic human resource management is to ensure that the culture, style and structure of the organization, and the equality, commitment and motivation of its employees, contribute fully to the achievement of business objectives.

Corporate strategy aims to establish sustainable competitive advantage (that includes superiority regarding cost position and product/service quality, and ability regarding meeting customers' demands), whereas strategic HRM informs it on the eligibility and achievability of the decisions on selected strategic directions with respect to the capacity and capability of the firm's human resources. Furthermore, strategic HRM feeds the overall corporate strategy by providing the workforce qualitatively and quantitatively with sufficient impetus to secure a firm's viability and to attain its business goals. Armstrong (1992) points out the interdependence between HR strategies and business strategies. As indicated by him, HR strategies:

> can play a proactive role by helping to form business strategies through culture management and by providing a framework of reference relating to human resources for those who create the business strategy . . . It can identify the human resource strengths and weaknesses of the enterprise so that business strategies are formulated. (1992, p. 47)

Several authors argue for the necessity of a 'strategic fit' between business strategy and HRM strategy (Armstrong 1992; Fombrun, Tichy and Devanna 1984; Guest 1989; Hendry and Pettigrew 1986; Miller 1989), but it should be noted that the role of strategic HRM in this equation is not a passive adoption of corporate strategy and configuration of a firm's HR in line with it. Unfortunately, in reality this reciprocity between HRM and corporate strategies is quite complex and hard to achieve, and requires an innovative process of strategic planning. As Legge (1989) puts it, to obtain a 'strategic fit', HRM issues should be integrated to corporate strategy because they form the underlying and facilitating ground for the achievement of strategic goals of the firms. Kaplan and Norton's (1996, 2001) 'Balanced Scorecard' model is an excellent example of an approach that integrates HRM to overall corporate strategy. The model refers to three main levels of perspective: the financial perspective (related to the financial outcomes and shareholder values) which is the fundamental priority of the corporate strategy; the customer perspective (related to the customers' satisfaction); and the internal (related to the internal operations) and learning and growth perspective. Strategies regarding the 'learning and growth perspective' underpin the previous two and deal with the HR issues. Hence, strategic HRM is indispensable for enabling effective and efficient internal operations which in turn promote customer satisfaction. In other words, it is the first ring of a chain that leads to achievement of the desired financial outcome targeted by business strategy. So, as argued by Hendry and Pettigrew (1986), the internal workforce of a firm is an invaluable strategic resource for gaining and maintaining competitive advantage, and may even become a 'competitive weapon', in Boxall and Purcell's (2003, p. 185) words, at the hands of a talented HRM strategist.

In such a scenario, then, what are the basic questions that a talented HRM strategist needs to deal with? According to Boxall and Purcell (2003, p. 49), three main questions within the scope of strategic HRM are:

1   What strategic choices in HRM (including key HR policies, practices and investments, and the overall system of these choices) are critical to a firm's performance?
2   How are managers in a firm making these choices – what processes are involved, including the analytical and political processes, and how are strategic HR choices connected to other strategic choices in the firm?
3   How could a firm's HRM become more effective – what could be done in HRM to improve the firm's relative performance in its industry, perhaps even to the extend of generating some form of sustained competitive advantage?

It is clear that a successful HR strategy that properly responds to the issue areas specified above would enhance the competitive position of a firm. So, strategic directions determined by the top management of a company draw the boundaries of the strategic choices related to the management of human resources. Armstrong (1992, p. 50) indicates that there are three main strategic directions for firms: an innovation-oriented strategy; a cost-oriented strategy; and maintaining/increasing market share. The first direction focuses on product development and aims to enhance the competitive position of a firm by innovation and differentiation. A firm adopting this strategy needs creative, committed and highly skilled human resources, which at the same time display high levels of flexibility and adaptability to change. The second strategy, which focuses on market maintenance and development, requires organizational stability. Here the aim of the strategic HRM is mainly in maintaining a committed and stable internal workforce. Lastly, a firm which adopts the third strategic direction tries to protect its competitive position in the market via cost-leadership. Under these circumstances, the most vital role of the HR strategy is to enable the efficient and cost-effective use of labour.

Although the focus and objectives of HR strategies vary in line with corporate strategies, Boxall and Purcell (2003) argue that it is still possible to mention three goal domains of strategic HRM: labour productivity; organizational flexibility; and social legitimacy. Labour productivity, they argue, can be measured against the criteria of cost-effectiveness (2003, p. 8). However, judging on the basis of a cost/productivity formula requires the human resource strategist to take into account the production system of the company and not to decide solely on the basis of wage levels. Namely, cost minimization cannot be equated with cost-effectiveness in all circumstances. For instance, a combination of high wages and highly skilled human resources is cost-effective in high-tech, capital-intensive production systems, whereas the reverse is true for labour-intensive, low-technology sectors. Boxall and Purcell put the argument as follows:

> In certain cases, where markets are very competitive and where technology is limited and the work is labour intensive, wage levels are decisive in the assessment of cost effectiveness . . . This is why so much basic apparel manufacture, footwear manufacture, and toy manufacture, has moved to low wage countries. On the other hand, more complex and capital intensive design function can usually be kept in high wage countries. (2003, p. 9).

The second goal domain of strategic HRM, organizational flexibility, refers to the capacity of a firm's human resources to adapt to internal and external changes. In recent decades, with the shift from Fordism to so-called post-Fordism which will be discussed later, and a rapidly changing external business environment in the era of globalization, organizational flexibility has become an indispensable prerequisite for the success of corporations, especially those operating internationally.

The third goal domain is social legitimacy, which in a sense is the acknowledgement that firms function in a societal context. Although levels of commitment to social legitimacy vary, an increasing number of firms are competing to gain reputation as 'equal opportunities employers' or as the 'best company to work for' (Boxall and Purcell 2003, p. 12). When customers and employees are considered among the key stakeholders together with shareholders, social legitimacy turns out to be a business issue rather than just an ethical consideration, due to its crucial effects on the level of commitment and satisfaction of employees, a firm's capacity to attract a productive and skilled workforce, and the level of responsiveness to the values and demands of customers. The issue of 'equal opportunities' is one of the key areas that may exemplify the goal domain of social legitimacy. MNCs operating in the European Union member states, especially, should display some commitment to equal opportunities since it is enforced through European legislation. Article 119 in the founding Treaty of Rome committed member states to equal pay for men and women, marking the beginning of a commitment to equal opportunities between men and women at the European level.

Furthermore, Article 3 of the Treaty of Amsterdam states that 'The Community shall aim to eliminate inequalities and to promote equality, between men and women'. And since the Essen Summit of 1994, promoting equal opportunities for women and men has been identified as a 'paramount task' of the EU in the area of economic planning and policy. In 1998, Employment Guidelines adopted by the Council in December 1997 placed the equal opportunities issue at the heart of European employment strategy. The four pillars of the EU point to employability, entrepreneurship, adaptability and equal opportunities. Similarly, the 1999 Employment Guidelines maintained equal opportunities as a specific pillar as well as calling explicitly for the first time for member states to mainstream equality in the first three pillars. Four main aspects that are focused in the guidelines regarding equal opportunities are: the gender mainstreaming approach in employment; tackling gender gaps in employment; reconciling work and family life; and facilitating reintegration in the labour market.

Then, the question is how strategic HRM will produce successful results in these three goal domains – labour productivity; organizational flexibility; and social legitimacy – and how will it be harmonized with the corporate strategy. There are two mainstream schools of thought that compete in answering these questions, and the next section briefly outlines main arguments.

GROUP ACTIVITY

Choose two companies, one which is nationally based, and other with international operations. Conduct a review of their HR policies and practices, and identify the key objectives of their HRM and business strategies. Discuss the relevance of strategic fit between HRM strategy and corporate strategy for both cases.

'BEST FIT' OR 'BEST PRACTICE': PARTICULARISTIC AND UNIVERSALISTIC APPROACHES TO STRATEGIC HRM

There are two competing theoretical approaches to linking HR strategy to business strategy: the 'best-fit' school and the 'best-practice' school. The first model holds a rather particularistic view when analysing the relationship between management of HR and corporate strategy. According to this approach every context has its own peculiarities which should be considered as reference points by HR strategists when determining the mode of HRM. Namely, for a HRM strategy which will provide a competitive edge to the firm, both corporate strategy and HR strategy need to be harmonized with the internal and external business environment. This is because ignorance of the context-specific characteristics may undermine the operation of the firm at all levels to a point of total frustration of its corporate objectives.

The 'best-fit' school therefore considers that a HRM strategy which is very successful and efficient in one context may produce poor and unintended results in another. So, strategies that seem perfect on paper may be even impossible to implement if they are produced without considering the specific features of the organizational context and wider external environment, both of which to a certain extent will be shaped by the socio-cultural and economic context that firms operate in.

The other main school of thought, the 'best-practice' approach, advocates the adoption of universal principles with respect to HRM strategies regardless of context. This approach argues that best practices in the area of strategic HRM should guide the strategic HR decisions elsewhere, and this would produce similar successful results for the firms. To put this in a different manner, Boxall and Purcell (2003, p. 47) indicate that this universalistic approach 'argues that all firms will be better off if they identify and adopt "best practice" in the way they manage people'.

The problem with the universalistic approach of the best-practice model mainly stems from the ignorance of the decisive role of the societal context (external environment) which also frames the organizational dynamics (internal environment). Hence, adoption of the best practices that are developed in one national context, mostly in the USA, in a different context may have adverse effects, especially for the firms operating internationally. Boxall and Purcell (2003, p. 64) point out the national variations in law, cultural norms and methods of labour management. For instance, with respect to the industrial relations systems which, to some extent, determine HR strategies in a firm, Appelbaum and Batt (1994) point to four different labour-management systems – 'sociotechnical systems' in Sweden, 'lean production' systems in Japan, 'flexible specialization' in Italy, and 'diversified quality production' in Germany, all of which significantly differ from the 'high-performance work systems' prevalent in the USA that have inspired most of the best-practice models in the literature.

Aside from the best-fit and best-practice schools, the 'resource-based view' has become influential in the strategic HRM literature since the 1990s. The resource-based view (RBV) directs attention to the management of inner resources of firms which are assumed to be unproblematic and easily reconfigurable by the previous market-oriented approaches. As pointed out by Boxall and Purcell (2003, p. 73): 'In the RBV, the quality of management process and of the firm's workplace culture are seen as major factors that explain differences in business performance'. However, the RBV is criticized by many authors because of its bold emphasis on a firm's human and non-human resources, and because it ignores the crucial impact of the external market conditions by isolating firms from the very contexts in which they operate (Boxall and Purcell 2003; Porter 1991).

Boxall and Purcell (2003) argue that both context and universalism have to be considered while deciding on HR strategy. As an alternative to the two mainstream market-oriented approaches (best-fit and best-practice) and the recently developed resource-based view, they propose a hybrid model for strategic HRM which takes into account both internal and external dimensions that have a role in the determination of successful strategies. Figure 6.1 combines the premises of resource-based view's internal analysis that focuses on a strengths/weaknesses perspective, and positioning models' external analysis underlines the opportunities and threats in the business environment (Boxall and Purcell 2003, p. 74).

Figure 6.1   *Internal and external dimensions of the strategic problem*

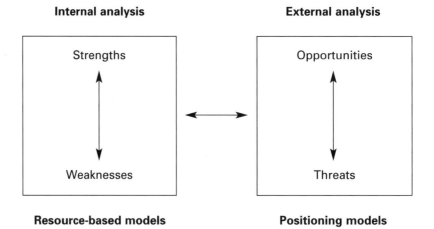

Source: Boxall and Purcell (2003, p. 74).

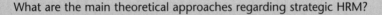

In this chapter, a similar hybrid model is preferred to explain the main issues regarding strategic IHRM. It is made explicit that in order to produce a successful IHRM strategy, both the internal and external environment of a firm should be taken into account. Hence strategic IHRM is seen as the linkage that, on the one hand, binds different levels of corporate management with HRM, and on the other situates the organization in the wider sectoral, national and international context. Within this framework, the national contexts of business operations have a crucial role to play for MNCs. For instance, Boxall and Purcell (2003, p. 6) emphasize the importance of the national context in the functioning of a corporation in general and human resources specifically, as follows:

> [N]ation states . . . exercise a major impact on the HR strategies of firms. Nations provide the resources for physical infrastructure, political-economic systems, educated workforces and social order . . . In exchange for the use of these resources, national governments impose certain regulations on how employees should be treated.

What are the main theoretical approaches regarding strategic HRM?

Choose an MNC and discuss if its strategic HRM approach conforms to any of the theoretical models identified above.

STRATEGIC HRM IN THE INTERNATIONAL CONTEXT: CREATING SYNERGY

Strategic IHRM does not propose a single 'magic' formula that guarantees success in global operations. Rather, its valuable contribution is the emphasis on the importance of contextuality regarding the applicability and efficiency of strategies themselves. It presumes the multiplicity of contexts and best strategies, so it is the role of human resource managers to creatively find the best fit between an external business environment and the internal organizational setting, so as to shape the company's human resource strategy which is also organically bound to its corporate strategy.

Strategic management of human resources on the international scale promises new issue areas for HR managers and strategists due to the increasing diversity of the cultural contexts. One of the main challenges to the overall strategic corporate management in MNCs is the need to ensure diversification and integration simultaneously in order to protect their existing markets and penetrate new ones in a rapidly changing and highly competitive global business environment. Phillips (1992, p. 34) stresses the balancing role of HRM in a MNC as follows: 'On the one hand, the organization must strive for consistency in order to build, maintain and develop its corporate identity, and on the other, it needs to adapt its methods of management to the specific cultural requirements of the host countries.'

For instance, with the globalization of markets and the internalization of competition, differentiation strategies became crucial for firms to hold competitive advantage in the international arena. The axis of a differentiation strategy both in terms of markets and products has increasingly become dependent on the consideration of cultural differences. This necessitates responsiveness and flexibility with regard to the cultural contexts in terms of consumers' demand for products and the supply of labour, as well as forming mergers and acquisitions with national companies. In their analysis of SHRM in a global context, Adler and Ghadar (1990, p. 243) indicate that the emerging circumstances force multinational companies to 'manage cultural diversity within the organization as well as between the organization and its supplier, client, and alliance networks. Attention to cultural differences becomes critical for managing both the firm's organizational culture and its network of relationships outside of the firm.'

Although cultural diversity, which becomes one of the most salient realities of today's business environment, may have adverse effects which resist change and continue to operate with their previously ethnocentric forms of management, it should be kept in mind that the very same challenge of diversity opens up new opportunities for business success. That is, strategic management of culturally diverse international human resources for a MNC may provide it with the necessary strengths for the successful implementation of corporate strategic goals, whether they be market penetration, product differentiation, innovation or integration.

Adler and Ghadar (1990, p. 253) make a similar point in summarizing three areas of organizational tension that stem from cultural diversity, and the ways to cope with these tensions:

> First, they [managers] minimize the impacts of cultural diversity when integration is needed. Second, they use cultural diversity to differentiate products and services when culturally distinct markets and or workforces must be addressed. And, third, they use cultural diversity as a primary source of new ideas when innovation is needed. (1990, p. 253)

Under these circumstances, strategic IHRM forms the very foundation of the ability of MNCs to respond to the demands of the international market by diversification and to protect the integrated structure of the corporation. So, in the face of increasing cultural diversity, strategic management of human resources has become one of the pillars of business agendas at the headquarters level as MNCs broaden their areas of operation globally.

The form of control exercised by the head office on local divisions is also identified as important in determining the direction of HR strategies in MNCs. Boxall and Purcell (2003, p. 212) indicate two important forms of control that need to be considered: forms of control under financial economies, and under synergistic economies. In the case of financial control, interdependence between strategic business units (SBUs) are loose; SBUs are to a large extend separated from the centre, operating decisions are decentralized and the main type of control exercised by the corporate office (or head office) on SBUs is 'budgetary`. With respect to HRM, this means autonomy of SBUs from the centre in their strategic decisions regarding HR issues, such as the number of employees, payment and reward systems, recruitment and training decisions. However, the financial freedom required for practicing the strategic HR decisions is quite limited under the financial form of control. 'Investment decisions are made by the corporate office and the operating budget often has no reserved area for HR issues . . . Short-run targets render long-run HR goals difficult to achieve, if not impossible' (Boxall and Purcell 2003, p. 213).

The second form of control is 'synergistic control'. 'Synergistic economies exist where common techniques, skills, or market knowledge are utilized across a range of products or services. These companies are capable of organizing around key values and are usually concerned that acquisitions match and enhance their business mission' (*ibid.*, p. 212). For instance, Boxall and Purcell argue that in the cases 'where the same tasks are carried out in each division . . . active management is aided by the movement of executives between divisions and countries . . . Managing knowledge worldwide allows for a process innovation in, say, Brazil to be tapped by the others'. However, they warn,

> This does not mean doing the same thing in the same way everywhere since differences in institutional frameworks and national cultures, and in particular histories and traditions of the operating unit, SBU or division, establish different contexts for policy implementation and innovation. The successful divisionalized firms, especially global ones, require strong performance but recognize the need for local diversity. (2003, p. 217)

Although there are still MNCs exercising strong financial control, the management trend is towards synergistic forms of control and 'the rise of firms such as ABB, the continuing success of Unilever and Canon, and resurgence of Ford over the last 20 years, point the way to new strategies in corporate control' (*ibid.*, p. 218).

In the synergistic integration form of control, HRM occupies strategic importance for the company. Whittington *et al.* (1999) in their research on change in European firms find that,

> The human resource function has become central to making the new forms of organization work. These new HR practices have two dimensions in the emerging model of organization: those concerned with supporting horizontal networking, and those with maintaining organizational integration. (Cited in Boxall and Purcell 2003, 218–19)

They further put forward that ability to manage change in structures, processes and boundaries varies with the national business systems. For instance, German firms which have matrix organizational forms and operate in the 'patient' capital market of Germany hold more innovative approaches to HR strategies when compared to British firms functioning in the short-term capital market of the UK.

In this emergent form of matrix-type organization in MNCs '[e]ach national and regional unit operates independently but is a source of ideas and capabilities for the whole corporation. National units seek to achieve global scale through specialization on behalf of the whole corporation' (Boxall and Purcell 2003, p. 219). In these organizations, the corporate centre holds the responsibility for managing the 'global network by first establishing the role of each business unit, then sustaining the system through relationships and culture to make the network of business units operate effectively . . . These types of firms are the most innovative in developing human resource strategies and more able to spread best practice from unit to unit' (Boxall and Purcell 2003, p. 219).

Phillips (1992) suggests that MNCs, by their very nature, bring together different national cultures under the same roof, which in turn posits the necessity of more flexible and less-centralized forms of organization that would allow the freedom and initiative to subsidiaries to develop their own local competences and excellence. This does not mean giving up general corporate objectives and principles common to all local branches of the MNC, rather it implies the 'recognition that in different locations people will use different paths and strategies to achieve them' (Phillips 1992, 3–4).

This section started with a discussion of the importance of managing, respecting and learning from cultural diversity in gaining competitive advantage for MNCs. The increasing need for a new form of control, that is synergistic control, was then put forward with a caution that which form of control will be more advantageous to the firm to a large extend depends on the overall competitive strategy of the firm and the distribution of tasks and operations between subsidiaries. Before ending the section, it is important to mention the main issue areas of strategic IHRM and the basic internal and external factors that would have effect on any strategic HRM decision for firms operating at the international level, that HR strategists need to consider when taking decisions.

Boxall and Purcell (2003, p. 60) suggest two main sets of factors that affect choices regarding HR strategies in a company: economic and technological factors, and social and political factors. The first set covers the sector and competitive strategy, technology of production, size and structure of the firm, state of business capital and general economic conditions; whereas the second refers to the supply of labour, expectations and power of employees, managerial capabilities and politics, labour laws and social norms, and the general educational level and vocational training system.

GROUP ACTIVITY

Identify three local branches of a MNC in your country. Compare and contrast the strategic HRM decisions at the level of these local subsidiaries, and discuss the impact of the national context of operations on the similarities and differences that exist between the local branches. Identify the overall strategic IHRM of the MNC of your choice.

IDENTIFYING LOCATION: STRATEGIES OF HRM IN MULTIPLE NATIONAL CONTEXTS

One of the competitive strategies of MNCs to expand their business is market penetration, which generally comes in the form of opening overseas branches and developing new markets in different countries. Strategic HRM has an important role with regard to decisions about the selection of locations in which new subsidiaries will be established, and there are several factors related to HRM that will affect the performance of the local subsidiaries. Levels of unionization, strength of unions, national industrial relation systems and national labour laws are among those factors that vary across nations and play an important role with regard to the identification of location. These issues are broadly discussed in Chapter 5 of this book. The investigation in this section focuses on the effect of the labour supply on the IHRM strategies regarding the determination of a location to establish a new subsidiary.

According to Horwitz, Kamoche and Chew (2002, p. 1024), 'cross cultural variation in the labour market and skills supply for addressing the market needs is an important consideration of MNCs in the decision regarding foreign direct investment'. So, conducting a preliminary research on the availability of a labour supply with the necessary skills to run the operations of the MNC's local branch is one of the first steps in choosing a country of location. The quality and quantity of the human resources needed for opening a new subsidiary depends on the corporate strategy and the specific objectives attached to the new branch. To exemplify, if the strategic objective behind the decision to establish a new branch is cost-effectiveness rather than product differentiation, countries with low wage levels would be the priority for the MNC. In recent decades it has become a common practice of MNCs to transfer their production plants to developing countries from industrialized countries where labour costs are higher. This shift of production from developed to developing countries is one of the reasons behind the retrenchment of manufacturing and enlargement of the service sector in the developed regions of the world.

However, if the firm is protecting its market position and competitive advantage in the market by the strategy of product differentiation and innovation, wage levels would be a secondary concern against the availability of certain skills. In this case the general education level and facilities/opportunities of vocational training of the host country becomes decisive when considering the possibilities of location. As Boxall and Purcell (2003, p. 61) remind us '[F]irms are "embedded" in societies which regulate and influence them while also providing social capital of varying quality'. They further indicate that 'It is wrong to assume that a good workforce is readily available when the skill requirements of the firm are advanced and specialized. High-skill industries can only survive in particular countries if that society generates sufficient numbers of people educated in the relevant science and technology' (*ibid.*, p. 192).

Besides these skill and labour-cost considerations, it is also crucial to recruit a committed and motivated core internal workforce. Enhancing motivation and commitment among employees is necessary for efficient utilization of their skills and capacities. In that sense, the human capital of the workforce is a necessary but not sufficient condition for building an internal human resources pool with high levels of creativity and productivity. HR strategists need to take into account that working is an interactive social process, and group dynamics affect the level of performance. Hence, creating an organizational structure and culture that is harmonious with the strategic HRM objectives is an indispensable part of any strategic HRM policy. 'Firms need talented and functioning leadership teams, along with a motivated and capable workforce which can reliably execute its work processes and deliver on promises to consumers' (*ibid.*, pp. 194–5). The challenge of this point for international HRM strategies is the effect of national cultures on the perceptions, attitudes, expectations, behaviours and work habits of individual employees, and on the group dynamics. The issues of cultural diversity and organizational culture are discussed at length with several examples in the next section.

GROUP ACTIVITY

Choose a MNC and recommend a location for a new branch considering the basic strategic HRM issues facing the company. Justify your recommendation in relation to the local HR context and business strategic directions available to the company. Substantiate your argument with factual information on the MNC and the country of your choice.

STRATEGIC MANAGEMENT OF AN INTERNATIONAL WORKFORCE: 'THINK GLOBAL, ACT LOCAL'

Organization of work has gone far beyond the early twentieth-century Taylorist style of highly planned organization of labour processes of the mass-production era. In the highly competitive global market, firms increasingly need to adopt organizational principles of, to use Piore and Sabel's (1984) term, 'flexible specialization' which allow a wider space for cost-reduction and diversification/innovation simultaneously. This development, associated with a decline of unionization, the increasing prominence of individual voices in collective bargaining, the transfer of plants and Fordist production methods to low-wage developing countries, and diversification/individualization of customer demands, has lead to the shift to 'human resource management'. The emphasis is put on the strong corporate culture and teamwork to organize the multi-skilled, flexible workforce which is rendered highly committed, satisfied, motivated, productive, creative and innovative (Schoenberger 1997; Procter and Mueller 2000).

Among the reasons for adopting a flexible form of organization by firms, Boxall and Purcell (2003, pp. 112–13) indicate the need to reduce unit labour costs 'since fewer people, working better, improve efficiency'; to respond more quickly to costumer needs 'since employees are more likely to be in direct contact with customers'; and to increase the product or service quality or to decrease the levels of defect 'since quality is built into the work processes of "right first time" and workers solve problems as they occur'. 'Thus', they conclude, 'the operational requirements of "quicker, better and cheaper" can only be delivered by new forms of work organization' (*ibid.*, p. 113). In their work on competencies in UK business, Kandola and Pearn (1992, p. 66) point to the shift from a 'parochial outlook' and 'procedure-bound' approach, to 'company commitment' and 'innovative and open-minded' thinking which are generally considered as the positive outcomes of flexible forms of work organization.

Within this framework, the problem is about the strategies of creating flexible, motivated and capable human resources that will form efficient work teams that display high levels of performance and commitment. As discussed throughout this chapter, one of the basic features which differentiates IHRM from HRM in a single national context is the issue of cultural diversity. It is pointed out by many authors that creating a strong corporate culture which increases the performance and commitment levels of employees is not a simple task in culturally diverse organizational settings. Accordingly, it is one of the most complicated issues in strategic international HRM. It requires a sensitively planned HRM strategy for taking the advantage of cultural diversity among employees and managing the movement of an internal workforce across national boundaries.

MANAGING DIVERSITY

As opposed to the relative cultural homogeneity of enterprises operating in a single country, the internal workforce of MNCs consists of employees from different cultural backgrounds. As Horwitz, Kamoche and Chew (2002, p. 1019) indicate, 'the complexity involved in operating in different countries and employing different national categories of employees rather that any major differences between the types of HRM activities and practices, is a key variable differentiating domestic and international HRM'.

The diversity of the workforce posits pitfalls as well as creative opportunities for HRM strategists. Among the necessary skills of HRM managers of MNCs are recognition of cultural differences, understanding foreign cultures and the aspirations of other nationalities, an ability for cross-cultural interaction and synergy as well as technical and managerial capabilities (Adler and Ghadar 1990; Phillips 1992; Torrington 1994; Simons *et al.* 1996; Elashmawi and Philip 1993). Barham and Rassam (1989, p. 149) give a shorthand description of successful international managers as those who are 'able to act locally, but to plan and think strategically and globally'.

The Vice-President of Exxon Chemical Europe, John G. Holloway, says 'The capability to switch international teams with underlying communication problems into high performing teams which fully tap the creative dimension of their diversity, is a prime source of competitive advantage' (quoted in Phillips 1992, p. ix). As is made clear in the quotation, creating a team of employees with diverse skills and from different nationalities is increasingly recognized as a way of enhancing creativity at both individual and organizational levels. For instance, the international strategy of Apple Computers is a successful example of a rather flexible use of HRM which allows room for local differences in management, while not abandoning the fundamental values of the company. The head office of Apple allows its subsidiaries enough space and freedom to decide on local HRM strategies which are in conformity with local business practices and styles. What is more inspiring in Apple's case is the commitment of the corporate management to the idea that by recruiting host-country nationals in the local branches they can operate more efficiently and be able to capture the complexities of international markets (Phillips 2002, pp. 30–1). So, local knowledge turns out to be an asset that adds value to the corporation in general.

However, if not managed effectively, the national diversity of a workforce may easily become a factor that destroys the organizational fabric and minimizes the individual employees' performance. In order to reveal the 'creative dimension of diversity' and to avoid the potential conflicts that may stem from having a human resource pool that consists of different nationalities, MNCs need to be able to create a corporate culture valuing, respecting and learning from diversity.

The corporate culture of a firm may be regarded as part of its social capital that contributes to the creation of financial capital. Several authors argue that the social aspect of internal and external business operations, which is very often neglected in business and academic circles, indeed creates directly or indirectly an economic value. Collier (1998, p. 7) defines social capital as 'a subset of the processes which generate externalities'. In similar vein, Schiff (1999, p. 2) argues that 'social capital . . . may generate benefits by raising utility and by rising output by reducing the cost of transacting business due to higher trust and enforceability of sanctions'. What then is social capital? The most classical and broad definition of the concept is given by Putnam (1993, p. 36) as follows: social capital is 'features of social organizations, such as networks, norms and trust that facilitate coordination and cooperation for mutual benefit'.

Creating a trustworthy organizational culture with some common set of norms and values is a prerequisite for raising the performance, commitment and motivation of employees and transcending communication problems which are one of the major sources of conflicts especially in the case of MNCs. Stereotyping on the grounds of nationality frequently undermines communication in international teams and leads to misunderstanding and conflict. This, in turn, implies that 'power and effectiveness of international management relates directly to the quality of communication achieved' (Phillips 1992, p. 46).

Research findings suggest that organizational cultures that enable effective communication between employees, and that encourage team work, discretional activity, involvement by employees in problem-solving and decision-making, positively affect the performance, motivation and satisfaction of employees which in turn increases customer satisfaction and profitability of the firms (Appelbaum, Bailey, Berg and Kalleberg 2000; Becker, Huselid and Ulrich 2001; Boxall and Purcell 2003). Namely, organizational culture as a part of a MNCs social capital provides a competitive edge and is an indispensable medium for the diffusion of corporate objectives at all levels and ranks of the firm. One of the tasks of strategic IHRM is to create a corporate culture that would be accepted by employees with different national cultural backgrounds. For that reason, IHR managers should handle assumptions and generalizations about the effective management of their workforce with caution. Several authors point to the ethnocentric tendency persisting in MNCs' decisions to adopt HRM strategies and practices that are developed in the Western context, and investigate the traps involved in imitating these principles that are mostly inappropriate outside of that context (Blunt and Jones 1992; Kamoche 1993; Wasti 1998). For instance, an organizational culture based on employee involvement, which is indicated as one of the factors fostering motivation and satisfaction, may face resistance by workers in societies that value status differences or, to use Hofstede's (1980) typology, societies with a large 'power distance'. Elashmawi and Philip (1993, p. 73), investigating basic features of corporate cultures in different national contexts, state that 'in most business situations, the Americans would come with a competitive attitude. The Japanese, conversely, value group cooperation in the pursuit of success. An Arab will make compromises in order to achieve a shared goal between the parties'.

Similarly, motivating factors display variety across national culture (Phillips 1992). For example, it is argued that managers whose leadership styles are based on a blend of professionalism and friendliness are able to effectively motivate their subordinates in an American context, whereas counselling, mentoring and persuasion are the main motivators for Japanese employees. In contrast to both cases, in Arabic organizational cultures authoritative manager figures who at the same time assume parenthood roles are a motivating factor (Elashmawi and Philip 1993, pp. 168–9).

It is important to conclude this section with a caution. Strategic management of culturally diverse workforces in multiple national contexts is not a simple task that can be guided by universal principles or short-hand formulas. Sensitivity towards acceptance of, respect for and learning from cultural diversity are among the basic prerequisites of successful strategic HRM. However, the IHRM strategist should also avoid culture 'fetishism', that is differences between cultures should not be exaggerated. Because, such an exaggeration is another reflection of cultural stereotyping, which is as ethnocentric as the ignorance of cultural differences. So, the very first task of IHRM strategists is to develop an understanding of the new culture he or she encounters, and the process of understanding a culture would begin with unlearning of the stereotypical assumptions.

> **?**
>
> What are the impacts of national cultural diversity on strategic IHRM issues?
>
> Take an example of a MNC and discuss how diversity regarding nationality is managed in two local branches of that MNC. Compare and contrast diversity management strategies and the resulting organizational culture in each case.

MANAGING TRANSFERS

One of the most crucial areas that strategic IHRM should handle is creating the most effective workforce composition of parent-country nationals (PCN) and host-country nationals (HCN). Horwitz *et al.* (2002) suggest that there is a correlation between the management styles of MNCs and PCN–HCN composition. According to them 'Ethnocentric MNCs place expatriates in key executive positions, centralizing parent-company control in decision-making. In polycentric and regiocentric MNCs, subsidiary host nationals manage foreign operations. Geocentric MNCs aim to staff positions worldwide with the best recruits regardless of nationality (Horwitz *et al.* 2002, p. 1023).

Both categories of employees have very important strategic functions in the operations of MNCs. Host-country employees and managers fulfill the very important functions of carrying the local expertise to the MNC 'not only technically, but in the field of communications with local institutions . . . The local manager in a global corporation has to operate as an insider in his market, and has to feed information regarding local cultures to his company, so that products can be adapted to local cultural values' (Elashmawi and Philip 1993, p. 241). On the other hand, transfers of employees from the parent country which take place generally in the form of expatriation, have two important strategic roles: carrying the corporate culture and values, and technical expertise, to local subsidiaries, and feeding the corporate centre by providing them with local knowledge (Bonache and Fernandez 1999; Boxall and Purcell 2003; Brewser and Scullion 1997; Punnet and Ricks 1992). Torrington (1994, p. 90) indicates that

> the attraction of using expatriates is that they are completely familiar with the parent company products, processes, conventions and control systems. Many expatriates are also appointed because of their technical expertise. When starting a new venture in a strange land, it is comforting to have your 'own man on the spot'.

Similarly, Schuler *et al.* (2002, p. 47) indicate that protecting company interests and building local talent are among the reasons of international assignments.

However, expatriation is generally a costly practice and there is the risk of failure due to the cultural differences (Schuler *et al.* 2002; Black *et al.* 1999; Torrington 1994). Despite these risks of expatriation, MNCs may easily ignore the vitality of cultural awareness to their performance. This attitude results in inadequate preparation, only in the forms of 'briefings', of the managers before the international assignment (Phillips 1992; Rothwell 1992). In general, inadequate preparation and insufficient training is to a large extent associated with high rates of expatriate failure. Many authors suggest that the high level of failure among American expatriates is due to relatively short training programmes lacking the necessary orientation on cultural sensitivity and intercultural communication skills (Dowling *et al.* 1999; Noble 1997; Torrington 1994).

Phillips (1992, pp. 181–2) argues that selection of expatriates for a foreign assignment is an issue that should be handled carefully. He advises MNCs to follow a step-by-step procedure for managing international transfers. The first step is 'careful selection and screening of managers to be moved'. He argues that the interpersonal skills of the managers would be at least as important as their technical skills in an international assignment. The second step is cross-cultural training and preparation that will also include information on local customs and social aspects, of the expatriates before and during the assignment. He also indicates that it is crucial for international managers to develop 'an appreciation of the different styles of management, communication and decision making prevalent in the host country' (Phillips 1992, p. 182). The operational issues about international recruitment and selection and expatriation are investigated further in the next chapter.

GROUP ACTIVITY

Choose three MNCs. Identify expatriation strategies and PCN–HCN composition in each case. Discuss the similarities and differences between the MNCs of your choice, and substantiate your argument with factual information.

A CHALLENGING AGENDA FOR IHRM STRATEGISTS: MERGERS AND ACQUISITIONS

One of the reflections of globalization on business operations is the increasing number of mergers and acquisitions (M&As) transcending national borders. Operations of nearly all of the world's leading enterprises in different sectors take place in multiple national contexts (Hubbard 1999). For instance, '39% of the Ford Motor Company's employees worked outside the United States, N.V. Philips of Holland had 79% of its employees located outside Holland, and 43% of ICI's employees worked outside the United Kingdom' (Phillips 1992, p. 1).

One of the reasons behind the preference of MNCs to penetrate new markets through M&As is the strategic value of timing and learning for business success, as indicated by the resource-based view. Boxall and Purcell (2003, p. 76) suggest that 'Directors of the firms often feel they cannot make a mark in a new sector (or a new region) without buying an established player who has built up the necessary client base, employee skills and operating systems'. So, in the decisions related to mergers and acquisitions, the local firm's experience, and social capital, become a valuable asset. However, as further pointed out by them 'Becoming an integrated multinational . . . developing networks and powerful international systems of knowledge building, exchange and intellectual capital, often via acquisitions, is a daunting task' (*ibid.*, p. 224).

Coordination of the subsidiaries is a crucial issue for MNCs. As pointed out in the previous sections, there is a trend towards synergistic forms of control from economistic control. However, it can still be argued that there is a typology of methods of coordination depending on the nationality of the parent company. Torrington (1994), referring to the work of Bartlett and Ghoshal, states that there are three main traditional approaches to coordination: Japanese centralization, American formalization, and European socialization. He summarizes the argument as follows:

The typical Japanese approach is where a strong headquarters group maintain for themselves all major decisions and frequently intervene in the affairs of overseas subsidiaries, . . . [whereas in the American formalism] power is vested . . . in formal systems, policies and standards . . . In the European companies . . . there has been a reliance on key, highly skilled and trusted individuals. These people were carefully selected and developed a detailed understanding of the company's objectives and methods . . . [they] were despatched to manage the subsidiaries, so that the headquarters and the subsidiaries were both strengthened. (Torrington 1994, pp. 101–2)

However, argues Torrington, as companies become more global rather that international, the need for new and more sophisticated methods of coordination becomes urgent.

In cross-cultural mergers and acquisitions, the more powerful party may appropriate a dominating role (Horwitz *et al.* 2002, p. 1022). When the corporate cultural values of the companies display divergence rather than convergence, each value becomes a source of cultural friction and the simplest operations that may have been realized in an easy manner previously, such as conducting meetings, motivation, training and so on, become sites of conflict and misunderstanding. To avoid conflicts and to utilize the capabilities and strengths of both parties involved, a more synergistic form of coordination needs to be realized. HRM strategies should be developed to blend the strengths of the organizational cultures and human resources of the merging companies. Elashmawi and Philip (1993, p. 3) argue in a similar manner as follows: 'Whenever a merger, acquisition or joint venture is formed by two existing companies, two or more distinct organizational cultures must be combined. It is ineffective when one entity simply tries to impose its own culture upon another. It is more productive to seek cultural synergy between and among the systems involved.'

An example of a successful merger is Rhone Poulenc Agrochemicals. In 1987, French MNC Rhone Poulenc bought the American agrochemical company Union Carbide. Two key principles were set for achieving structural merger: giving precedence to both international and local levels, and motivating all staff members to increase overall efficiency. Leaders of the group decided that a 'spirit of mutual acceptation and of respect for the cultural specifications of the various countries that the group was set up in' would be the motto during the merging of employees (Mutabazi 1994, p. 171). Accordingly, 'This ethical choice was later to guide the development of a cultural fusion within the daily functioning of the enterprise and so lead to staff motivation and a feeling of complementarity between subsidiaries and between individuals' (*ibid.*). Rhone Poulenc Agrochemicals succeeded in combining integration and differentiation strategies together, and moved up from sixth to third rank at the international level.

However, nearly half of all M&As fail to realize their initial premises 'in the sense of having either an inability to provide shareholder value greater than the sum of the previous two companies, or an inability to maintain market dominance, achieve promised cost reductions, or manage synergies between the new firms effectively' (Boxall and Purcell 2003, p. 220). Strategic problems regarding HRM issues play an important role in the failure of M&As (Hunt *et al.* 1987; Cartwright and Cooper 1992; Boxall and Purcell 2003), because, very often, cultural and organizational issues are subordinated to financial issues during the process (Elashmawi and Philip 1993). However, the acquisition process has a very crucial human dimension which should not be ignored due to the fact that utilization of tangible resources of a company is only possible given the availability of capable and productive human resources.

As asserted by Boxall and Purcell (2003), uncertainty generated in acquisitions may result in employees feeling violated in the psychological contract with the employer. The perception of breaches of the psychological contract and feelings associated with it 'typically lead to a withdrawal of support for the organization and a reduction in discretionary behaviour and motivation' in the case of individual employees (*ibid.*, p. 221). 'In an acquisition, this psychological breach can occur on a large scale, covering groups of employees leading to distinctive, and for the acquirer, damaging consequences of withdrawal of trust and commitment . . . People often feel powerless and suffer from anomie' (*ibid.*, p. 221).

'To have a psychological contract must mean that employer and employee share some common understandings that go beyond what was written in their employment agreement' (*ibid.*, p. 153). In the process of international M&As, together with the uncertainty stemming from change there are also feelings of insecurity and a state of anomie associated with the 'internationality' of the operation. To explain more openly, common cultural understanding forms the very basis of the psychological contract between employer and employee. In a sense, corporate organizational cultures are part of national cultures and working cultures in each national context rooted in the wider cultural structure of society. To exemplify, the Confucian values of Japanese culture have a strong effect on the perceptions of people about their jobs and employers. Phillips (1992, p. 9) states:

> In Japan, the employing organization is seen as a kind of society to which employees belong, rather than just a place they go to work . . . employees very often make a lifelong commitment to their employing organization, which is seen as an extension of the Japanese family . . . conformity and tradition are more highly esteemed than individuality and opportunism.

So, in the Japanese context, in most cases, a lifelong commitment to the same employer by employees, and paternalistic protection of employees by the employer, are unspoken and unwritten presumptions of any employment contract, in addition to the other features of the psychological contract that vary with the specific corporate cultures in consideration. An international merger or acquisition undermines this very basis of the psychological contract and leaves employees in an insecure, ambiguous and uncomfortable state.

Some of the questions in the minds of employees that lead them to feel insecure are:

■ How will their position/career/salary be affected?
■ Who (or which company) will manage them?
■ What will be the changes in the organizational culture and relationships?
■ How will their level of involvement and responsibilities be affected?

The HR strategist should not allow these questions to be left unanswered, and during the process of merger or acquisition, strategies for resolving potential conflicts between the staff of merging companies, countering resistance to change on the part of employees and creating a new corporate culture which will reestablish a motivating, secure and stable organizational environment should be given priority.

What is the role of strategic HRM decisions on the success or failure of international mergers and acquisitions?

Take an example of an international merger or acquisition. Identify the HRM strategies that are adopted during and after the merger or acquisition process. Discuss the impact of strategic HRM decisions on the success or failure of that international merger or acquisition.

Case study 6

KOSHITA MANUFACTURING TECHNOLOGIES

Koshita Manufacturing Technologies is a large-scale Japanese firm specializing in the production of automobiles. It has a 23 per cent of the domestic market and 12 per cent of the East Asian market. Its international business experience is limited to local sales offices in other East Asian countries, and R&D and production functions are completely realized within its national borders.

Koshita is a cost-leader in the Japanese automobile industry. The main business strategy is penetration of domestic markets and developing market share by penetrating different segments of Japanese society. To this end, it diversifies its products according to the needs and demands of the different social strata of Japan. It presents a wide product range to its domestic customers.

The dominant form of HRM in Koshita is hierarchical and paternalistic. A strong corporate culture, which establishes a family-like relationship between employees, is a vital element of its HRM strategy. It has a highly committed and motivated core workforce that implements the main operations of the company.

In 2001, Koshita executives decided to internationalize the firm's operations and to develop their markets overseas in order to protect their competitive advantage. As the location of their first international subsidiary, they choose Egypt due to its low labour-cost advantage. They recruited Japanese employees for all the managerial positions, and formed a highly skilled workforce with the necessary technical skills provided by Japanese and Egyptian nationals. The entire population of unskilled and semi-skilled workers in the production plant, however, is composed of Egyptians.

As their HRM strategy, they adopted their 'best-practice' approach aiming to produce efficient and effective results with high levels of performance, commitment and motivation; the approach having been one of the strengths of the firm in the highly competitive business environment of Japan. However, in a short time it became apparent that the performance levels of both the Japanese and Egyptian employees were in steady decline. So, opening an overseas subsidiary to raise the firm's level of cost-effectiveness turned out to be a costly experiment for Koshita.

Analysing the situation from a HRM perspective, it is found that Koshita's HR managers' ignorance of the importance of working in a different culture had a great role in the failure. The strategy of adopting 'best practice' that worked well in Japan proved to be fatal in the Egyptian context. It is now understood that the overall low performance level of the Egyptian employees stemmed from a lack of motivation and commitment rather than skill deficiencies. What is more interesting is that according to the assessment results, the performance levels of the Japanese expatriates were also very low. This was found to be due to their inability to fit in with the Egyptian culture and their loss of a sense of belonging to a large family in their workplace, due to their conflictual and implicitly hostile relationships with their Egyptian colleagues.

Case study discussion topics

1 Based on the theoretical approaches developed in this chapter on strategic aspects of HRM, how would you evaluate Koshita's experience of internationalization? Discuss the premises of the 'best-fit' and 'best-practice' schools with reference to the above case.

2 Discuss the strategic IHRM issues of identifying location, managing diversity and managing transfers in the case of Koshita Manufacturing Technologies.

3 If you were the HRM strategist of Koshita, what would be your recommendations?

SUMMARY

This chapter has situated strategic IHRM in the context of global business management by investigating the linkages between corporate strategy and HRM, and by summarizing the main theoretical approaches to strategic HRM. Strategies for managing international human resources in the three crucial domains for MNCs – identifying location, managing cultural diversity and international transfers, and managing mergers and acquisitions – have also been examined.

Through the case study, the importance of strategic IHRM issues for the operation of MNCs has been revealed.

Chapter seven

Operational Aspects of International Human Resource Management

Olympia Kyriakidou

Learning outcomes

After reading this chapter, you should be able to:

- Explore the operational aspects of IHRM.
- Analyse the main dimensions behind discrimination and bias-free selection.
- Understand the role of criterion bias and bias in measuring performance constructs.
- Design bias-free selection processes.
- Analyse the different approaches to diversity training and outline their advantages and disadvantages.
- Understand the problems and reactions of expatriate managers.
- Analyse the different selection and training policies and programmes for expatriates.
- Develop effective methods in selecting and training expatriate managers.

INTRODUCTION

Theoretically, international business and HRM have been the pioneer fields that have provided insights into managing an international workforce and diversity. Diversity, in this case, has emerged as a need for survival and success. According to Adler (2002), organizations have to consider diversity training, both domestically and internationally, to a much greater extent than ever before. The previous chapter has highlighted the significance of management of diversity. Some important reasons for this include: (1) Increasingly, more organizations are operating in the global arena, with people, goods and services coming from and going to many different countries; (2) the cost of not having appropriate diversity training can be very high; and (3) the types, frequency and number of intercultural encounters in organizations are increasing greatly around the world.

Organizations that recognize the need to fully develop all members of their workforce in order to remain competitive, are responding by implementing a variety of different initiatives to manage a diverse international workforce. Managing diversity means establishing a heterogeneous workforce to perform to its potential in an equitable work environment where no member or group of members have an advantage or a disadvantage (Torres and Bruxelles 1992). Managing an international workforce includes a process of creating and maintaining an environment that naturally allows all individuals to reach their full potential in pursuit of organizational objectives (Shaw and Barret-Power 1998). Diversity management emphasizes building specific skills, creating policies and drafting practices that get the best from every employee. It assumes a coherent environment in organizations and aims for effectiveness, productivity and ultimately competitive advantage. This chapter, therefore, will explore the operational aspects of diversity management principles in the key human resource functions of recruitment and selection, training and development, with which an organization can effectively manage workforce diversity.

International HRM, however, is not only limited to the management of an increasingly international and heterogeneous workforce, but is also concerned with the increasing number of specialists and managers specially selected by their companies to take their particular skill abroad. During the past two decades human resource managers in multinational corporations have been plagued by a persistent, recurring problem: significant rates of the premature return of expatriate managers. The inability of expatriate managers to adjust to a host culture's social and business environment is costly in terms of management performance, productivity in the overseas operation, client relations and operational efficiency. There are also invisible costs due to a manager's failure overseas: the loss of self-esteem and self-confidence in the expatriate's managerial ability, and the loss of prestige among one's peers. This chapter, therefore, will explore the problems and reactions of expatriate managers who work in foreign counties, will underline the need for effective selection and training policies and programmes for expatriates, and explore the main issues behind the development of effective methods in selecting and training expatriate managers.

GROUP ACTIVITY

How might we conduct a bias-free job and organizational analysis that suits an international and diverse workforce?

RECRUITMENT AND SELECTION

In this section, we are interested in discrimination at the entrance to organizations. This is what Terborg and Illgen (1975) call 'access discrimination'. It is assumed that, one way or the other, selection is necessary to employ personnel, and that for all the parties concerned, that is applicant, employer and society, it is desirable that non-discriminating and valid tools for personnel selection are used.

Statistically speaking, discrimination is distinguishing between individuals or groups in a reliable way. Thus, the literal meaning of the word discrimination has no negative connotations. In fact, tests are developed to distinguish between individuals or groups. Therefore, different test scores between two groups *per se* do not mean that the test is in favour of the group with the highest scores. The test may simply reflect the actual existing differences. Nevertheless, score differences may be a sufficient reason to look for the possibility of selection bias (Hofstede *et al.* 1990). Although the technical meaning of discrimination is neutral, its general meaning has the negative connotation of unfair behaviour towards an individual or group. It then refers to holding back an individual or a group on biased grounds.

Discrimination can be distinguished into direct discrimination, indirect discrimination and a so-called discrimination effect (Jahoda 1983). Direct discrimination means that irrelevant elements are taken into account deliberately to influence the selection decision; for example, individual qualities that have no clear functional relationship with the criterion performance, such as ethnicity, gender and background, are applied in the decision process. The word criterion is specifically used for any kind of measure of individual performance in work or education (see Table 7.1). It is hard to say how frequently this type of discrimination occurs, because it is generally not openly acknowledged as such and the discriminating institution or person would not often openly admit one of these irrelevant dimensions to be the true reason for rejecting an applicant. This gap between such discriminatory practices and workplace discourses that conceal them is a result of the growing recognition that direct discrimination on the basis of arbitrary criteria such as sex, race, nationality, disability and sexual orientation, is both unethical and increasingly unlawful.

Referring to indirect discrimination, the irrelevant characteristics do not affect the selection decision, yet the result will be that a group of applicants sharing a particular characteristic will be at a disadvantage as a result. This is, for example, the case when a test can predict the future performance of a particular group better than that of another group. This is a paradoxical situation: it means that even when ethnicity is not involved in the selection decision, that nevertheless as a result of the selection process members of one or more minority ethnic groups may be discriminated against. For example, a height criteria of 'two meters or taller' for selection will have a disproportionate effect on people from regions or countries where the average height is lower, effectively and indirectly discriminating against them.

For all that, a selection procedure that is free of direct and indirect discrimination may nevertheless put certain groups or individuals at a disadvantage. This is what we call a discriminating effect. It occurs when the characteristics upon which the selection is based correlate with irrelevant characteristics. When a certain level of education is required for entry to a job, and there are two groups differing in average level

Table 7.1   *Definition of criterion*

A criterion is 'a canon or standard' against which something is evaluated or judged. This definition suggests that criteria are measures of critical aspects of performance for the advertised job and provide the means to discriminate between effective and ineffective performance along the performance dimensions. A criterion will specify exactly what an employee should be doing, with respect to each required job dimension (i.e. job dimensions refer to decision making, communication skills, cognitive ability, while a criterion refers to the level of cognitive ability required by the job).

Source: Bailey (1983).

of education, it will be clear that one group will have more drop-outs than the other. This effect would work against diverse international groups.

The design of a discrimination-free selection procedure hinges on criterion development through the development of appropriate, bias-free identification, definition and operationalization of performance criteria. Following Jensen (1980), the term bias is used in a strictly statistical sense. It is defined as 'systematic errors in the criterion validity or the construct validity of test scores of individuals that are associated with the individual's group membership' (1980, p. 375). Although bias is often associated with culture bias, bias against any type of group membership can also be considered. For instance, bias towards age, gender, social class and religion can be investigated. When research shows that a test is biased against a specific group, it obviously does not mean that the test is biased for other classifications: the existence of gender bias does not imply culture bias, and so on.

GROUP ACTIVITY

Identify the elements of, and design a fair and discrimination-free performance appraisal process for, managerial career development.

Criterion bias

Criterion bias is defined as the discrepancy between measures for work performance (the actual criteria) and the employee's real value for the organization (the ultimum criterion) (Schmitt 1989). It means that in a systematic or consistent way something else rather than the ultimate criterion is being measured. However, a practical problem is that one can never have the scores on the ultimate criterion. One can work with estimates at best, which in turn need to be unbiased.

Studies that investigate racial influence on the rater in relation to that of the subject confirm that there is a suspicion of bias in performance ratings. Kraiger and Ford (1985) did a meta-analysis on 74 studies with Caucasian raters and 14 studies with African-American raters to investigate racial ratee effects in performance ratings. They found small, yet significant mean correlations between the race of the subject and that of the rater. An interesting part of this analysis was that the possible influence of five moderators was taken into account: rating training (yes/no), type of training (behaviour/trait), rating purpose (administrative/research), experimental setting (laboratory/field), and the composition of the workgroup (percentage of African-Americans in each study). The first three variables do not appear to have any influence on the size of the racial effect. The experimental setting, however, does. A racial effect was found in field settings, but not in laboratory settings. Moreover, racial effects tended to increase as the percentage of African-Americans in the workforce decreased.

More evidence about the presence of criterion bias can be found in studies in which international groups are compared with respect to differences in performance level on the basis of objectively defined measures and subjective ratings. Ford, Kraiger and Schechtman (1986) collected data from 53 studies with African-American and Caucasian employees, in which both objective and subjective criteria were used. With respect to both types of criteria significant racial effects were found. However, group differences for objective and subjective criteria were equal. The correlation between group membership and criterion score was .20, independent of criterion type, the white employees getting the higher scores. So far, these results could imply that there is no bias since the results on the objective and subjective measures run parallel. In order to further examine this, three types of criteria were classified: performance indicators, absenteeism, and cognitive criteria (training and job-knowledge tests). The relationship with race was the lowest for absenteeism. The relationship with racial group was slightly higher for the performance measures; a significant difference between the correlation coefficients of the objective and subjective measures was found. The racial effect was lower for the objective indicators. The cognitive criteria showed the highest relations. This type of measures revealed a significant difference between the relations of objective and subjective indicators with race as well, but here the objective measures showed the highest correlation. Thus, the differences between African-American and Caucasian employees on objective cognitive criterion measures were even greater than on the subjective measures.

Assuming that objective criteria are unbiased performance measures, this analysis may lead one to conclude that subjective criteria show little bias. From research on prediction bias, using subjective criteria, and not revealing any differential prediction, one could conclude that predictors for international groups are fair even when subjective measures are used as the criterion. According to Ford *et al.* (1986) this conclusion needs further explication. First of all, differences on ability tests tend to be greater than for work performance, with the exception of job-knowledge tests where the differences found tend to be the same as on ability tests. This could imply that this type of predictor and this type of criterion measure a construct that is related to international groups, in addition to the intended objectives of measurement. Alternatively, one could argue that in the actual work situation international, minority or majority group members can compensate for lower skills by other characteristics such as work experience and motivation. Thus, the effect of compensation may be greater with work performance criteria than with cognitive criteria.

Finally, we have to bear in mind that actual work performance measures may be biased as well. Although this subject has not been systematically investigated, it could be that differences in performance between subgroups are due to differences in working conditions between the two groups, whereby the conditions for the minority group would be worse than for the majority group, as minority group can be assumed to be working with older equipment, working in less successful districts and high-risk jobs. It could also be that employees from minority groups cannot fully use their abilities because of external factors in the work situation that are beyond their control. One of these factors may be sabotage by majority-group members as is mentioned by Sikking and Brasse (1987), who, however, found no such discrimination effect in their study which was done in the Netherlands.

Reviewing the research on criterion bias one may conclude that the use of ratings as a measure for performance may put minority-group members at a disadvantage, since raters will for the greater part belong to the majority group. Although this effect is relatively small and the ratings appear to be partly determined by actual work performance, nevertheless action is called for in order to prevent this kind of bias as much as possible. This can be done, for example, by using behaviour-oriented scales and the formation of multi-ethnic rating teams. With respect to objective criteria, American research on African-Americans and Caucasians rather consistently shows higher scores for the majority group. The degree of difference varies according to the type of criterion measure used. So these measures are by no means interchangeable and each individual measure by itself cannot be considered a proper indicator for the ultimate criterion. In sum, it appears that additional research into the validity of criterion measures determining the criterion construct is needed.

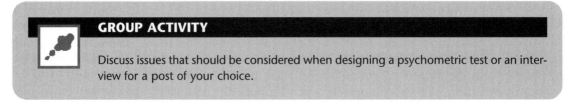

GROUP ACTIVITY

Discuss issues that should be considered when designing a psychometric test or an interview for a post of your choice.

Bias in measuring the construct

This approach to the problem of selection bias does not primarily focus on the degree to which a test over- or underpredicts with respect to a specific external criterion, but on the characteristic of the test itself and the interpretation of the test scores. The central issue here is whether the test refers to a theoretical concept or construct in the same way in different cultural groups. The importance of this approach, which can be seen as complementary to the study of prediction bias, lies in its explanatory character. Finding that the meaning of a test changes in a certain direction when it is administered to individuals and groups with different cultural backgrounds will more readily lead to hypotheses about biasing factors and to recommendations for adapting the instrument or the administration procedure.

Test bias is not primarily a characteristic of the test as such, but is linked to the test interpretation. If person 1 with cultural background X answers more test items correctly than person 2 with cultural background Y, this could simply be seen as an empirical fact which did not require any consideration about the possibility of test bias. However, a problem is created when, on the basis of this difference, one concluded that person 1 ranked higher than person 2 with respect to some general personality characteristic. A problem certainly arises if this characteristic is held to be stable and/or genetically based.

In the past, researchers have expended considerable efforts constructing so-called 'culture-free tests'. It was thought to be possible to eliminate the influence of environmental factors on test performance and to draw conclusions about differences in inborn potential irrespective of the cultural background of the persons taking the test. However, for cognitive ability tests at least, these attempts have never been very successful. Cross-cultural test research has provided us with many examples of cultural groups not possessing the specific skills presupposed by standard ability tests to a sufficient degree.

The main question here refers to the validity of the construct or attribute for the cultural groups concerned. Does it make sense, for instance, to apply concepts like spatial ability or arithmetic reasoning outside the Western cultural system in which they originated? Inspired by ideas from cultural anthropology, a number of investigators have argued that cognitive functioning is conceived as an adaptation to specific cultural and ecological requirements and should be defined in terms of these requirements. Cross-cultural comparisons of test performances in this view become practically impossible. For an overview of the discussion about this topic we refer to publications by Berry (1972), Jahoda (1983) and Poortinga and Malpass (1988). We will confine ourselves here to a pragmatic approach in which an attempt is made to formulate psychometric criteria for the comparability of test scores, taking the universality of constructs as a point of departure.

A good example of this approach is the work carried out by Poortinga and Malpass (1988), which draws a distinction between different levels of comparability. For total test scores the distinction is drawn between functional equivalence and score equivalence. Functional equivalence relates to the requirement that the test qualitatively measures the same attribute in the different groups. When dealing with more than one test to which this requirement applies, the testable condition follows that the relationships between the tests are the same in the groups concerned. Score equivalence implies that the test should measure the attribute on a quantitatively similar scale in the distinguished groups; when there is more than one test, the requirement of similar regression coefficients follows.

The functional equivalence of measurement instruments across different cultural groups has been studied relatively often. Comparison of factor structures is one of the most appropriate methods. An advantage to the comparison of separate correlation coefficients or correlation matrices is the possibility of starting from an appropriate theoretical framework, which makes the assumption of equal relationships between theoretical concepts a less arbitrary one and creates the possibility of interpreting changes in meaning. Among the intelligence theories based on factor-analytic research, both the hierarchical model by Vermon (1950) and Cattell's (1963) theory of ability have shown their cross-cultural applicability, while most of Thurstone's (1938) 'primary mental abilities' have also been recovered in divergent cultural groups (Irvine 1979).

GROUP ACTIVITY

Identify some of the key issues/problems surrounding selection biases.

Trace the steps involved in a comprehensive and bias-free development of a performance criterion of your choice.

Nevertheless, the political and demographic drive to facilitate diversity at work by eliminating selection biases may be challenged by an unspoken, and perhaps even unconscious drive to maintain traditional demographics in the workplace and to accept diversity only in the shallowest of terms. Highly bureaucratic and mechanistic organizations have traditionally thrived on sameness, and the principles of management in the past were generally seen as being based on the concepts of standardization and homogeneity. And the ways in which managers achieve control in the workplace are still seen by many of the major organizational theorists as being based on standardization of work outcomes, work processes or skills. Moreover, 'the desire for social certainty causes decision makers to prefer to work with individuals that they perceive to be similar' (Kanter 1977). Recent studies on 'homophily' or a 'preference for sameness' (for example Ibarra 1993) indicate that there continues to be a 'desire for social certainty' in organizational settings of today.

However, while managers may experience a need for control, this is also accompanied by a need to perform and achieve results. Building a business case for diversity is likely to be one of the most persuasive ways of promoting and encouraging diversity across occupations and hierarchical levels (Cox 1991). Apart from achieving a discrimination-free selection process, training is one of the most widely used strategies in effectively managing diversity in the workplace. Wentling and Palma-Rivas (1998) found that training and education are considered the most effective international diversity initiatives used by multinational corporations. At this end, the present section will examine formal diversity approaches and provide examples from the literature of several successful diversity initiatives in organizations operating in international settings.

GROUP ACTIVITY

Devise a selection process using whichever techniques are most suitable for a particular job you are analysing. From your findings suggest how you might devise a selection process that is free of bias.

APPROACHES TO DIVERSITY TRAINING

Diversity training has been categorized in different ways. One perspective looks at four different classifications: (1) sensitivity training, (2) dissonance creation, (3) cultural awareness, and (4) legal awareness (Nemetz and Christensen 1996).

- *Sensitivity training* is designed to sensitize individuals to feelings provoked by discrimination. Content tactics include separating individuals by characteristics like eye colour, and then arbitrarily discriminating against a group to illustrate the underlying belief that all individuals are hurt by discrimination. For example, men are separated from women, and women are empowered through role-playing to sexually harass men. This strategy is used to illustrate the belief that men victimize women.
- The *dissonance creation* approach is based on purposely creating cognitive dissonance with the hope that the target audience will resolve inconsistencies by changing attitudes and ultimately behaviours. Tactics range from requiring an individual who exhibits initial prejudice to write an essay showing the absurdities of stereotyping, to requiring an individual who shows initial prejudice to debate in favour of the idea that the dominant group is oppressive.
- *Cultural awareness training* provides an exploration of cultural differences. Tactics range from discussing stereotypes and unintentional slights to building consensus on ways to avoid stereotyping. Cultural awareness training also separates the oppressed from the oppressive while encouraging the former to express their feelings to the latter.

Measuring progress in accomplishing the desired outcomes is critical to diversity programme effectiveness. Tsui and Gutek (1999) focus on two broad categories of desired diversity programme outcomes: task and social awareness. Although assessing task outcomes has been an area of focus, along with using organizational performance measures (e.g., increased profit, fewer customer complaints) and demographic indicators (e.g., increased representation of underrepresented groups, reduced turnover), there is a need for assessing the efficacy of programmes regarding social outcome dimensions, such as increased awareness or awareness development. In this sense, how can we measure awareness development?

Cultural awareness is fundamental since the values of a particular culture can generate conflicts forming around the crucial issues of leadership, organization and communication in a company trying to operate as a true diverse organization (Trompenaars 1993). Hampden-Turner and Trompenaars (1994) argue that cultural values might influence our preferences towards how power and authority are distributed, how people and systems come together to get things done, as well as our preferences about the methods and manners of sending and receiving messages. Trompenaars (1993) puts forward a process, which he calls reconciliation, in order to help us work through the conflict and tension that can be caused by cultural differences. When not leaving them in constant tension, he proposes to recreate a dialectical process whereby the opposites are synthesized (as a result of creative thinking) into a new element or attribute. The process begins by recognizing differences; continues by a search for similarities (the questions here are: What do we have in common? What is our common goals?); and creates solutions or outcomes which utilize the most appropriate elements of the opposing cultural dimensions to get acceptance of the policy outcome and implementation.

This process is not so different from the creative synthesis required to discover a 'win–win' solution in negotiation (Fisher and Uri 1981) or the method of dialoguing in conflict resolution (Walton 1987). Managing conflict can mean finding a resolution or controlling the conflict so that its negative consequences are decreased. In this sense, an essential precondition of engaging in this process is a commitment to the ongoing relationship despite the differences and discomfort it causes. This is where the idea of dialogue enters. Dialogue means that the parties directly engage each other and focus on the conflict between them, including aspects of the relationship itself (Walton 1987).

- Finally, *legal awareness* training is based on explaining discrimination laws. Content includes describing various activities that violate the law with an explanation of the consequences of the violation. Content also includes discussing unfairness and bias in laws and the injustice present in white-male-dominated justice systems.

GROUP ACTIVITY

How can self-directed learning on diversity be operationalized in a business setting?

A second perspective identifies five categories of diversity training. These include: (1) introduction to diversity, (2) focused awareness, (3) skill building, (4) sexual or other forms of harassment, and (5) integrated diversity training (Gentile 1995).

1   The first category, *introduction to diversity* and its implications for business generally and one's own firm in particular, is used by 40 per cent of US companies in their training programmes. Introductory training usually includes the presentation of demographic statistics, a brief overview of historical approaches to diversity in organizations, descriptions of distinctions between affirmative action and valuing diversity, provision for basic self-awareness building, and exercises to help individuals see ways in which they may unconsciously harbour and act upon various stereotypes. The purpose of this type of programme is to begin to develop a shared

definition and vocabulary around diversity, to share the organization's rationale and goals, and to create a sense of positive interest in further individual training.

2   The second type of training is in-depth, focused *awareness development*. These programmes feature more individual and small-group interactions. They pursue an understanding of the nature, functions and prevalence of various stereotypes in the organizational setting. Sometimes they will focus on race, gender or particular ethnic groups. The purpose of these programmes is to expand individual under-standing as a means to changing behaviour in relation to other employees and those in the business environment.

3   A third type of training is the *skill-building* workshop. It is increasingly being recog-nized that specific competencies and skills are necessary in order to work success-fully as members of a diverse group. People who are not equipped with these will be less able to develop the integrating group processes that are characteristic of highly effective diverse groups. Developing integrating competencies and skills in a diverse group should not be an attempt to make it more homogeneous; rather these capacities should create a mechanism where individuals can retain their dimensions of diversity (which are inherently valuable for a variety of group tasks), while at the same time avoiding such damaging processes as dysfunctional inter-personal conflict, miscommunication, higher levels of stress, slower decision-making and problems with group cohesiveness. Such a training workshop is designed to teach specific communication skills such as listening across differ-ences, conflict resolution, interviewing, and mentoring with an emphasis on the ways gender, race, culture or other differences may affect the process.

GROUP ACTIVITY

Some organizations have begun exploring structured dialogues on diversity. The theory and practice of dialogue provides a process for opening up conversation that enhances awareness and understanding of controversial and divisive subjects. In the instances of structured dialogue processes, the dialogue process is designed to enhance individual growth through personal development and understanding, rather than focusing on diversity programmes' traditional objective of organizational or work-group effective-ness.

Specify specific skills needed in order to work successfully as members of a diverse group and associate them with relevant theories.

Moreover, Mazneski (1994) uses Blakar's (1984) theory of communication to suggest some important features that trainers should introduce in the design of diversity training programmes. Blakar's theory states that a broad competence for effective integration is achieved through the development of important commu-nication skills. These skills are in turn based on the existence of some key precon-ditions: a shared social reality between group members; an ability to 'decentre' or to consider viewpoints that may differ from one's own; motivation to communi-cate, ability to negotiate and endorse contracts of behaviour and ability to attribute difficulties appropriately. Developing people's abilities to create such preconditions might form the basis of a competence and skills-based training programme. In addition, by helping people to explore these preconditions it is likely that additional knowledge about the contextual requirements of group interaction will be put into practice.

4   Another training technique in this category targets the workshop for specific minority groups within an organization. For example, some companies have developed programmes for middle-management-level women who are trying to counteract the effects of the perceived 'glass ceiling'. This type of programme can have a negative impact if members of the targeted group are perceived as being less prepared than others are to advance within the organization or if the targeted group is perceived as getting special assistance or attention. Some organizations have avoided these problems by having members of the targeted group develop these workshops for other members as a function of a special support network. Skills communicated in such workshops are useful to all employees and may be offered more effectively as part of generally available programmes (Gentile 1995). Finally, training could be provided on sexual or other forms of harassment. Such programmes usually focus on communicating the legal definition of harassment and the organization's policies and practices for dealing with such occurrences. Sometimes these efforts provide discussion where conflicting feelings and concerns about the definition of harassment can be aired.

5   Diversity training can also be provided in the form of integrated diversity training. Such programmes integrate appropriate diversity issues into the course of pre-existing and new training efforts that target specific functional skills or business goals. For example, in a customer-service training programme the particular challenges and opportunities of serving a diverse customer base can be introduced. Integrated efforts such as these are able to continually link diversity to business activities. Integrated diversity training can ensure that diversity issues are raised often and in varying forums, making it more difficult to compartmentalize and dismiss them.

GROUP ACTIVITY

During the skill acquisition process, what kind of things might be found particularly difficult? Why do you think this is? What might aid/hinder the process?

Wentling and Palma-Rivas (1999) identify a large number of goals related to increasing personal multicultural effectiveness. Some of those cited included: provide awareness-building; promote effective intercultural communication; improve morale; build trust in all employees; develop understanding and respect for differences; help employees understand their strengths and weaknesses; reduce differential treatment; and build skills needed to more effectively work within a diverse workplace. Skill training should also be provided with specific information needed to create behaviour changes that are required to effectively manage and work within a diverse workforce.

Some of the goals frequently mentioned by the experts related to increasing organizational effectiveness included: connect the diversity training to the organization's strategic goals; and improve organizational culture. According to diversity experts, an organizational climate that emphasizes fairness, equity and promotes trust, respect and understanding among all employees, motivates individuals to maximize their individual performance and contributions to an organization's mission for effective diversity management.

In summary, the components of effective diversity training programmes may be listed as follows:

1 commitment and support from top management;
2 included as part of the organizational strategic plan;
3 programmes meet the specific needs of the organization;
4 utilize qualified trainers;
5 combine with other diversity initiatives;
6 mandatory attendance;
7 create inclusive programmes;
8 provide trust and confidentiality;
9 require accountability; and
10 conduct evaluation.

Finally, most diversity initiatives (not necessarily the most successful ones) rely almost exclusively on training to instil the concepts and skills needed by the workforce to handle differences (Burkhart 1999). However, the current research cautions against developing training programmes without first creating a strong set of goals to guide the process. Organizations must initially decide if their goal is merely to expand individual awareness of differences, or to change the culture (that is attitudes, values, practices, language, and so on) of the entire organization. From this perspective training is either individually motivated or systems motivated. Individual training is similar to the intercultural training that is conducted by government agencies for their employees overseas, and for employees of transnational organizations. While this type of training acknowledges differences, it does little to evoke significant resistances among participants, and is easily and inexpensively delivered to an audience. The primary disadvantage is that it does not go far enough to encourage any long-term change. It depends on the possibility that individuals will conduct themselves differently once they understand that others may have different worldviews. The primary focus is on empathy as a means of guiding behaviour; skills training is not at the heart of the approach.

GROUP ACTIVITY

Recall an instance of transfer difficulty that you have experienced yourself after a training session. (1) Describe the instance. (2) What were the critical areas of difficulty with transferring your skills/knowledge? What would have facilitated/supported the transfer process in your view? What could you have done better or differently to facilitate transfer?

On the other hand, a systems approach to diversity directly addresses issues of dominance and difference. 'It recognizes that racism, sexism, and other forms of oppression are not just matters of individual bias and prejudice, but have taken root in the culture of the organization at every level' (Burkhart 1999). Unlike the individual training focus, systems training addresses underlying discrimination that often makes for discomfort and resistance on the part of the dominant group. In addition to creating awareness, this format entails important skills training to change the traditional power dynamics in an organization. Because the change is at a cultural level, much of the training is initially targeted from the top down, which assumes there is an up-front commitment from top executives and managers. This programme is a three-part process. The first phase includes developing awareness and building commitment to change. The second phase builds the framework for change at all levels of the organization. Communication is a key channel for successful, continued change. The third phase allows for institutionalization or the integration of the new cultural norms and roles into the organization.

Finally, most studies of successful diversity training efforts find that training is only one component of productive change. Change must be part of an overall strategy that includes defining goals, measuring and assessing change, skills training and accountability (Frost 1999). Thus, top management involvement and support are critical for long-term change as well as embedding training within a larger change effort. Rather than simply committing to valuing diversity, companies must create an atmosphere of inclusion, fairness, openness and empowerment that can support diversity initiatives.

GROUP ACTIVITY

Taking all the points that have been discussed so far, design a holistic programme of diversity management.

EXPATRIATE MANAGERS

It is extremely difficult to ascertain the number of expatriates living in any one country. Figures are unreliable for several reasons: some countries can and do attempt to keep reliable records; other countries are loath to disclose the precise number of nationals living abroad; others might be prone to exaggerate the number for political reasons. Furthermore, expatriates are made up of a very diverse and heterogeneous population of individuals: businessmen and women, diplomats, military personnel and students, as well as a host of others who have left their country of birth for a wide variety of reasons. Hence, research in the area is scattered and limited.

The first issue to be confronted will be to attempt to address the problems and reactions of expatriate managers and discuss the concept of culture shock from a psychological perspective. The important issue of selecting and preparing expatriates for their move will then be considered and different methods for reducing expatriate stress will be discussed.

What are the costs and benefits of international job assignments? How do people adjust to international job assignments? Is there such a thing as the 'international manager'?

Experts talk much about culture shock, which is a sort of shorthand for individuals' early and profound experiences in a new culture. The concept implies that the experience of living in a new culture is an unpleasant surprise or shock, partly because it is unexpected, and partly because it may lead to a negative evaluation of one's own and/or the other culture.

Bock (1970) described culture shock as primarily an emotional reaction that follows from not being able to understand, control and predict another's behaviour. When customary experience no longer seems relevant or applicable, people's usual behavior changes to become 'unusual'. Lack of familiarity with both the physical setting and the social environment have this effect, as do the experiences with the use of time. In this sense, culture shock is seen by a number of writers in the field as a stress reaction where salient psychological and physical rewards are generally uncertain and hence difficult to control or predict. Thus, a person is anxious, confused and apparently apathetic, until he or she has had time to develop a new set of cognitive constructs to understand and enact the appropriate behaviour. In the business world, where for instance a manager has been successful and developed all the requisite skills for dealing with peers, subordinates, supervisors and clients in his/her own culture, all or many of these skills, strategies and techniques may become ineffective or irrelevant in the new culture. Hence, the anxiety and confusion until new techniques, skills and concepts are learned.

Culture shock includes the individual's lack of points of reference, social norms and rules to guide their own actions and understand others' behaviour. This is very similar to the attributes associated with alienation, which include powerlessness, meaninglessness, normlessness, self and social estrangement and social isolation. Certainly, many poorly adapted expats react to their new environment like alienated people do in their native environment. As a result, people seem to lose their self-confidence, trust of other and ability to innovate (Adler 2002).

Most of the investigations of culture shock have been descriptive, in that they have attempted to list the various difficulties that expatriates experience, and their typical reactions. Less attention has been paid to explain for whom the shock will be more or less intense; what determines which reaction a person is likely to experience; how long they remain in a period of shock, and so forth. The literature suggests that all people will suffer culture shock to some extent, which is always thought of as being unpleasant and stressful. However, this assumption needs to be empirically supported. In theory, some people need not experience any negative aspects of shock, instead they may seek out these experiences for their enjoyment, self-development and personal growth (Adler 2002). Culture shock is seen as a transitional experience which can result in the adoption of new values, attitudes and behaviour patterns.

Thus, although different writers have put emphasis on different aspects of culture shock, there is by and large agreement that exposure to new cultures is stressful. Fewer researchers have seen the positive side of culture shock, either for those individuals who revel in exciting and different environments, or for those whose initial discomfort leads to personal growth. The quality and quantity of culture shock has been shown to be related to the amount of difference between the expatriate's culture and the culture of the country they are visiting or working in. These differences refer to the many cultural differences in social beliefs and behaviours.

What kinds of individual differences might impact on expatriates' experiences? How can international assignments be used to enhance management development?

Furnham and Bochner (1986) have offered eight different explanations for culture shock and evaluated the power of each 'theory' to explain the phenomena. Briefly the eight explanations are:

1   Culture shock is the psychology of loss and the phenomenon is akin to that of grief or grieving. Therefore, it is experienced by most people but depends mainly on how much one loved, and was attached to, one's country of origin.
2   Locus of control-type beliefs in fatalism or instrumentation best predict culture shock. The more fatalistic, the less adaptive people are.
3   Social Darwinism or selective migration forces are some of the best predictors of culture shock. That is, the more carefully migrants are self-selected or selected by other forces (economic) for their ability and strength, the better they will be able to adapt.
4   Realistic expectations about what will be encountered are the most important factors in adaptation. The closer the expatriates' expectations about all aspects of their new life and job approximate to reality, the happier they will be.
5   Culture shock should be seen as, and calculated by, negative life events, such that the more actual change people experience and have to adapt to, the more likely it is they will experience culture shock. The sheer number of major life differences experienced is a good (negative) predictor of adaptation and happiness.
6   The better, both quantitatively and qualitatively, one's social support network of friends, family and co-nationals, the better will be one's ability to overcome culture shock.
7   Value differences between native and foreign culture are the most powerful predictors of adaptation and shock. The closer one approaches the fundamental values and behaviours that drive them, the easier it is to adapt.
8   The actual social skills one possesses in dealing with people from the native culture are the best predictors of adaptation and shock.

Furnham and Bochner (1986) attempt to point out the insights and limitations of each 'explanation', favouring the latter four as having most explanatory power. Certainly, each explanation has important implications for how one deals with culture shock and the psychological effects of change and transition.

RECRUITING AND TRAINING EXPATRIATE MANAGERS

For effective performance in overseas work assignments, a lot of researchers have concentrated on how to prepare potential expatriates for overseas transfer. For instance, Lanier (1979) recommends seven steps to be taken in preparing personnel:

1   A well-planned, realistic pre-visit to the site (country).
2   Early language training prior to departure.
3   Intensive study on issues such as history, culture and etiquette.
4   The provision of country-specific handbooks, including useful facts.
5   Efficient, explicit provision of intercompany counselling facilities.
6   Meeting returnees for 'old-hand' tips.
7   Notification of personnel office and spouses' committee on arrival.

Sievenking *et al.* (1981) stress the importance of orientation programmes prior to expatriation, which aim to do such things as:

■   Develop an understanding of personal and family values so that employees can anticipate and cope with the inevitably unsettling emotions that accompany culture shock.

- Develop an appreciation of the important ways in which the host culture will differ from the employee's own culture, so that the employee can guide his or her behaviour accordingly.

- Show the expatriate how he or she can be rewarded in ways in addition to income and travel, such as novelty, challenge and the opportunity to learn new skills.

- Help expatriates anticipate and begin to plan for hardships, delays, frustrations, material inconveniences and the consequences of close living and working with others.

- Help expatriates to anticipate that, although they may have been superior employees in their own culture, they may need to gain greater satisfaction from experiences other than those that are work-related.

In a more considered and thoughtful paper on the selection and training of personnel for overseas, Tung (1981) outlines a contingency approach and notes four types of factors crucial to success in foreign assignments: technical competence on the job; relational abilities (social skills); ability to deal with environmental constraints (government, labour issues); and the family situation.

Tung outlines five types of training programmes: area studies (giving extensive background knowledge); culture assimilation (testing cross-cultural communication); language training; sensitivity training (focusing on affect); and field experiences in a microculture. These programmes have very different emphases and can be costly and inefficient. A study of 26 organizations showed that many used language training and environmental briefing (both non-psychological), but very few used a culture assimilator (a training programme examining cultural differences in attribution), sensitivity training or field experience.

Tung offers a contingency approach of coping with the process based on a sensitive selection process. He argues that no one test, selection criterion or training programme is appropriate for all job categories, and a contingency framework states that in practice there is no one criterion that could be used in all situations. Rather, each assignment should be viewed on its own. In each instance, the selection of the 'right person' to fill the position should be made only after a careful analysis of the task (in terms of interaction with the social community) and the country of assignment (in terms of the degree to which it is similar/dissimilar to that of the home country), and the personality characteristics of the candidate (in terms of the candidate's and spouse's ability to live and work in a different cultural environment) (1981, pp. 77–8).

Many articles quite recently have concentrated specifically on multinational corporate policies for expatriates, most of which appear to accept, somewhat uncritically, lists of traits and abilities that supposedly distinguish successful expatriate managers. It is uncertain to what extent there is research to support these lists, or indeed whether they are simply hypotheses or 'intuitions'. Moreover, there are more serious problems: how to measure these variables, the relationship between them, which are the most powerful predictors of which expatriate behaviour, and so on. Nevertheless, such attempts to understand the problem do provide a rich source of hypotheses which one may test.

More recently, in an empirical study, Harvey (1989) looked at the problems in repatriating corporate expatriate executives. In his study of over 175 members, less than a third had repatriation programmes, although over three-quarters had programmes before expatriation. Those programmes that did exist tended to stress legal, organizational and economic issues rather than 'psychological' issues and problems. The disorientation and dissatisfaction experienced by many expatriates indicates that the issue of selecting and preparing both ex- and repatriates is at last meriting the attention and research it deserves for many reasons, not least of which is the cost of poor decision-making.

One major aim of preparing expatriates is to prevent or correct stereotypes of other people or countries. Stereotypes, like other forms of categories, can be helpful or harmful depending on how we use them. Effective stereotyping allows people to understand and act appropriately in new situations. A stereotype may be helpful when it is:

- consciously held: the person should be aware that they are describing a group norm rather than the characteristics of a specific individual;
- descriptive rather than evaluative: the stereotype should describe what people from this group will probably be like (actual behaviour) and not evaluate those people as good or bad;
- accurate: the stereotype should accurately describe the norm for the group to which the person belongs;
- the first best guess about a group prior to having direct information about the specific person or persons involved;
- modified: based on further observation and experience with the actual people and situations. To this extent, however, it is not a stereotype.

REDUCING EXPATRIATE STRESS

Attempts to reduce ex- and repatriate stress and to improve the skills and coping mechanisms of those preparing to move have been at the centre of research in this area. Opinions differ as to which is the most effective method. Few would disagree with the idea that men and women working in culturally different environments require some sort of orientation programmes, and many techniques are available which differ according to theoretical orientation, length and type of training, and personnel involved. For instance, Brislin (1979) has listed five non-mutually exclusive programmes: self-awareness training (in learning about the cultural basis of one's own behaviour); cognitive training (in being given various facts about other cultures); attribution training (learning the explanation of behaviour from the point of view of people in other cultures); behaviour modification (individuals are asked to analyse the aspects of their culture that they find rewarding or punishing); and experiential learning (actively participating in realistic simulation). Furnham and Bochner (1986) have examined some of these in greater detail, as follows:

Information giving

The most common type of cross-cultural orientation usually involves providing prospective expatriates with specific information about their new culture. Prospective expatriates are presented with all sorts of facts and figures, about topics such as the climate, food, religious customs and anything else the trainer may consider important. However, the effectiveness of such illustrative programmes is limited in four ways. First, the facts are often too general to have any clear and specific application, except when discussing tax or organizational structure; secondly, the facts emphasize the exotic, yet tend to ignore the mundane but more commonly occurring happenings; thirdly, such programmes give the false impression that a culture can be learned in a few easy lessons, whereas all that they mostly convey is an often misleading and superficial picture, which does not reveal the culture's hidden agenda; and, finally, even if the facts are remembered, they do not necessarily lead to action, or to the current action. If cognitive informational training is to be of any particular use, it must be combined with some sort of particular experiential learning in the appropriate setting – amusing lectures, helpful guidebooks and well-prepared videos are not enough.

Cultural sensitization

Programmes based on this approach set out to provide trainees with information about other cultures, as well as how to heighten their awareness about the cultural bias of their own behaviour, and how the practices of their society differ from those of the host country. The aim is therefore to compare and contrast the different cultures, look at various behaviours from the perspective of each society, and thus develop a sensitivity to, and awareness of, cultural relativity. This view holds that very few human values, beliefs and behaviours are absolute and universal, and that what a particular individual believes to be good and true will depend on the norms prevailing in that person's society, norms that other societies may reject. Such programmes often operate at two levels: they aim to achieve self-awareness about the modal values and attitudes that are typically held by members of one's own society; and to gain insight into one's own personal traits, attitudes and prejudices. Cultural sensitization and self-awareness programmes, being essentially cognitive techniques, suffer from many of the same limitations as information-giving.

> **?** What are the limitations of each approach?

Intercultural (social) skills training

Although there are various different approaches to social skills training, they share various elements in common. The first is an assessment or diagnosis of a particular problem (for example assertiveness) or situations (for example chairing meetings) that the person has or is likely to encounter. The second stage is an analysis or discussion of the elements in these problem areas, possibly followed by a modelling exercise where a trainer enacts the role. This is turn is followed by a role-play by the trainee, with critical feedback at length following each practice. The number, range and variety of contexts in which the role-plays are enacted add to the generalizability of the training. Trainees are also encouraged to do homework exercises between role-play and feedback sessions.

The advantages of the intercultural skills approach include the following:

■ Training procedures are based on a specific theory, thereby avoiding vague statements about 'mutual understanding' and instead emphasizing behavioural skill deficits.

■ 'Practical' aspects are covered in the sense that the approach has at its centre everyday, common, as well as business, situations which, nevertheless, cause friction, misunderstanding and interpersonal hostility. This avoids vague statements about culture shock by attempting to quantify social difficulty on various dimensions and then reduce it.

The disadvantage of this approach is that, because of the systematic nature of such programmes, they are likely to cost more, intrude into and disrupt the activities of the institution whose members are being trained, and require an interdisciplinary team of trainers.

GROUP ACTIVITY

Identify a problem of your choice that an expatriate is likely to encounter and design an intercultural skills intervention taking into consideration both structural and psychological dimensions. What are its objectives? Who and how will it be managed?

Finally, Black *et al.* (1992) have come up with various important policy explanations for dealing with expatriate businessmen and women. For instance, in order to prevent employees 'going native', they recommend only a limited time away from the organization; sending only managers with strong organizational ties, and having good sponsor links. On the other hand, to avoid sending managers who 'leave their hearts at home' and do not adapt, it is preferable to send younger managers, facilitate cross-cultural adjustment and provide cross-cultural training. The ultimate aim of any organization should be to create 'dual-national' or 'multinational' citizens who need to be carefully selected, trained and rewarded.

Case study 7

THE AGENCY

The organization is a 3,200-employee US government agency, whose mission is scientific and extremely technical in nature. A primary focus and priority is given to technical issues. Technical proficiency is highly valued, and the Agency has enjoyed a history of leading in technical competence. The high focus on technical competence has greatly de-emphasized the importance of 'people' issues, leaving the perception that mediocrity on people issues is acceptable. As a result, the Agency has faced difficulty in recruiting and retaining employees. This compounds the issue of not having a representative workforce, and has brought the larger issue of workforce diversity to the forefront. A 1997 employee-opinion survey and focus groups conducted in 1998 and 1999 also increased attention to diversity issues.

Since 1997, the Agency has conducted many diversity-programme initiatives, addressing all three areas of diversity-programme objectives (e.g., demographic representation, awareness and sensitivity, systemic culture change). Specific initiatives have included training programmes; the establishment of a multicultural advisory team; the initial development and timely revision of a diversity management plan; diversity 'celebrations' with educational speakers, ethic food, and entertainment representing different cultures; and several seminars that dealt with specific aspects of diversity in the workplace. At the same time, human resource development (HRD) officers responsible for the implementation of the diversity initiatives identified a number of values and ideologies that assisted the success of these initiatives.

■ **Viewing managing diversity as a priority**. Managing diversity was the priority for the government Agency to convey the message that actions are taken in the best interests of the effectiveness of the teams of the company and the organization as a whole.

Leaders were evaluated for their success in building and maintaining a diverse workforce. Doing so underlined the intelligence of efforts to develop appropriate skills in working with multinational staff. Equally, the agency realized that they should embed multinational leadership skills at lower organizational levels acknowledging their strategic significance. This reality required senior leaders to mentor subordinates and model the skills and sensitivities that enhance multinational team cohesion. The importance of having a strategic plan for the success of their diversity initiatives was recognized by everyone in the organization. Strategic planning led to the success of diversity initiatives because it provided guidance, made management staff reactive, and avoided shortsightedness. Moreover, strategic planning emphasized the development of long-term initiatives, avoiding the danger of having 'one-shot' diversity initiatives that are likely to disappear with time. The importance of strategic planning was reflected in the words of the HRD officer: 'Strategic planning did not allow diversity initiatives to become a fad.'

■ **Learn from other organizations but import with care**. Throughout the organization, there was the strong belief that there is no single recipe for managing diversity and that what works in one organization with a different staff profile in terms of culture may not work in another organization. In this sense, strategies for managing diversity had to be focused in consideration of the particular organization's needs and personnel. Leaders championed the implementation of diversity initiatives. Top leaders played an important role in diversity initiatives through their guidance and continuous support. They influenced implementation of new policies and facilitated information flow at all levels. Leaders at lower levels likewise could see the new measures put into practice, serving as models for other staff. Moreover, the diversity initiatives were integrated into the organization's goals and prior-

ities and there was a clear link of the diversity initiatives to the agency's strategic plan. The HRD officers had to coordinate several initiatives simultaneously and they argued: 'Diversity initiatives really do work, but they do not stand alone. If you implement just one initiative, you are not going to get the rest of what needs to happen; meaning, you don't have the good foundation in place.'

■ **Have people personally committed to diversity**. 'I think what has been successful is the energy and the commitment you get from people in the organization. We have people that at different levels wanted to be involved because they are really committed and recognize the importance of respect and inclusion. Because they are committed, they can also connect diversity with its impact on teams, and also can understand how important it is for an organization to utilize everybody. We have people functioning as champions in the workplace and they are really trying to raise issues around diversity whenever they can.'

■ **Provide training as an ongoing education process and set high expectations for all staff**. Well-designed training was necessary to promote and maintain a workforce. Research suggests the importance of training in managing and valuing diversity in order to increase awareness of diversity-related issues such as cultural biases and cross-cultural sensitivity, and in building essential skills for cultural interactions. The aim here was to promote behaviour change in favour of chosen organizational/operation/team values rather than attempting to change personal beliefs, and to find ways to encourage cooperation despite differences. Training and education was considered an effective tool to assist in removing barriers, such as people not understanding the value of diversity, slow involvement, resistance to change and unwillingness to participate. Diversity training was a way to communicate the importance of diversity and its impact on the organization. Communicating the value of diversity was reported as a way of preventing failure of diversity initiatives.

■ **Listen and watch, patiently**. Understanding others involves taking the time to actively listen and to watch for potential cultural factors that may be interfering with a member's ability to function successfully. Moreover, recent work with international organizations points to the role of patience as an important quality of global leaders.

■ **Emphasize the importance of trust**. Dialogue between members of a multinational workforce is a process of learning rather than a product of conflict statements. As people with different values, beliefs and traditions come together in dialogues, they rely on each other for help in their struggle through their biases and assumptions. Because this was sensitive and could be threatening at times, the extent to which people were comfortable with sharing and learning depended clearly on their perception of psychological safety in their group/team.

■ **Organizational policies should not interfere with diversity initiatives**. HRD professionals indicated that at the beginning out-dated organizational policies did not accommodate the changes taking place in the diversity workplace and did not allow the proper implementation of the diversity initiatives. In this sense, the Agency had to revise organizational policies and procedures that supported diversity and helped the organizational culture continually adapt in response to the changing workforce. Moreover, the agency had to reconsider the organizational context and the organization of task and reward structures in order to promote interpersonal cooperation and coordination.

■ **Be prepared to implement organizational change**. The strategic management team of the agency followed specific steps in implementing fundamental changes in how the organization operated for diversity initiatives to be successful: (a) they established a sense of urgency by relating external environmental realities to real and potential crises and opportunities facing their organization; (b) they formed a powerful coalition of individuals who embraced the need for change and who could rally others to support the effort; (c) they created a vision to accomplish the desired end-result; (d) they communicated the vision through numerous communication channels, and (e) they empowered others to act on to the vision by changing structures, systems, policies and procedures in ways that facilitated implementation.

■ **Watch out for backlash**. Finally, diversity programmes had to be carefully evaluated and their performance and fit to the Agency's strategic objectives had to be assessed at different critical points. The strategic team planned for and created short-term wins by publicizing success and building momentum for continued change. At the same time, they consolidated improvements and changed structures, systems, procedures and policies that were not consistent with the vision. Finally, they managed to institutionalize the new approaches by publicizing the connection between the change management of the diversity initiatives and organizational success.

Case study discussion topics

Reflecting on the case study above and the theoretical discussions in the chapter answer the following questions:

1 If you were the training director of a large corporation, what steps would you take to maximize transfer of diversity training among your employees?

2 What is the role of the wider supporting organizational context and culture on the effectiveness of diversity training initiatives?

3 What elements of the organizational context and organizational structure could support the successful implementation of diversity training initiatives?

SUMMARY

This chapter has explored the operational aspects of diversity management principles in the key human resource functions of recruitment and selection, training and development, with which an organization can effectively manage workforce diversity. The chapter then turns our attention to the increasing number of specialists and managers specially selected by their companies to take their particular skills abroad. Reviewing the relevant literature, the problems and reactions of expatriate managers who work in foreign countries have been explored, underlining the need for effective selection and training policies and programmes for expatriates and exploring the main issues behind the development of effective methods in selecting and training expatriate managers.

Chapter eight

International Careers

Yehuda Baruch

Case study by Yehuda Baruch, D.J. Steele
and G.A. Quantrill

Learning outcomes

After reading this chapter you should be able to:

- Understand individual perspectives of international careers.
- Relate to organizational management of careers within the global context.
- Analyse theoretical frameworks of international management of HRM.
- Identify the variety of strategic options for managing expatriation and repatriation.
- Understand the impact of organizational IHRM on obtaining and retaining its people globally.

INTRODUCTION

Today, most of the corporations listed in *Fortune 500* have global operations in a considerable number of countries. The leading ones, most notably IBM, are typically used to demonstrate the archetype of global corporation. Nevertheless, most of the companies which operate globally come from around the globe, not all are American, not all are as large as IBM. Still, all need to manage their human resources internationally. As will be demonstrated in this chapter, the IBM model is not necessarily the best strategy for them to follow.

The processes of moving out from a country-based to a global-based operation are reflected in a shift in career systems and their management. Career paths cross national borders, and this implies a complexity of the system, coupled with a need for flexibility from both individuals and their employing organizations.

INTERNATIONAL CAREERS

MacLuhan (1960) introduced the label 'global village' into modern management and everyday jargon. Forty years later, many companies indeed perceive the globe rather than their home country as their playing field. This implies for the business, the market, and the labour market. Operating across geographical borders on a regular basis has become the rule rather than the exception, in particular for large, 'blue chip' companies. From a career-management perspective, this means that people need to manage and be managed beyond both geographical and cultural boundaries. Few would challenge what has by now become the 'bread and butter' of MNCs executive careers. Global managers are needed to provide answers for the challenges of global management (Cornelius 1999, p. 215; Sparrow and Hiltrop 1997). Firms look for such 'global' managers, be they 'home', 'host' or 'third-country' nationals.

It is important to unpack some of these terms. Home country is the country where the main operation was established, where the headquarters of the firm is situated, and where strategies are defined. In short, where the control is. Moreover, the distinct organizational culture is determined or strongly influenced by the home-company (and national) culture. It is typical that employees, mostly managers and professionals, who work in the home country, will be sent as expatriates to the host countries, as companies seek to expand their operations across national borders and as global competitiveness intensifies (Arthur and Bennett 1995; Drucker 1999, p. 61). Host countries are countries where the home company ('mother company') operates. They will employ mostly local, host-country nationals (and some expatriates). There may also be some employees who are 'third-country' nationals – people who moved from an altogether different country to work for the company. Some of them may have moved from an operation in one host country to another host country. Companies invest in the development of future global leaders who understand the operation of diverse teams and who take up the challenge of cross-border mobility (Conner 2000), in order to ensure competitiveness in the international market. Of course, not every manager is expected to be international, but 'a small core of international employees will be key to a successful globalization' (Shackleton and Newell 1997 p. 82).

One clear definition missing in the literature of international management of people is that of a 'Global Manager'. Practically, there could be several meanings to this label:

(a)   An expatriate manager (Black and Gregersen 1999);
(b)   A manager who works across borders (Bartlett and Ghoshal 1992); or simply
(c)   A manager in a company that operates across borders.

The last option is too all-encompassing, making the majority of large firms' employees 'global managers'. The first two, however, are valid to a certain extent, and indicate a distinction which exists between the expatriate, the globetrotter and the 'travelling manager' (Baruch 2004). The expatriate is an employee who works in an overseas subsidiary of a company, for a considerable period of time, and is usually accompanied by direct family (when it exists); the 'travelling manager' is a manager who operates across borders as a routine, but has a base in one country, usually the country where the core operation and the headquarters are located. In their roles within MNCs, they need to hop among different locations around the globe. Moving from the firm level to the general global village, we can see many other 'specimens' or categories of global managers, such as agents, merchants, solicitors, who perceive the whole world as their field of operation.

ARE THERE GENERIC OR SPECIFIC INDIVIDUAL CHARACTERISTICS OF GLOBAL MANAGERS?

Some scholars have tried to define what a global manager is. Borg and Harzing (1995) attempted to profile the 'international manager' using both Tung's (1981) and Mendenhall and Oddou's (1985) criteria. According to Tung, there are four groups of variables that determine success of a global manager. These are (a) technical knowledge and job skills; (b) interpersonal relationships; (c) ability to cope with environmental constrains; and lastly (d) the family situation. Mendenhall and Oddou referred to a different set of dimensions: self-orientation (including self-esteem and self-confidence); features that enhance a manager's capability to interact effectively with host-nationals; the ability to perceive what the locals have in mind; and the ability to deal with cultures that are very different from their own.

In contrast, Baruch (2002) claims that these as well as other possible sets of variables that define success for international managers are essential for the success of all managers, both local and international, thus concluding that 'there is no such thing' as a global manager. Still Baruch recognizes that there is what he termed, a 'global mind-set', the readiness and willingness to work within a global environment, to accept differences, and benefit from such diversity. Baruch argues that while the concept of globalization is a contemporary business reality, the idea that there is a certain template into which one should fit in order to be a successful global manager is flawed. If one would try to profile an 'international manager' in terms of personality (for example *The Big Five*, Goldberg 1990), it would be difficult or impossible to point out specific attributes that will distinguish a person more inclined to succeed in an international career from those who are doomed to fail. It seems that, all in all, what can make an individual a 'global manager' is more a state of mind, which embodies an openness and willingness to cross borders – geographical and cultural – as part of their career (Baruch 2004). As a result, it is not surprising to find that global assignments present managers with great challenges, and that HR procedures to identify and select people for international assignments are not readily available.

Can you be a global manager? Do you wish to be a global manager? Does your organization need you to be a global manager?

What qualities and specific circumstances that you believe you possess would make you a successful global manager? What qualities and specific circumstances that you believe you possess might prevent you from becoming a successful global manager?

Are these your inner qualities? Your job-related competences? Your personal and family status and circumstances? Will you be interested in global assignment(s)? What can you gain from them?

Are you working for a global organization? Does your organization prefer to use home- or host- (or third-) country national managers?

PSYCHOLOGICAL CONTRACTS, NEW PSYCHOLOGICAL CONTRACTS, AND GLOBAL PSYCHOLOGICAL CONTRACTS: CAREER PATHS AND CAREER PROSPECTS IN MNCS

Today's business and economic environments are characterized by perpetual changes, one of which is the blurring of business-related borders. As businesses operate around the globe, so do people, and hence career systems are not restricted by geography. The organization needs to choose and keep the right mixture of employees for global assignments, and part of the process is the need to develop new psychological contracts in line with contemporary business culture (Rousseau 1996).

The idea of a psychological contract was originally suggested by Levinson and his colleagues in the early 1960s (Levinson, Price, Munden, Mandl and Solley 1962). In layman's terms, the psychological contract is 'The unspoken promise, not present in the small print of the employment contract, of what an employer gives, and what employees give in return' (Baruch and Hind 1999). It refers to the informal reciprocal agreements between employers and employees. Such a contract is fundamentally different from the formal, legal employment contracts in their context and expected impact. The concept was reintroduced to organizational studies and developed later by Kotter (1973), Nicholson (1985) and others. A change in the psychological contracts occurred in the 1990s, with new business realities within the context of transition creating new psychological contracts (Rousseau 1996; Robinson and colleagues, 1994, 1995).

The issue of global HRM, in particular of expatriation, can be placed within the framework of the psychological contract and the emerging new psychological contracts (Guzzo, Nooman and Elron 1994). Viewed from this theoretical perspective, expatriation is a specific case of the employment relationship. Guzzo *et al.* argue that these relationships will be relational rather than transactional, and the nature of the relationship might also be influenced by individual characteristics. However, the direction of the impact is not simplistic or linear. For example, Baruch (2004) noted that age may have two contradictory directions; that is, young people, especially without children, may agree for expatriation more willingly; and again, older people whose children have left home may be more mobile (unless caring for elderly), while middle-aged people might find it problematic. Such U-shaped relationships are not simple for detection. Moreover, age is associated with the level of hierarchy, and people destined for expatriation are typically senior members of staff. To add to the complexity, not too many top executives are required to lead overseas operations, but rather a number of mid-level managers take on such roles.

Gender and marital status are further individual demographic factors considered relevant to global HRM. Ample evidence indicates that most expatriates are men, and Markham (1987) has noted that women are less willing to accept relocation, a tendency that could be stronger when overseas relocation is involved. Organizations need to be realistic in assigning female managers to overseas posts. In certain cultures female managers may face barriers in the shape of local employees who might be reluctant to collaborate, or even legal obstacles for employment. However, as the Japanese case shows (Taylor and Napier 1996), the argument is not that simple. Taylor and Napier suggested a plausible explanation for their finding that American female expatriate managers were fully accepted by the local businesses. Their argument was that in Japan, US female managers were accepted first as professionals, as American and as managers, and less as females, practically eliminating the gender bias one might expect in the Japanese context which is characterized by persistent forms of gender segregation.

In today's society, career systems must accommodate marital status as well as caring responsibilities of employees. This is clearly relevant for expatriation, when several different factors may pose an obstacle for overseas assignments. Dual-career couples, single parents, people with care responsibilities for elderly relatives or with teenage children pose challenges for the system. A study on the issue of selecting dual-career couple employees for international assignments (Harvey 1996) found their relational commitments to pose a major obstacle for employees' readiness and willingness to accept expatriation. For dual-career couples, the implications of international assignment for one would severely disrupt the career prospects of the other. If both are professional or managers, they will find it hard for one of them to leave their job or to trail a spouse while the other is on assignment. In the past, a typical case would have been to send the male managers to international assignments while their wives were placed in secretarial roles. Today it is difficult to find suitable roles to answer the career aspirations of highly educated dual-career couples.

Bearing in mind the domestic and cultural considerations together, the case of immigration can also be relevant in the context of global management. Leong and Hartung (2000) indeed included the issue of immigration and the way multicultural communities interact within a different cultural realm. Focusing on people of Chinese origin who grew up in a Western culture, they discuss the way career interventions (for example counselling) would be influenced by the target population, and argue for the need to move from a multiculturalism based on demographics to one based on mind-sets.

A combination of individual values and needs, organizational approaches (see further) and national culture is manifested in Baruch's (1995) push–pull model. This model is based on Lewin's field theory (1951), and takes into account the economic, legal and cultural realms (see Figure 8.1). Whenever an expatriation-related decision needs to be made, which involves a move across borders, there will be two forces operating within the employee' mind, in conflicting directions. One is to pull the employee into moving to the new place, and the other one to push him or her back. Each person will make the decision according to the strength of these forces, and these forces operate in all three realms. For example, the organization may increase the pull factor by offering high economic incentives or by indicating the positive implications for future career prospects. A push factor might be a strong dislike to the culture of the host country, or even its physical climate. There are many legal constrains relating to the movement of people across borders, such as the need for a work permit, or which people can work in specific countries. Cultural forces can pull people too – for those looking for adventure, some exotic places would have an appeal, whereas for other people the same place may cause resentment. Thus organizations need to analyse in advance the prospects of people accepting or refusing global assignments, according to the prospects of their expected agreeableness for such moves.

Figure 8.1   *Push and pull model*

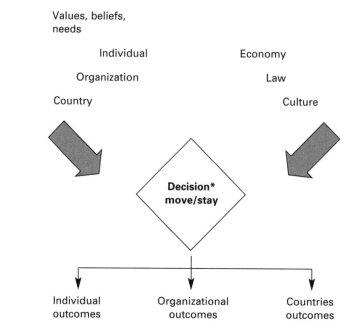

Values, beliefs,
needs

Individual   Economy

Organization   Law

Country   Culture

Decision*
move/stay

Individual   Organizational   Countries
outcomes   outcomes   outcomes

* Can be taken in each level – usually the person.

Source: Baruch (1995, p.316).

Assuming you will work for a global enterprise. After two successful years in a managerial role, you will be asked to take up an assignment for two or three years in,

1   The USA – will you agree willingly, will you agree reluctantly? Will you refuse such expatriation?
2   Tanzania – will you agree willingly, will you agree reluctantly? Will you refuse such expatriation?
3   Russia – will you agree willingly, will you agree reluctantly? Will you refuse such expatriation?

Explain your reasons for each case.

Different national managerial cultures

There is an assumption that national cultures and conventions would not necessary be applied or easily translated elsewhere. A vivid example relevant to international career management is the question, 'Which are the most important criteria for managers to gain success?' Schneider and Barsoux (1997, p. 144) compared and contrasted different answers. They argue that, in the US culture, the right answer is drive and ability. In France, it would be whether or not the manager attended one of the *Grand École* for their studies. The German model emphasizes technical and functional competence, whereas in the UK what matters is classical education and a generalist approach. The Japanese approach values qualifications from top universities, compliance and loyalty (this may be relevant also to other Far Eastern societies). As a result, arguably, the development of career systems must take into account such differences, and even then the managers will face challenges that stem from sub-cultural factors such as differences in their managerial cultures and assumptions.

The Hamburger Discipline

The following illustrative case was provided by Dan W., an American executive who worked for Mobil Oil (now Exxon-Mobil) as an expatriate in several countries, including Japan, Germany, the UK and, of course, the USA. It illustrates the diversity of metaphorical hamburgers that global managers experience in different national contexts:

When you work in the US and make a mistake, your manager will call you up to his/her office. At first you will be told something along the lines 'we know how good you are, valued by the company, and that usually your work is fine'. (Lower bun). Then will come the 'meat':

'Yesterday you have acted in such and such manner, which is not according to our policy . . .' and so on. So a warning or comment will be entered into the file. Then the manager will say 'we do know that it was a one-off event, and we value your work, and wish to leave this behind us'. That is the upper bun. You got your 'balanced' hamburger.

However, if you work in Germany, most probably your manager will call you up to his/her office, and will tell you exactly and to the point: 'Yesterday you have acted in such and such a manner, which is not according to our policy . . .'. So a warning or comment will be entered into your file'. That's it. Just 'meat'.

On the other hand, if this would happen in Japan, your manager will call you up to his (probably not her) office, and will tell you something along the lines 'we know how good you are, valued by the company, and that usually your work is fine'. Then he will go on, praising your work, providing more nice positive comments, and will send you out (just the buns). Nevertheless, you will know, you will know indeed, why you were called up.

What are the implications of the Hamburger metaphor in international management of HR and careers?

Source: Baruch (2004).

First, within each country, people can well recognize the method of disciplinary action, and how severe it may be. Second, these methods are highly dependent on the national culture. Third, if managers are unaware of such differences, a problem will emerge when people from different cultures are working together. Imagine that a manager with the German culture orientation is placed in a Japanese company, and is called for the Japanese version of a disciplinary procedure. He or she will probably never get the message. Or even worse, a Japanese manager stationed in Germany is

Table 8.1   *Borg's (1988) classification of stages of expatriation*

	Single global assignment	Multiple global assignments
Ending up abroad	Naturalized	Cosmopolitan orientation
Ending up at home	Local orientation	Unsettled

told off 'the German way' by the local manager – this might lead to immediate departure of the worker or other severe consequences.

Of course, the Americans feel that their way is the right one (at least one must admit that it is balanced). But the question is not who is right. What matters is that the message needs to be delivered and understood, wherever the company operates. Waiting until after the assignment might be too late. Cross-cultural training before an assignment takes place is essential, and a one-off workshop will not be sufficient for more than raising awareness.

Moving on from the metaphorical illustration of cultural differences, the typical progression in and out of organizations varies significantly across countries. As presented above, in the UK and the USA, people may enter the organization either to the rank and file, and then develop their careers from within, or directly take up managerial positions (for example via graduate recruitment) and develop, or be headhunted into executive positions. In Germany and Japan the entry point will almost exclusively be to the lower echelons. In Japan, congruence, compliance and obedience are crucial for promotion. In many Western cultures being confrontational (such as playing the Devil's advocate) is a better way to introduce oneself to top management.

The problem for global management of careers is that the same multinational company operates across a variety of cultures and career systems, and still needs to obtain and retain the right people, applying a set of coherent policies and 'best practices'. However, 'best practice' in one place may not be considered as such in another. Thus one major challenge for international career management is to become 'Glocal' – being global in strategy, but adaptive to local situations, finding the right balance across the different operations, and setting a policy that will take into account the strategy of the organization as well as the local requirements. Another major challenge is the management of expatriates and their expatriation and repatriation process.

Is finding a person for an international assignment a sufficient consideration? Not according to Borg (1988), who looked at the stages involved in the process of expatriation. He identified four categories for such a classification (Table 8.1). The interesting outcome of his study is that only 38 per cent of the 200 managers he examined had only a single global assignment and returned to their homeland and home organization. The rest either stayed in the country where they were sent (25%), or moved to a global career with several consecutive global assignments; either staying abroad (22%) or returning home (15%) after such multiple assignments.

WHAT IS FAILURE, HOW MANY FAIL?

One indication for the problem career systems face when dealing with international assignments relates to failure. The literature indicates that failure rates are high.

Failure may be defined as early return, poor performance on assignment and lack of learning from the international experience. Several studies have tried to analyse the failure rate of expatriation, but one problem with these studies is the lack of clear identification of the meaning of failure. As indicated above, some studies consider early return or preplanned departure from the role as failure, but a more comprehensive approach should take into account the level of performance (or lack of it) while on assignment. Lastly, a wider approach would also take into account repatriation failure, and an overarching definition of failure should include leaving the company after repatriation, as Black and Gregersen (1999) argue. Leaving the organization soon after repatriation imposes both a heavy cost and business risk (Selmer 1998), may amount to significant numbers – as much as half of the expatriates, as reported by Baruch, Steele and Quantrill (2002). Their findings are in line with the revelation of the phenomenon that between 30 to 40 per cent of expatriates leave their companies within two years of repatriation (Dowling, Schuler and Welch 1994; Stroh 1995).

In addition, the context of the host country of the MNC will have an impact on the prevalence, the nature and the level of success/failure of expatriation. A possible interpretation for the discrepancy in the literature on failure rates may be due to perceived and real differences among cultures. There is empirical evidence that failure rates in Europe and Japan are lower than those for US companies (Tung 1988; Scullion 1991; Harzing and Ruysseveldt 1996), and one of the possible explanations is the preparation process and the level of training that companies provide.

Repatriation

One of the problems that people may suffer upon return is termed a reversed cultural shock (RCS) (Rodrigues 1996). Under such a phenomenon a person returning to his or her home country and home organization can suffer a different cultural shock than that experienced on expatriation. The reasons are dual: people change, in particular through being exposed to different ways of doing things which they may appreciate better than the old ways in the home country. Second, the home country and the organization may have moved in certain directions while the expatriate was away. Culture, equipment, people, procedures and more can be altered within a time period of three to four years, typical for expatriation.

Several factors may influence the emergence of RCS. At the individual level these may be issues of age, gender, marital status (as demographic factors), profession, tenure, career stage, past experience in expatriation, and level in the hierarchy (as organizational and professional issues). At the organizational level, issues such as training, mentoring, policies, socialization procedures and the intensity of contact during expatriation would influence the prospects of RCS. A strong RCS may lead to premature exit from the organization, or lower levels of satisfaction and performance, which can be coupled with a long adjustment period. A smooth repatriation process would lead to quick readjustment, increased satisfaction, and willingness for further expatriation in the future. The level of the cultural gap between the home and host countries can play a significant role in both the type of shock and the level of expectations.

GROUP ACTIVITY

Imagine that you are preparing yourself for the repatriation surprise. What will you do if, upon repatriation, you find that:

■ Most of your former peers and superiors have left while you were away.
■ You have been deleted from the HR system.
■ Your place in the career development system has been taken by others.
■ The role formerly designated to you for your return has disappeared due to restructuring.
■ You cannot easily readapt yourself (and family) to cultural changes that have happened at home.
■ Your job is no longer involved with strategy-making – you have returned to become a small cog in the machine of operations.
■ Your mentor has moved elsewhere or quit.

Now, what will you do, *while on expatriation*, to *prevent* the above or their consequences from occurring?

Whatever may be the cause for expatriate failure, its costs for the employer are considerably high compared to failure in a local, conventional job. The real cost should relate to the lost training, the relocation costs, and to the indirect costs of loss of reputation and further difficulties in finding a replacement.

From the individual to the organizational level: relevance for career systems

Three organizational models of global management of people will be discussed in this section: these are models developed by Perlmuter (1969); Bartlett and Ghoshal (1989); and Baruch and Altman (2002). The earlier part of this chapter dealt with the issue from an individual perspective, but expatriation is more a managerial issue that should be cared for as part of an organizational career system. Moreover, some of the concerns relating to expatriation relate to the national level, including its legal system. It is the combination of economic and social factors which has caused global competition to increase and global operations to widen their scope. Subsequently, there has emerged a surge and acceleration of labour movement and traffic in the shape of expatriation and repatriation (Laurent 1986; Porter 1989; Porter and Tansky 1999). Moving on from the individual issues, the organizational level of analysis provides a different perspective to the management of international careers and the introduction of international assignments to the portfolio of organizational posts.

One seminal classification of strategic approaches to global management strategy was offered by Perlmutter (1969), who differentiates among global organizational configurations: *ethnocentric* (home-country oriented), *polycentric* (host-country oriented) and *geocentric* (worldwide-oriented) orientations. Later, Heenan and Perlmutter (1979) added the *regiocentric* option. The reason for the wide acceptance of this taxonomy (ethnocentric, polycentric, geocentric and regiocentric) is the good fit that it has had with the American international outlook in the second half of the last century. Under the ethnocentric model, most or all of the decision-makers in the host operation will comprise people from the home country, sent as expatriates from the headquarters. The reasons for opting for such a strategy can be a lack of trust in local people, a need for strong control by the mother company, or a lack of market experience on behalf of the mother company. It could also stem simply from lack of technological or specific know-how in the host country. While these may be strong reasons, a lack of knowledge of local culture and ways of working might hinder the success of the home-country managers. Another problematic result is the host-country managerial cadre's different perceptions of their careesr. Such an approach limits their developmental options, which might cause them to move elsewhere.

The polycentric model favours locals being appointed to managerial positions. This leaves locals with ample developmental options, helping to reduce the costs of expatriation and the length of time it takes for an expatriate manager to adapt to local conditions. Under particular circumstances it also helps to overcome local political hurdles and sensitivities. The major problem here becomes coordination across the global operation in different countries where the mother organization operates, and the possible difficulties in terms of contact between the home and host companies. Different operations might suffer possible detachment. This is in contrast to the ethnocentric approach, which aims to transfer the home culture to the host-country operation.

The geocentric model seeks to overcome the problems of the first two models. It suggests that nationality shall not inform appointment decisions in a MNC. The best person who fits the job will get it, no matter what his/her nationality is. While in principle this option sounds like a best-practice approach, this model is quite utopian or idealistic in the sense that it may take many years before such a model can be fully applied worldwide.

The regiocentric model is an attempt to compromise and divide the operation into several regions, wherein people will move according to the ethnocentric model, but not across different regions. This model allows for host nationals to develop their careers further than in the polycentric model, but in fact the barrier is not eliminated, just moved to the regional level. It might serve as a good intermediate strategy until the MNC can move on to the geocentric approach.

Another influential framework was later suggested by Bartlett and Ghoshal (1989). Their categorization classifies organizations according to a two-dimensional matrix. One dimension is the level of integration, and the other is the level of responsiveness. This matrix forms 'a four-quadrant model' with the following labels for each quadrant: *international* (low on integration and responsiveness), *global* (low on responsiveness, high on integration), *multinational* (high on responsiveness, low of integration) and *transnational* (high on both). The taxonomy offers an alternative and complementary approach to that often featured in the literature. For example, Bartlett and Ghoshal's concept suggests a stages-based model, where firms can develop and improve their strategy up to the final *transnational* stage.

In contrast, a model suggested by Baruch and Altman (2002) argues for five distinct options, each with their relative advantages and disadvantages. The options are grounded in practice, and can match organizational strategies in globalization for both the business and the HR function.

Baruch and Altman's (2002) five options offer different models or approaches for organizations to adopt in managing expatriation and repatriation. These are based on several dimensions – values, time, global vs local focus, individual vs company criterion, and nature of the psychological contract. Each option implies a different organizational approach to the management of careers and the meaning of an international assignment as a part of a person's career within the organization. The five options are:

1 The **Empire** or **Global**. This is the archetypal large global MNC, with an established reputation in expatriation management. The corporate philosophy of the 'empire' considers expatriation as integral to organizational life. Both individual and organizational expectations bear upon it when planning careers, and periods of expatriation are inevitable parts of career paths for any executive. Some may not wish to be expatriated, but this will deviate from the norm and thus exclude them from the mainstream career paths. For the 'empire', globalization is not a goal as such, it is an inherent property and part of the organizational ethos. The company will have a comprehensive set of procedures and practices in place. Moreover, people in the company as well as those joining would expect expatriation to be at the core of their professional and managerial careers.

2 The **Colonial** or **Emissary**. The 'colonial' company has established overseas markets with a long-term view as to its international aspirations; however, it is firmly rooted in a particular culture and this serves as its repository ideology, power base and expatriate source. It is characterized by an organizational culture indoctrinated with an ingrained obligation – a sense of duty backed with high commitment and loyalty. Under the 'colonial' option some people may be asked to accept an expatriate role, and in line with the ethos 'for God, King and Country', they are not expected to refuse.

3 The **Peripheral**. This model fits companies operating in peripheral geographies, where expatriation experience is most desirable. Here expatriation would be a means to benefit employees. Globalization for the 'peripheral' company is an expansion strategy, as local markets are insufficient to offer growth. Or indeed the company may have, by design, targeted itself as export-oriented. What seems to be different in the 'peripheral' option is that people will be queuing up to get the chance of expatriation; both individuals and the employer will perceive this as a perk.

4 The **Professional**. The 'professional' strategic option is based on buying-in knowledge and expertize. Its goal is to concentrate on home-country strengths and keep their people within specified geographical borders. Hence the ideology drives towards outsourcing cross-border activities, and delivery through people external to the company. These may be local people, or Trans National Company (TNC) specialists. The company prefers to use external people, in effect outsourcing the expatriation process.

5 The **Expedient**. This approach is for newcomers to the global scene, and characterizes most firms in the process of developing policies and practices for expatriation and international management. Drawing on an *ad hoc* and pragmatic approach, the 'expedient' option involves more of a 'mixed-bag' approach, which is evident in a wide range of companies entering globalized markets or wishing to become global players.

The five options are posited as ideal-type models, while in reality organizations have to respond pragmatically in managing expatriation processes. Therefore one often encounters mixed variants, which are hybrids of two or more options. The variations among these options are expected to be mirrored in the career systems and opportunities embodied in each option of the model. In the Empire, the career prospects for managers are truly borderless. For the Colonial, executives may be expected to contribute a service of a few years for the company's sake, while in the Peripheral the motive to embark on an international career would be based on individual eagerness to explore the world. The Professional option involves a market-led career, and some people would be life-long expatriates, moving among companies that need their services and are ready to pay for them. In the Expedient, the career overseas is an exception and involves negotiations with the company about future prospects, especially following repatriation. Table 8.2 summarizes some of the features of Baruch and Altman's model.

This approach supports a strategic alignment of HRM with business strategy (Gratton *et al.* 1999; Holbeche 1999), and provides benchmarking for the strategic choices companies need to make in directing their policies and practices. The set of options reflects the variety of cultural perspectives of a global economy at the onset of the twenty-first century. The main contribution of Baruch and Altman model's is of breaking the mould of any one 'best' model that all companies should aspire to. Such models might fit many of the well-known blue-chip MNCs, but not every player in the global market.

Are there any global companies at all?

Many MNCs aspire to be a transnational, i.e. borderless company, but Hu (1992) claims that in fact there exist only national companies, that operate across borders. The fact remains that in most cases most of the employees and operations or the management and headquarters are located in the mother country (Nestlé is a well-known but rare exception to this rule). Can you think of any companies from your own country that can really be considered purely global?

International career trajectories

Expatriation is the clearest manifestation of globalization from a HR perspective (Brewster and Scullion 1997; Porter and Tansky 1999; Selmer 1996). Theuerkauf (1991) suggested that for the global organization, career planning right from the recruitment stage, throughout the way to the top, should consider international assignments.

There are four key elements in career management and expatriation: choice of candidate, pre-posting preparation for the executive and family (both taken care of prior to the expatriation), support and maintenance of relations with the home organization while on the assignment, and the facilitation of a smooth return to the home base upon completion (Mendenhall, Dunbar and Oddou 1987; Zetlin 1994).

Globalization will continue to foster cross-border careers. Although political trends and legal changes may help or hinder its implementation, the growth of international trade suggests that international careers will prevail in the future.

What are the issues that a HR consultant should direct in providing advice to female managers seeking a global career route? In what ways may such advice be different for male managers?

Based on a review of the literature, identify the relevance and significance of the emerging themes in the practice and theory of global career systems, for companies operating in your country.

Table 8.2 Expatriation and repatriation dimensions of HR

Option	Strategy						HR Practice			HR consequences		Level of analyses*	Examples**
	Philosophy/ ideology	Goals/ aims	Policies	TNCs	Time-org. dimension	Time-ind. dimension	Recruitment & selection	T&D	Career development: retention	Advantages	Challenges		
Empire/ Global	Life-style: the expected career pattern	Globalization as a key org. characteristic	Established	Non-issue	Long-term	Short-term	Internal (enforced)	Regular, ongoing	Integral career path	Steady flow of candidates, ongoing learning	Managing the flow	The firm	Nestlé, Exxon, Lafarge
Colonial/ Emissary	Cultural agent: organizational long-arm	Expansion: branching out	Developed	Frowned upon	Long-term	Mid-term	Internal (normative)	Regular, specific	Loyalty and long-term; relational	Long-term commitment	Maintaining attachment, low turnover	The firm & national/ cultural	Sony, Vivendi, Matsushita
Peripheral	Expatriation as a perk	A growth strategy	Evolving	Undesirable	Variable	Ad hoc, usually short-term	Internal (desired)	Ad hoc	Distributive justice as an issue	Easy to recruit	Difficult to repatriate, 'politicized'	The firm & national	Ericsson, Corus, Jypex
Professional	Foreign legion: annexed for expat. missions	Segregate between 'internal' and 'external'	Outsourcing	Common	Mid-long term	Mid-long term	External	Buy-in	Contract-based relationships	Cost-effective, flexible	Lack of commitment, high turnover	The firm & the individual	Gillette, KPMG, Teva
Expedient	Opportunistic: reactive	Responsive to emergent opportunities	(Lack)	Possible	Ad hoc	Ad hoc	Internal or external	None (time & budget constraints)	Exceptional case; dealt as per need	Unstable, flexible	Managing the chaos	The firm & the individual	NU, Brintons, Barclays

Source: Baruch and Altman (2002).

Notes: * Level – while the stress in our framework is on the organizational (firm) level, we acknowledge that other levels of analysis apply; for example, the Professional is individual-oriented in its practices whereas national location (geography and mentally) would play a significant role in the Peripheral option and national culture in the Emissary option.

** While many of the prototypes chosen need no presentation, in particular the Globals, others may be less known to the US readership. Even within the Globals, one example is Lafarge, a French construction company with more than 65,000 employees, most of them outside France; at Lafarge being expatriate is a condition for getting into the upper echelons of the firm.

Case study 8

MANAGEMENT OF EXPATRIATION AND REPATRIATION FOR A NOVICE GLOBAL PLAYER*

Yehuda Baruch, with D.J. Steele and G.A. Quantrill (FinCorp)

With 12,000 employees in the UK, based in a regional city, FinCorp represents a typical 'Expedient' option, which, as argued, is quite different from the strategic choice many giant MNCs would take for managing expatriation and repatriation. After more than two centuries of existence, first as a local firm, then a national one, the company is striving to become a player in the international market. It has the vision to become a leading international provider of insurance and related financial services, principally within the European Union. This means that it needs to break the mould, to go outside the boundaries of the UK.

It is clear that FinCorp cannot adopt the approach, policy or strategy of well-established MNCs. The company is a relative novice to the global market (although it has small subsidiaries operating in the Far and the Middle East). It is relatively small in both size and level of business conducted outside the UK. Lastly, and perhaps most significant, the company lacks a global-oriented culture. Being different, it needs a different approach, one that will match the organizational strategic aims and enable the breakthrough sought for. However, even by the mid-1990s, FinCorp has not yet developed a culture of internationalization. Objection to being expatriated was accepted, even expected in many cases, as globalization was not yet part of the company culture. Thus there was a need to 'buy people in', and sometimes individuals were even recruited from outside the organization and

---

* Extract from a paper first presented as Baruch, Y. Steele, D.J. and Quantrill G.A. (2002) 'Management of Expatriation and Repatriation for Novice Global Player', *International Journal of Manpower*, 23(7), 659–671.

expatriated after a short induction (socialization) period in the UK.

Operational perspective: the decision to move into international markets

FinCorp started as a local group, and saw the UK as its target market for the first era of its operation. Competition in the UK has become fierce. Overseas companies have penetrated the UK market, mostly since the 1980s, increasing competition and globalization. Following a corporate strategy revision in the 1990s, FinCorp amended its business strategy to regard its home market as Europe rather than merely the UK. The already existing overseas operations were not to be abandoned but reexamined. However, the operation size was small compared to those of global players. The actual number of expatriates in the 1990s consisted of some 30 British nationals stationed overseas on a continuous basis.

Managing expatriates: the FinCorp experience

The company motto is:

1   People are the top priority.
2   There is never a perfect candidate.

First, FinCorp values its employees, and realizes that the success of the operation is due to the people who operate the business rather than just the company name, financial assets and operational procedures. Second, with a relatively small pool of possible candidates for expatriation, compromises have to be made, especially in the early stages of globalization. Without the culture of a MNC it was clear that many employees would not naturally welcome the idea of moving from their home-base to the unpredictable risks of an overseas assignment. In some cases external people were recruited for specific assignments, and were sent overseas after a short period of induction into FinCorp. The issue of repatriation has been given even less attention than that devoted to expatriation.

The basic guidelines for using expatriates were:

(a) *Specific business needs* – seconding people with specific skills and/or experience, in cases where the destination operation lacked these skills (typical cases: actuaries, IT specialists and accountants).

(b) *Development* – appointing promising managers to provide them with experience of management, autonomy and self-sufficiency.

(c) *Control* over overseas operations, keeping the subsidiary in line with the UK operational direction. This has meant that normally the personnel involved would be senior managers.

How has the relative importance of these guidelines changed over the years? The main underlying reason for expatriation was and remains the need for specific business skills. A considerable change was reflected in the increase in importance for the developmental aspect of expatriates, compared to significant reduction in the role as a control mechanism. This change in policy is reflected, for example, in the readiness and even willingness to appoint locals as the CEOs of subsidiaries, in particular in Europe. It is also a reflection of the evolving culture of the company.

These policies and priorities set by the company were acknowledged and appreciated by the expatriates via the way they were reflected during the interviews. When asked 'why did the company need expatriates?' responses included 'The company wished to have people representing their professional competence and cultural difference.' As one expatriate put it: 'They needed a Brit . . . to install values and philosophy.' Asked 'Was that directed to fulfil a business need?', the answer was: 'Yes, to bring the company and the UK actuary system to a newly acquired subsidiary, and to introduce financial disciplines.'

The formal selection process

Selection criteria for expatriates may include elements of openness, persistence and resilience, interest in other people and cultures, combined with empathy, sensitivity to cross-cultural factors, respect for all that is different, role flexibility, a tolerance for ambiguity and communication skills (preferably coupled with knowledge of languages or an ability to acquire them within a short time frame). Support for the family should also be considered a prerequisite. Luckily for the company, most cases did not involve dual-career couples, which imposes additional severe constraints on HR policy. FinCorp expect the dual-career issue to increase in the future (in line with Harvey, 1996). In the past spouses have been offered jobs, where available. However, increasing numbers of employees form a part of a dual-career couples (i.e. the spouse, usually the wife, has their own separate full working career). The company has already experienced a case of an employee rejecting expatriation as the partner's aspirations were not being met. Such experiences are expected to become more common.

In the 1980s, selection was based on exceptional cases of employees – those who were willing, but not necessarily suitable. Subsequently induction was inadequate. Expatriation was 'sold' to people to persuade them to accept it, and financial incentives played a major part in the deal. As a result unrealistic job expectations were the norm during both expatriation and repatriation. Prospects on return were overstated. Upon return the organization did not deliver, and frustrations arose, often leading to departure, which meant losing the investment made by the company.

The question FinCorp faced was how to establish a clear, manageable selection process that would recognize the variety of challenges mentioned above (family considerations, realistic job preview, and, in particular, expatriation as part of a comprehensive career development path). It is not easy to develop formal procedures to measure and evaluate such qualities. Indeed, in the early stages there was no formal process, and trial-and-error paved the way forward. The key aspects sought were technical ability and the likelihood of acceptance; and, to a lesser degree, adaptability and attitudes. As experience was gained, both formal procedures and informal tacit knowledge were developed in the HR component of expatriation. Thus, for example, the process currently includes internal testing plus interviews, based on FinCorp's own experiences – not only at a professional level but also at a personal level.

The remuneration element

Remuneration can serve to help people accept expatriation. However, if this is the only reason for accepting expatriation, the prospects for success are slim. FinCorp had to start with a fair offer to people sent to 'less-desirable destinations' in terms of culture. The package for the Middle East was more generous, due to local taxation consideration as well as the environment. This policy and practice were indeed reflected during the interviews. No expatriate complained about the financial incentives and remuneration package. The danger is, of course, that upon return people have to readjust to normal levels of income and lose additional benefits such as school fees. Another risk is that an individual who spends too much time out of the UK is likely to become a 'professional' expatriate, and may be unable to readjust to the UK lifestyle. Another possible problem involves equity theory, which implies that expatriates in different locations (and also non-expatriate employees) will be viewed unfairly by their local colleagues due to the high salaries paid to them. A fine balance needs to be established between 'fair', 'generous' and 'lucrative'. The basic concept and philosophy ensures a fit between UK terms and conditions and the local ones, as well as the ability to readjust to former levels following repatriation.

The guidelines established by FinCorp with regard to their worldwide operations were to keep people at a similar earning level in terms of standard of living, accommodation, savings, pension schemes, and so on. The package needed to sound attractive and fair, but not to a level that it would be the sole factor in accepting the secondment. FinCorp uses a 'balance-sheet approach' – calculating the UK net disposable income and then applying the local cost of living. However, it is acknowledged that a differential cost for an expatriation exists, so expatriates will have to pay more in many instances as they lack local purchasing knowledge (Western brands, easy contact, lack of awareness where to shop in the new country). In destination countries where living costs are cheaper the remuneration package would be reduced. This is in contrast to the early days of embarking on international markets, when people were reluctant to agree to expatriation and were lured into the secondment by financial incentives.

The guidelines stated for today are that FinCorp will provide the employee with 'a salary which ensures that disposable income has the same purchasing power as in the UK and that people will not have a lower standard of living than a local employee with similar responsibilities' (company's *Employee Guide for Relocating Overseas*). The following factors are taken into account: living cost, taxation and social security, and local salaries for similar jobs. Other issues which can enable flexibility are the 'recognition of environmental and special factors relative to the location and the element of "promotion" of the new role'. Pension plans are maintained when possible or alternative arrangements made. Accommodation is comparable to that in the UK (with additional 'disturbance allowance' of one-month's salary, up to £5,000). Part of the salary may be paid in the UK, for example to cover mortgage payments or insurance premiums. In addition, the company encourages (and finances) the expatriates to have a consultation with one of the Big Five consultancy firms in relation to the tax implications of their packages. An additional financial benefit is provided in form of reimbursement of education fees. This is important since in some locations potential English schools can be limited or very expensive, and some expatriates opt to leave children in UK boarding schools. To alleviate the problems when returning to the UK, contributions continue for three years on a gradually reducing basis. Otherwise the repatriates may face school fees they cannot afford or having to return their children to state education. The company leaves these readjusting matters to the repatriates to solve.

Keeping contact and preparing for repatriation

There are several methods to ensure the expatriate is not detached from FinCorp and will not feel isolated. Yearly home visits, mail communication, a designated line manager to keep the person informed of developments at the headquarters – all these and other mechanisms are expected to be practised to ensure continuous contact. One such mechanism is the performance-appraisal process. Performance appraisal is conducted with the expatriate's mentor, in combination with the local system. FinCorp felt that the performance appraisal system needs to reflect both local and home viewpoints, and thus a dual concept of performance appraisal was developed comprising a two-tier approach to ensure fair appraisal.

The repatriation and the impact on later career are expected to be managed by the HR function. However, not all was as good as originally intended. In particular people were not prepared for the return: 'I was not prepared; my expatriation was due to be finished in July, but in May I still had no idea of my next job!' 'People in the UK decided, no one owes you anything', was the perception. A pressing issue here was the involvement and interaction between the HR function and operational units, especially as the theory was that expatriation should form an important stage in the career development of the individual (all expatriates were either managers or professionals with managerial roles). These experiences are in contrast to the more positive feeling of preparation for the expatriation, as quoted: 'although there were many surprises . . . I was well prepared – it was a good induction in the UK.'

Company support

The support can be divided into work- related and non-work-related aspects. People were advised in relation to their remuneration, taxa-tion, culture, physical move, health, renting-out their UK property and preparation for their new working environment. The prospective expatriate and their spouse were provided with training sessions to prepare them for the different culture, which included the availability of language training. This approach is in line with the already accepted notion that globalization means the need to overcome cultural rather than geographical boundaries (Adler 1984).

FinCorp recognizes that the induction for both expatriation and repatriation is about making people safe and comfortable, breaking barriers often caused by a lack of knowledge. Sending the expatriate for a pre-visit is just one example which has helped in preventing failures. The whole picture must be taken into account. Says a senior manager, 'you cannot focus on the employee, forgetting that if his wife (husband) are dissatisfied this will have strong implications on their performance and readiness to complete the secondment period'.

The problems that emerged in the interviews were mostly concerned with work-related aspects. The company policy is to call the expatriate for a 'home visit' once a year, to enable the expatriate to be updated on changes in the UK organization and market, and to hold career-planning sessions and assessments with UK managers. Although this policy was indeed practised, the actual bene-fits gained from it were perceived as minor, and the majority felt it was not arranged properly. Moreover, the return and resettling into new roles was problematic. Again and again people report that the experience they gained was not recognized and was somehow lost in the process. The hands-on management experience – the ability to run an autonomous business and make major decisions – was not fully utilized upon return. In several cases, restructuring of FinCorp meant that managers had left, positions were dismantled, and repatriates found there was no role waiting for them, sometimes not even phys-ical space to return to.

To conclude, the case, here is a quote from a former expatriate manager from FinCorp:

Try to re-incorporate overseas operations into a 'main-stream career concept', which should be part of a career development path at FinCorp. It is good for "calibre" people. This way a good, positive cycle will be developed. Do not let people return to old jobs, and be aware that for them it may be a new organization, especially following frequent changes. As their former boss might have gone or moved, a mentor can be a good replacement. Also half a year before return, one should come for meetings etc. Don't let them feel they have lost the place in the queue.

References

Adler, N.J. (1984) *International Dimensions of Organizational Behavior* (Belmont: PWS-Kent).

Harvey, M. (1996) 'Dual-Career Couples: The Selection Dilemma in International Relocation', *International Journal of Selection and Assessment*, 4(4), pp. 215–27.

Case study discussion topics

1 Indicate how the case of FinCorp might match the following: one of Perlmutter's four options; one of Ghoshal and Bartlett's options; one of Baruch and Altman's five options.
2 How does the case emphasize the significance and relevance of managing repatriation?
3 What advice would you give FinCorp in order to improve their record of expatriation?

SUMMARY

The chapter has provided the reader with a focus on international careers and their role for individuals, organizations and nations. It highlights the ways in which organizations should direct their career systems when opting for global operation. The chapter started from the individual perspective, looking critically at the possibility that there is a set of specific characteristics for global managers. It then examined the issue of global psychological contracts.

The general framework of the Push–Pull model was presented, to enhance understanding of individual career decision-making in the global context, in light of different national and managerial cultures. Moving on from the individual to the organizational, the chapter addressed the implications for HRM and career management when HRM has to operate across borders. The case study considers issues of remuneration, performance appraisal, training and development. Three prominent models and frameworks for understanding international careers from an organizational strategy perspective have been presented and discussed, for both expatriation and repatriation processes.

Chapter nine

Competencies of International Human Resource Managers

Moira Calveley

Learning outcomes

After reading this chapter, you should be able to:

- Define the concept of competencies.
- Identify the personal competencies required by an International Human Resource Manager.
- Understand the complexities involved in managing human resources from an international perspective.
- Use a case study example to identify issues of importance and concern when managing people in an international setting.

INTRODUCTION

Chapter 1 discussed how the development of communication and transportation technologies widened the geographic imagination and allowed for the development of business beyond traditional geographic areas. It reminds us that there has been a growth of international, transnational and multinational companies and how this has encouraged companies working in an international environment to strategically change and develop their business and management practices.

There are now millions of people living and working abroad for their companies; for example, it is estimated that over two million Americans are in this situation (Joynt and Morton 1999). Many multinational organizations are huge and operate in a number of different countries; for example, in 2000 McDonald's had more that 25,000 restaurants in 116 countries and employed approximately 1.5 million people (Royle 2000). Indeed, 'the world of work is controlled increasingly by multinationals' (Lewis *et al.* 2003, p. 37), with the United Nations Conference on Trade and Development

(UNCTAD) estimating that there were 63,000 multinational organizations in 2000, with 15 of the top 100 employing more than 100,000 people (Leat 2003). It is not surprising, then, that multinational companies are beginning to understand the importance of the resourcing and development of their human resources (Holden 2001), and the importance of people management is becoming increasingly more recognized. It is also now recognized that the malfunctioning of human resource management (HRM) systems can have far-reaching consequences for organizations (Holden 2001). This chapter will explore how the role of the human resource manager is also developing as they acquire the requisite competencies to deal with a global workforce.

The growth of international and multinational organizations has meant that International HR managers have to deal with people of different nationalities on a daily basis; they interact in more diverse and dynamic environments than their counterparts who are responsible for single-country operations. This does not necessarily mean that they travel widely, but the increased use of telecommunications technology such as electronic mail systems and video-conferencing brings workers from different countries closer together. Indeed, even at the micro-level of the local workplace, the diversity of nationalities employed by organizations has brought about a need for HR professionals to understand and appreciate different cultures in the workplace. It is important to note, however, that as Dowling *et al.* point out, the 'management of diversity within a single national context may not necessarily transfer to a multinational context without some modification' (1999, p. 4).

Joynt and Morton (1999) argue that as companies operate on an international basis, business functions need to develop the skills, knowledge and experience needed to help their business succeed in this environment. They go further to say that it is particularly so for the HRM function as 'effective people management is essential . . . because international expansion and operation place additional stress on resources, particularly people' (Joynt and Morton 1999, p. 7). Joynt and Morton also identify a number of areas in which international human resource management (IHRM) differs from domestic HRM:

- being responsible for a greater number of functions and activities;
- requiring a broader perspective;
- greater involvement in employees' lives;
- having to change emphasis, because the employee mix of parent- and host-country nationals varies at different locations and over time, distance and cultures;
- greater exposure to problems and difficulties;
- coping with a greater number of external influences; and
- having to consider greater overall complexities in decision-making (*ibid.*, p. 10).

It is imperative that HR managers have the right knowledge and skills – competencies – which they can employ in the management of human resources. Clearly, as evidenced by Joynt and Morton's (1999) list above, there are a number of areas in which IHR managers are required to develop their knowledge and skills to a greater depth than they may need when managing in a local environment. From an international perspective, it is essential that their competencies can be utilized not only within the home country of the HR manager, but also across national boundaries. The IHR manager is someone who needs to be able to manage across a number of different countries, regions and cultures simultaneously.

Competencies

So what are the competencies needed by the IHR manager? Firstly it is necessary for us to understand what competencies are in general and then consider these in more detail from an international perspective.

Boyatzis is widely recognized as developing the idea of competency which he defines as 'an underlying characteristic of a person which results in effective and/or superior performance in a job' (1982, p. 21). Maund (2001, p. 152) defines competency as 'the knowledge, skills and personal qualities needed to carry out a task, and how such attributes are applied'. It is not the intention here to consider the debate surrounding the notion of competencies; however, it is clear that competencies are seen as the work-related behaviours which are identified as being necessary for successful job performance. In this chapter we will be looking at competencies as the knowledge, skills and personal attributes required by a HR manager.

GROUP ACTIVITY

Make a list of the competencies you think are required in order to successfully manage the HR function.

COMPETENCIES OF THE HUMAN RESOURCE MANAGER

Although competencies can be generic for all management functions, there are arguably some which are HR-specific. Schuler *et al.* (2001) suggest that as HR professionals are becoming more actively engaged with the strategy formulation of the organization they now need a broader set of competencies. These authors (2001, p. 128) provide a comprehensive list which they examine under four main headings:

Business competencies
- Industry knowledge
- Competitor understanding
- Financial understanding
- Global perspective/knowledge
- Strategic analysis
- Partner orientation
- Multiple stakeholder sensitivity

Leadership competencies
- Strategic visioning
- Managing cultural diversity
- Creator of learning culture
- Planning and decision-making skills
- Value-shaper

Change and knowledge-management competencies
- Network-building
- Designing and working in flexible structures

- HR alignment
- Managing and learning knowledge transfer
- Consulting/Influencing
- Group/process facilitation
- Organization development/effectiveness
- Managing large-scale change

Professional/technical competencies
- Staffing
- Performance management
- Education/development
- Remuneration/reward systems
- Employee relations
- Employee communications
- Succession planning
- Union relations
- Safety/health/wellness
- Diversity management

GROUP ACTIVITY

From the above list identify the competencies which you think are generic to all management functions and those which you think are HR-specific giving reasons for your choices. Identify any competencies you feel should be added to the list.

What are not explicitly included in Schuler *et al.*'s (2001) list, although to some extent implied, however, are the 'soft competencies' which include 'managing people and dealing with one's own and other people's feelings' (Weightman 2001, p. 11). As we will see below, the 'softer' competencies, which incorporate good interpersonal and communication skills, are essential for human resource management, both at a domestic and international level.

The Schuler *et al.* (2001) list gives insight into the growth of competencies required by HR professionals who become actively engaged in the strategic development of an organization. Whilst the authors question whether it is possible for anyone to have all of these competencies, it does show how HR managers are required to have a broad overview of the working of the organization. Torrington (1994) states that although many of the competencies required by management do not change regardless of whether they are taking an international perspective or not, there are some competencies that need to be developed in order for a company to sustain effectiveness in an international market.

If the list of competencies required by IHR managers is as extensive as Schuler *et al.* (2001) state, and these need to be developed further for HR managers operating in an international environment, then this is no small task. The following section will consider the extent to which competencies of HR managers need to be expanded and developed in order to operate on an international basis.

What competencies do you think an international human resource manager needs?

COMPETENCIES OF THE INTERNATIONAL HUMAN RESOURCE MANAGER

Rugman and Hodgetts (2003, p. 351) state that IHRM strategies 'involve consideration of staffing, selecting, training, compensating and labor relations in the international environment' and that provides a good starting point for considering the competencies required by the IHR manager. Further, Dowling *et al.* (1999, p. 4) suggest that 'the complexity involved in operating in different countries and employing different national categories of employees rather than any major differences between the HRM activities performed' is the key variable that differentiates international and domestic HRM. This view is shared by Paauwe and Dewe who state that it is the way in which HR activities are performed which gives rise to differences between countries (1995). So, if the HR functions to be undertaken are similar in different countries, what then are the different competencies needed by an international human resource manager?

Torrington argues that in order to operate in an international environment people need to 'think international' all of the time (1994, p. 17). Most IHRMs will operate from the corporate centre of their organization; this may be in their own country or they may themselves be expatriate workers (see Chapter 7) living abroad. In this environment, it is necessary for them to 'think globally, but act locally' (Torrington 1994) and it is being able to think from an international perspective which is perhaps the overriding competency required by IHRMs. However, 'thinking globally' requires the development of a number of different competencies. IHRMs need to demonstrate 'cognitive complexity' (Barham and BerthoinAntal 1994; Schneider and Barsoux 2003) whereby they are able to see 'several dimensions in a situation rather than only one and to identify relationships and patterns between different dimensions' (Barham and BerthoinAntal 1994, p. 235).

In this section we shall consider the various competencies needed by the IHR manager under specific headings, but it is important to note that skills and attributes are not mutually exclusive and cannot be considered as such.

There are a number of different situations in which IHR managers can find themselves involved in managing people. For example, they may well have the responsibility for employment relations in the parent company head office with overseas operations, or they may be in their home country working in a foreign firm. Although different organizations will have different structures, if a HR manager is acting in an international capacity then it is likely that the organization is either an international or multinational organization. The structure of the organization may be:

1 Centralized – decisions made by the corporate head office are implemented at the local level; managers report directly to the head office. The HR manager is directly responsible for HR issues on a global basis.
2 Decentralized – strategic decisions are made by the corporate head office but operational decisions are made locally; there is a local management team who report to the company board. The HR director is ultimately responsible for all HR issues.

These typologies broadly fit with Perlmutter's (1969) ethnocentric and polycentric approaches respectively (Holden 2001). Regardless of the management approach, whether centralized or decentralized, HR policies and practices are the ultimate responsibility of the IHR manager. From the centralized perspective he or she needs to take a 'hands-on' approach and will therefore require an in-depth knowledge of issues which affect the day to day functioning of the management of human resources across all operations. If the approach is decentralized, then the HR manager will need to take local situations into account whenever corporate-level decisions are made which affect human resources in any one of the global operations.

Whatever the situation, clearly there are challenges here for the HR manager who has to develop effective HR policies and practices in each of the business operations. Some of these policies and practices may be distinctive to the individual organization and some may have to be developed and implemented on a global basis.

Organizational knowledge

One of the most fundamental and obvious areas of knowledge for the HR manager is that of the organization itself. It is clear that if the HR manager is to operate on an international basis then he or she must be aware of operations throughout the world. This wider perspective allows for smoother and more effective development of corporate policies. As Dowling *et al.* state 'it is difficult to advocate international HRM policies if one is not fully appreciative of the importance of the firm's international operations to its overall profitability and competitiveness' (1999, p. 20). If the company is a large multinational, then there may be a large number of different areas and functions and possibly diverse operations; it is therefore far more complex than a domestic organization.

Some of the reasons for the complexity involved in developing knowledge of the international or multinational organization will be discussed further below; however, it is important to remember here that organizations do not exist in a vacuum. Therefore, the local and national environments in which organizations operate need to be taken into account when HR decisions are made. In order to ensure that all HRM policies and practices are aligned, it is necessary for the IHR manager to have a thorough understanding of the organization's corporate strategy. He or she needs to be aware of future investment and divestment plans as these have an impact on HR planning – recruitment and selection; training and development; succession planning, and so on.

Knowledge of the business environment requires an understanding of the environmental setting of each section of the organization for the HR manager to gain a full understanding of the organization itself. It is necessary to understand the various economic, political and legal systems in operation as these impact upon the HR functions. The HR manager also needs to be aware of the demographics of the local labour force, local employment relations, management styles and local politics as well as customs and traditions:

- ■ *Economic.* The economic environment in which organizations operate can vary widely, not only between countries and regions, but also across them. For example, economic development in the Asia Pacific region has been uneven with some areas developing at a faster rate than others (Ng and Warner 1999). This has implications for the IHR manager who needs to have an appreciation of whether a particular practice can be adopted region-wide or whether the practice needs to be tailored for the different regions. The economy of a country is influenced either directly or indirectly by the political standpoint of the government.

- *Political.* The IHR manager needs to have an understanding of the political system in operation in the country in which their employees are based, as governments shape and influence the framework for employment relations. For example, the national government can have an impact on the management of organizations as we saw in the 1980s in the UK and the USA, when there was a drive towards the use of market forces (Hollinshead and Leat 1995) in the promotion of flexible labour markets. On the other hand, in Germany employment relations since the end of the Second World War have been based on a corporatist approach (Bean 1994) which acknowledges the role of all parties (government, employer and trade unions) in the employment relationship and sees the free market as an inadequate mechanism in promoting social equity (Leat 1998).

- *Legislation.* Employment law is always a complex area for the HR manager. However, for the IHR manager it is more so as they need to be aware of the different legislations in different countries. For example, in Japan the law on dismissal has been established on the assumption of lifetime employment (Eaton 2000). Across Europe, employment law is increasingly influenced by the European Court of Justice, and indeed in Britain this is one of the most significant factors influencing the development of employment regulation (Willey 2003). In some countries, such as France (see below), the labour market is highly regulated and it is a statutory requirement that employers consult with employees when making decisions about issues such as plant closures. (See Eaton, 2000, for an insight into comparative labour law.)

- *Employment relations.* This is closely linked to the above points as it is associated with the economic and political environment of the country involved and integrated with employment legislation. The way in which employment relations are approached is to some extent determined by the approach of the government. As we have seen above, governments may take an interventionist approach as in the case of France, or they may prefer to allow companies greater freedom in determining their own employment policies and practices as is the case in the USA (Hollinshead and Leat 1995). Japan, for example, has a strong state influence in employment relations (Ng and Warner 1999). Systems of employment relations have therefore developed in different ways in different cultures, and an understanding of how they developed is important for the HR manager to understand the system itself.

  The government's approach to trade unions also influences employment relations in a country. As discussed above, the government may take a corporatist approach which encourages trade union involvement at all levels, which means that at the local workplace level wages will be set through the collective bargaining mechanism. The human resource manager will be responsible for negotiating with one or more trade unions in deciding pay settlements. This negotiation may be influenced by factors outside of the immediate workplace, for example national economic strategies. If the company is involved in collective bargaining at industry level (that is where all companies in a particular industry agree to pay levels) then the wage settlement will need to take this into account. Contrary to this, in the USA employers are seen to go to great extents to avoid trade union involvement (Eaton 2000).

  Not only does the role of trade unions have to be taken into account, but also in some countries works councils (for example in Germany, the Netherlands and

France) have to be consulted with regard to business and employment issues (Hollinshead and Leat 1995).

As the employment relations system may vary widely between countries, then the IHR manager must be able to produce policies which allow for local interpretation and adjustment in practice. As Dowling *et al.* have identified, for multinational organizations employment relations policies 'must be flexible enough to adapt to local requirements' (1999, p. 233).

■ *Management style and local politics.* This is linked very closely with employment relations. Although the organization at a corporate level may wish to have a commonality of management styles, this may not always happen in practice for a number of reasons. Managers at the local level may give 'lip service' to corporate management by agreeing to implement practices but then not doing so; they may adjust the practices to suit their own needs or desires. It may well be the case that practices have evolved over time or are subject to local cultural factors and local managers may be reluctant to make changes.

The IHRM needs to be aware of the local and micro politics. Doyle (2001, p. 410), in his discussion on management development in general, states that managers are frequently confronted by 'political' factors and that managers must therefore achieve 'political competence'. He goes on to say that in order to do this, managers must understand the power relations in an organization. He argues that 'a politically competent manager can contribute to organizational effectiveness. Equally, politically incompetent managers can hamper and "damage" organizations as well as themselves' (2001, p. 411). The IHRM may be responsible for employees who have been the subject of a merger or (possibly hostile) take-over; tensions may exist between the centre and the local operation. The local manager may well feel that he or she 'knows best' and resist what they may see as 'interference' from the IHRM. The IHRM will need to draw upon a number of competencies, including political, in order to ensure the smooth integration of central policy.

Brewster and Larsen argue that in Europe there is now a widespread drive 'to give line managers more responsibility for the management of their staff and to reduce the extent to which personnel or human resources departments control or restrict line management autonomy in this area' (2000, p. 196). This is a further challenge for the IHR manager who has to oversee such devolvement of responsibility and, whilst to some greater or lesser extent taking a 'back-seat' in people management at the local level, ensure that company practices and procedures are fully adhered to and followed.

■ *Labour market demographics.* The make up of the labour market is an important issue which HR managers need to take into account, as it can affect both current and future human resource planning strategies. For example, the growth in the number of women entering the labour market throughout Europe has meant that there has been an increase in the demand for part-time and flexible working patterns. Despite the increase in female participation in the labour market there persists a gender pay gap with women across Europe earning 20 per cent less than men (EIRO 2001a). Both these issues are of concern to IHR managers who need to ensure equal and fair treatment of all workers.

Another international labour market issue that HR managers need to take account of is the ageing population. Statistics show that there is a fairly universal ageing population (Australian Bureau of Statistics 2003) which needs to be considered in human resource planning.

This section has identified how IHR managers need to have an in-depth knowledge of the environments in which their organization operates. To this end, they need to develop their learning and knowledge skills and to keep their knowledge updated. These skills need to be complemented by good interpersonal and communication skills as discussed below.

GROUP ACTIVITY

There is a dynamic relationship between the organization and its environment. Consider this relationship and discuss how, from a people management perspective, an organization may affect, or be affected by, the environment in which it operates. Think about this in relation to multinational and international organizations that you know.

Practical skills

The HR manager needs to have a thorough knowledge and understanding of the everyday HR practices such as recruitment and selection and training and development, and for the IHR manager how these may differ between countries. Staffing problems are likely to be more complex than in domestic firms, and if the policies and practices are inappropriate then this can lead to major difficulties.

It is not the intention here to discuss individual practices, but it is useful for us to consider some examples of the differences in practices across countries. We have already considered above how pay may be negotiated collectively through the involvement of trade unions; however, it can also be negotiated at an individual level and may be linked to individual or company performance. Interestingly, despite the long tradition of collective bargaining in Germany, there has been an increase in the use of variable pay in recent years (Kurdelsbusch 2002). This is seen to be partly attributable to the influence of multinational organizations, and both trade unions and works councils have been involved in the process. The HR manager responsible for operations in Germany would clearly become involved in developing these practices, drawing upon a number of skills to do so.

What competencies would the IHR manager draw upon when involved in changing a pay settlement system in a highly unionized organization in a country such as Germany?

When considering pay settlements, the IHR manager not only requires knowledge of the organization's own policies and practices, he or she needs to understand local employment and taxation laws, have a knowledge of currency fluctuations and inflation rates and an understanding of the local labour market and skills shortages. At the same time, the pay strategy needs to fit with the overall business strategy of the organization whilst attracting and retaining the right staff.

Another area in which practice may differ at the local level is that of recruitment and selection (R&S). It is a well-known mantra of HRM that R&S aims to ensure that 'the right person is in the right place at the right time'. For the IHRM, this can mean recruiting both within and across national boundaries. When a position becomes vacant a decision has to be made as to whether this can be filled through internal recruitment, which may involve relocating an individual with all the associated personal issues and costs, or advertising the job externally. A number of factors need to be taken into consideration which will not be discussed here; however, again it is important that the IHR manager takes into account local customs and culture and also ensures that the R&S practice is fair, ethical and equitable. Here again, a knowledge of legislation and local labour markets is vital.

An example of problems with introducing a common policy for R&S is that of psychometric testing which is surrounded by controversy in the UK and Australia (Dowling *et al.* 1999) and was banned in Italy in 1970 (Sparrow and Hiltrop 1994), although now it appears to be more widely adopted there (*Europa* 2003). For the IHR manager the question must be asked whether psychological testing can be used in multicultural settings, whether they can be 'culture-free' (Sparrow 1999a). Other R&S issues for consideration are that in Germany works councils have to be consulted about some aspects of R&S (Torrington 1994), whilst in Japan there is fierce competition between companies in recruiting graduates from the more prestigious institutions (Schneider and Barsoux 2003). Again, the IHR manager needs to have full awareness of these issues when implementing centralized policies and practices at a local level.

Interpersonal and communication skills

It is clear that a manager working with people needs to have good interpersonal and communication skills. Indeed, Morley *et al.* argue that effective communication is 'at the heart of effective human resource management' (2000, p. 147). For IHR managers in particular, who need to ensure that company policies and practices are aligned across different countries, interpersonal and communication skills need to be finely developed. As Barham and Antal point out, for international managers it is necessary 'to be able to enter into the minds of people operating out of different perspectives from their own'; the authors go on to say that this 'depends critically on the capacity for active listening' (1994, p. 235) as communication is, of course, a two-way process.

Communication can take a number of forms. It might be verbal or written; it may be on paper or electronic; it may be face-to-face or via a telephone – the list goes on. Importantly for HR managers, it can also be individual on a one-to-one basis or it can be collective involving a number of people. If there are works councils and/or trade unions involved, then the IHR manager would need to develop their consultation and negotiation skills. Indeed, according to Morley *et al.* 'communication through representative bodies continues to be a growth area in most northern European countries (2000, p. 155). In many cases, communication will be company-wide and that means that all employees must receive the same communication at the same time. This can be a mammoth task for an HR manager.

GROUP ACTIVITY

Imagine that an organization is cutting jobs across the world. What are the issues faced by the IHR manager when it comes to communicating this to the workforce? What are the competencies that she or he must draw upon in order to ensure the smooth running of the process?

With issues such as redundancy and plant closures, as we shall see with the M&S case study later, it is imperative in some countries (the Netherlands, France) that works councils and/or trade unions are consulted, whilst in others (USA, UK) this is not the case. A communication regarding redundancy needs to be received by all workers simultaneously in order to avoid confusion and uncertainty. It may need to be communicated in a number of different languages, and time zones also need to be taken into account. For example, if the redundancies affect London, Paris and New York, then the communication would need to be in at least French and English and published to coordinate three different time zones. This has to be done without any 'leakage' of the information. It may be that the HR manager communicates electronically by e-mail or, due to the seriousness of the issue, they may choose to write letters to all employees. The former may be easier to ensure a common receipt time (barring system failures), but the latter may be seen as more sensitive and personal. For the latter it would be necessary to have the letters ready to be distributed within the workplace at a set time. The manager is then able to choose a time when all workers are in the workplace at the same time and have the letters distributed simultaneously.

Clearly, and as the above example shows, good communication is a vital part of managing people effectively. For the IHRM, the ability to speak a foreign language can also be seen as a distinct advantage.

Language skills

It is now frequently suggested that English is the universal 'business language' (Dowling *et al.* 1999; Torrington 1994), and Torrington goes as far as to say that 'international managers must have fluent English, whether it be their native tongue or not' (1994, p. 19). However, it is also recognized that the ability to speak two or more languages is seen as a huge advantage when managing on an international basis (Dowling *et al.* 1999; Schneider and Barsoux 2003; Torrington 1994). Indeed, Dowling *et al.* report that US multinationals are not only requesting business schools to include foreign language studies in their curricula, but also giving preference to graduates who have studied languages; they have also found a similar trend in the UK and Australia (1999). Clearly, organizations in the English-speaking countries are seeking to become more bilingual.

It would be unrealistic to expect a person to be fluent in a number of languages; however, fluency in another language would be a clear benefit for the IHR manager for a number of reasons. An obvious benefit is the ability to communicate with employees in their native tongue. This can help avoid misunderstandings as meanings are lost in translation, but it can also help to explore more deeply the feelings of the other person. In issues of importance to HRM, which are often personal and sensitive, this is vital.

It is also important that the IHR manager does not face a disadvantage in negotiation or consultation situations with trade unions and works councils. If the IHR manager is English-speaking but negotiating with, say, a Dutch trade union, then she or he may be disadvantaged as the union representatives are likely to be at least bilingual. The trade union representatives can communicate with each other in their own language which excludes the HR manager. In the same vein, the home nationals will have access to information and data which may be published in the domestic language and which may lose meaning and emphasis when translated.

Finally, it can also be argued that understanding a language helps one to understand the cultural aspects of a country; as Schneider and Barsoux point out, 'it is through language that we formulate thoughts and that we experience the world and others' (2003, p. 44). Such cultural awareness and sensitivity is, as we shall see below, an important competency for the IHRM to possess.

Cultural sensitivity

As discussed above, managers are increasingly dealing with a culturally diverse work-force, whether they operate in a domestic setting or on an international basis. Indeed, the importance of the role of culture is discussed widely in texts on managing people, and most authors draw to a greater or lesser extent upon the work of Hofstede who, beginning in the late 1960s, developed theories of national cultures (see for example Holden 2001; Parkinson 1999; Schneider and Barsoux 2003; Sparrow and Hiltrop 1994). Whilst it is not intended here to enter the debate on the meaning and defini-tion of culture, it is important to recognize that different values, attitudes and beliefs exist and these shape the culture in which a person exists. Cultural sensitivity is, there-fore, an essential competency for any manager of human resources, but arguably even more so for the IHR manager who will be concerned with employment relations across country and cultural boundaries.

Schneider and Barsoux talk about the 'seeds of potential cultural conflict and misunderstanding' in cross-border alliances and how managers need to recognize what they describe as 'symptoms of cultural malaise' (2003, p. 10). For the IHR manager, they not only need to have the skills to manage people of different nation-alities and cultures, it is also necessary that they are able to recognize where cross-cultural conflict is developing and draw upon their skill and experience to deal with such issues. Indeed, failure to take account of culture can have disastrous conse-quences for the organization (Schneider and Barsoux 2003).

Understanding the psychological contract

This may seem an unusual section to include under competencies; however, as evidenced by the growing literature on the concept of the psychological contract, this is an area where human resource managers need to develop their understanding and their skills in dealing with it.

The psychological contract is the implied contract between an individual worker and their organization. Unlike the formal contract of employment, the psychological contract is not written down but consists of the mutual expectations formed between the employer and employee (Cox and Parkinson 2003); they are 'concerned with the social and emotional aspects of the exchange between employer and employee' (Sparrow 1999b, p. 75). The psychological contract is based on mutual trust and respect and there can be serious consequences if there is a breakdown in the contract, with employees feeling anger and betrayal (Robinson and Rousseau, cited in Cox and Parkinson 2003). Sparrow talks about the breakdown of the psychological contract in the UK and the USA (1998), and in Europe and Japan (1999b), which emphasizes that the notion of the psychological contract is indeed global.

It is therefore incumbent on the IHR manager to be aware of the psychological contract and how this may develop between management and employees in different countries. To some extent, an understanding of culture will assist in this. However, as the concept is difficult to define – arguably it is not clear what the contract was until it was broken – this puts great demands on the HR manager. Indeed, all the skills discussed above have to be drawn upon to understand the contract and help maintain it in a positive way. No mean feat!

Case study 9

MARKS & SPENCER: from continental chocolates to continental closure

The company background

Marks & Spencer (M&S) is a well-known high-street retailer in the UK with stores nationwide. It was formed in 1894 by a partnership between Michael Marks and Tom Spencer, becoming a public company in 1926. During the 1970s the company began to expand on a global basis, opening its first overseas store in Canada in 1973 and in France and Belgium in 1975. In the late 1980s it acquired stores in the USA (which remained trading under the Brooks Brothers name) and opened stores in Hong Kong. By the mid-1990s, M&S had stores in around 30 countries worldwide, incorporating Europe, North America and Asia.

Known for its high-quality, good service and value for money, the company developed into a highly profitable organization, even branching out into financial services in 1985. M&S was to become one of the most profitable retailers in Europe. However, when recession hit the retail industry in the UK in the late 1990s, Marks and Spencer began to make the news as its profits dropped sharply.

In 1999 Marks & Spencer responded to the fall in profits by reviewing its management structure, stopping recruitment to its graduate training programme and reviewing its business operations. The first major overseas investment to go was in Canada, where in 1999 it closed its 38 stores, reportedly cutting approximately 900 jobs and paying around $35 million in severance payments and closure costs (Warson 1999). It also sold its Brooks Brothers stores in the USA in November 2001. It was, however, the closure of shops in France and Belgium in March 2001 that put M&S in the headlines as we shall see below.

M&S's approach to people management

The company takes a paternal approach to managing people and, although not without its critics, it is often viewed as a 'good' employer. M&S prided itself on introducing staff 'welfare' services in the early 1930s which included the provision of pensions, subsidized staff canteens, health and dental care, hairdressing, rest rooms and camping holidays. Such practices have continued over the years and the company works at being seen to be fair with people. For example, when it was decided to freeze graduate recruitment in 1999, as a gesture of goodwill they gave the equivalent of one month's salary (around £1,500) to each of the graduates to whom they had withdrawn their offer of employment (Welch 1999).

The company has promoted good human relations because, as Lord Sieff a former Chairman explained 'we are human beings at work not industrial beings' (1984, quoted in Blyton and Turnbull 1998) and 'good human relations at work pay off; they are of great importance if a business is to be efficiently run' (1990, p. 245, quoted in Blyton and Turnbull 1998). The company's approach to trade unions is that employees have a right to join one, but that unions are not recognized for negotiation purposes – except where legislation requires them to do so, as in mainland Europe. With good HR practices, M&S believe that trade unions are not necessary. However, although M&S have traditionally put a strong emphasis on personnel management, giving it strategic importance (Blyton and Turnbull 1998), Clara Freeman lost her position as Executive Director for UK stores and personnel in September 2000 as part of the management restructuring programme (Cooper 2000). An M&S spokesperson denied that the HR function was being downgraded as HR was being represented at executive level by the chief legal adviser and company secretary; nevertheless, a company analyst commenting on the situation suggested that 'personnel directors do not make money' (Cooper 2000).

Continental closures

In order to retrench and cut costs, in 2001 Marks & Spencer decided to close stores across Europe, and an announcement was made on 29 March that the shops in France and Belgium were to close. It is estimated that this restructuring involved around 38 stores in total and upward of 4,000 employees; in France the numbers were reported as 18 shops and 1,700 workers.

The announcement caused great controversy and uproar, particularly in France. It was alleged that managers were informed by e-mail and that the closure announcement took place only five minutes after the initial, informal, meeting with worker representatives, which reportedly did not constitute a consultation that conformed to the French work-code. The timing of the announcement corresponded with the opening of the London Stock Exchange, 8.00 am.

Although trade unions are not recognized by M&S in the UK (as discussed above), some French workers were. On their behalf, several trade unions filed a complaint against M&S claiming that they had broken French labour law by only informing the staff at the same time as they informed the UK Stock Exchange of the decision to close the stores. A French court later ruled that Marks & Spencer had acted illegally by not consulting with employees before announcing closure; the company were told that they had to suspend their plans until full consultation had taken place.

Marks & Spencer denied having acted in any way to contravene legislation in France, claiming that it was abiding by UK law and the rules governing listed companies. They argued that under these rules a quoted company has to inform the market of any major developments in its activities without delay. Further, they were only announcing that they intended to close stores by the end of the year. The implication is clearly that worker consultation would have leaked the news and this may have affected stock-market activity and share prices; as it was, M&S shares jumped 7 per cent on the day.

Marks & Spencer appealed against the ruling which was later overruled. However, the jobs were saved as the stores were bought by the department-store group Galeries Lafayette which,

as part of the deal, secured the jobs of the workers. Both trade unions and works committees in France were consulted prior to the deal.

Reaction to the closures

Following the announcement of the store closures, emotions were running very high. It was perceived that M&S were intent on restructuring due to a business crisis, but with little thought for the French workers. The French government encouraged trade union action against Marks & Spencer's decision: the labour minister called for a Europe-wide trade union protest; the Prime Minister, Lionel Jospin, described the company's actions in closing the stores as 'unacceptable' and called for the Labour Ministry to launch its own enquiry.

In protest over the closures, Marks & Spencer workers took to the streets. It was reported that more than 1,000 workers from across Europe protested outside the company's main UK store in London on 17 May 2001. There were also protests in Paris and at the European Parliament in Strasbourg.

In the UK, the French workers were supported by the Trades Union Congress (TUC), which supported the London demonstration. The TUC General Secretary was reported as saying 'M&S thought they could export the UK's easy hire-and-fire rules to the rest of Europe' (Benham and Freeman 2001). Contrary to this, an M&S spokesperson is quoted as saying 'We're convinced that we complied with all legal requirements . . . we're surprised by the reaction of the authorities' (*Guardian* 2001b).

French labour law, custom and culture

The French government takes an interventionist approach to employment relations. Their reaction discussed above was partly as a result of their drive to reduce unemployment in the country. Works councils were created by law in France in 1945 and are one of the channels of worker representation, the other two being workforce delegates and trade unions. In most companies these organizations coexist; however, works councils are playing an ever-increasing role. They are made up of elected employee representatives and they have the right to information and consultation which includes issues such as redundancy (EIRO 1998; Hollinshead and Leat 1995). It was the perceived failure of M&S to follow these consultation laws which caused unrest following the announcement of store closures.

Although not a direct result of Marks & Spencer's action but spurred on by it, the French government rushed through proposals to increase employment rights in order to protect workers' jobs. The resulting 'social modernization' bill included: the doubling of minimum redundancy pay; increased powers for works councils with regard to redundancy and a longer time period for consideration of redundancy plans; nine-month redeployment leave for redundant workers (EIRO 2001a).

One of the factors that M&S may not have taken account of in its decision to announce the shop closures the way it did, is the culture of the French people. The French are renowned for 'taking to the streets' to demonstrate for social and political reasons. In 1968, ten million people went on strike to demand a fairer form of capitalism which would create an economy to benefit all; in June 2003, people took to the streets to demonstrate over pension reforms. The French people believe that organizations have a social responsibility. Books of condolence were set up in M&S shops and were filled by people who had empathy with their fellow workers. The feeling of the people was perhaps summed up by French Prime Minster Jospin when he stated 'the employees who enriched Marks & Spencer's shareholders deserve better treatment. Such behaviour should be punished' (*Guardian* 2001b).

Source: Information was gathered from the following sources: BBC (2001a, 2001b); CNN (2001a, 2001b); EIRO (2001a, 2001b); Marks & Spencer (2003); *People Management* (2001); Guardian (2001a, 2001b, 2001c).

Case study discussion topic

1 From the Marks & Spencer experience described above, identify issues that can be learned by an international human resource manager.
2 What learning and knowledge skills will they draw upon?
3 What interpersonal and communication skills might be employed?
4 Imagine that you are the HR manager for a company in this situation, suggest ways in which you feel the company may have acted differently. Take into account cultural sensitivity and the psychological contract.

SUMMARY

The discussion above has taken us through the complexities of the competencies required by an international human resource manager. As has been discussed, these cannot be seen as discrete entities but are interlinked and related.

As can be seen from Schuler *et al.*'s (2001) list, the competencies required by an HR manager are many and varied. In this chapter we have taken this further and discussed the depth of the competencies required. As we discussed in the introduction, organization managers are working in ever-growing, more complex areas; the HR manager may encounter different values and cultures even when working in a domestic environment. Moreover, in order to manage across a variety of countries, cultures, languages and, in some cases, business operations, the IHR manager requires a greater depth of knowledge of both the business operations and environmental settings than their domestic counterparts. As we have identified, there is a dynamic relationship between the organization and its environment, with each affecting and being affected by the other. It is this that the IHR manager needs to be aware of and take into account when discussing, advising, consulting, persuading or negotiating with other parties in the employment relationship, whether this is other senior management, line managers, government representatives or worker representatives.

The chapter has also discussed how HR practices may not be easily transferable to other countries and systems of employment. Again, the different knowledge and skills of the IHR manager are entwined as he or she needs to be aware of local country and cultural practices and how these may affect, or be affected by, organizational policies and practices.

We have also seen how interpersonal and communications skills become increasingly important as an organization grows across national and international boundaries. This is especially important when we take into account the many different languages and cultures which need to be recognized. IHR managers need to have a deep sense of cultural sensitivity in order to be able to understand and take account of the feelings and actions of employees. This is especially relevant with regard to the psychological contract which is often fragile and easily broken. Even with awareness of ones own culture and language, the managing of the psychological contract is extremely difficult, and to do this across cultures is at the best very complicated and at the worst almost impossible. Clearly, in order to become a successful IHR manager it is necessary to draw on a number of different skills at any given time, indeed to employ cognitive complexity (Barham and BerthoinAntal 1994; Schneider and Barsoux 2003).

Chapter ten

Challenges Facing International Human Resource Management

Mustafa Özbilgin
Case study by Niccola Swan

Learning outcomes

After reading this chapter, you should be able to:

- Identify the key challenges facing IHRM today.
- Recognize the impact of globalization and its implications for the international management of people.
- Examine various puzzles within of IHRM that are facing its professional practice and theory.

INTRODUCTION

Human resource management (HRM) has advanced into new realms of professional and academic legitimacy, and penetration of its discourse into these domains at institutional, national and international levels has been both rapid and unyielding. Its persuasive and pervasive discourse achieved global appeal as it captured the essence of neoliberal internationalization that has left its legacy in our times. The global take-up of HRM principles, particularly in multinational, transnational and international firms and joint ventures, has engendered puzzles when faced with the complexity of the cross-national and cross-cultural encounters. In this framework, international HRM (IHRM) has gained legitimacy, emerging as a response to unpack such puzzles. This chapter examines the contemporary challenges that are facing IHRMs including the challenges presented by globalization, demarcations of HRM, its local versus universal perspectives, ethical considerations and professionalization.

GLOBALIZATION AND IHRM

Increased international trade has engendered cross-national encounters of unprecedented nature and scope, deeming management of people from different cultures an essential ingredient for corporate success. The impact of globalization has been explored in earlier chapters, which in exploring the dynamics of IHRM in the context of globalization have presented an operational view of globalization. What needs to be restated is the exploitative and imbalanced movement of international capital across national borders, often in pursuit of cost-minimization. This is characteristic of the field of IHRM, which hosts a wide spectrum of perspectives often leading to polarization of prognosis and diagnosis of, and prescriptions for, people-management problems. Furthermore, the increased diversity of demographic backgrounds of people, partly owing to the internationalization of workforces, adds to the complexity of challenges facing people management today.

The endemic interest in productivity, performance and effectiveness in a world of increased global and cross-border competition informs every venue of work, organization and employment today. HRM has become both an outcome and a vehicle of these discourses. However, these trends also warrant critical insights. From a cynical perspective, HRM's explicit promise to individual workers, to offer an alternative mechanism of voice through accommodation of their expectations in organizations, has been very instrumental in concealing its broader promise to employers, that is competitive advantage and increased productivity through effective management of people. Bourdieu (1998, p. 31) condemned the pervasive nature of this discourse, as well as its ultimate emphasis on shareholder value, and explains that,

> in France, instead of 'the employers' [*le patronat*] they say 'the vital force for the nation' [*les forces vives de la nation*]; a company that fires its workers is 'slimming', with a sporting reference (an energetic body has to be thin). To announce that a company is sacking 2,000 people, the commentator will refer to 'Alcatel's bold social plan'. Then there is a whole game with the connotations and associations of words like flexibility, *souplesse*, deregulation, which tends to imply that the neo-liberal message is a universalist message of liberation.

The spread of the neo-liberal ideology has been widely blamed for a general move away from collectivism towards individualism, from collective voice through trade unions to the individual voice through the use of sophisticated HRM approaches in industrialized societies. Therefore, individualization of employment relations is a reality which remains largely uncontested in industrialized societies; so is the uptake of IHRM approaches in international firms. Workforce heterogeneity, partly induced by internationalization, in increasingly individualized organizational settings, and the way such heterogeneity may contribute to or inhibit organizational performance, creativity and innovation have become key concerns for practitioners and researchers of IHRM. Management of diversity, in its full spectrum of demographic variations, is now considered a key challenge and a strategic concern for many multinational companies.

GEOGRAPHIC, ECONOMIC AND LINGUISTIC IMAGINATION OF IHRM

It is argued that IHRM, as an academic area of writing, faces three major challenges in its geographic, economic and linguistic imagination and reach (Özbilgin 2002, 2004).

First, human resource management is a manifestly 'Western' concept, originating in and dominated by empirical and theoretical knowledge from North American and Western European countries. Similarly, the majority of IHRM texts are written by authors from this cultural and geographic area, displaying a kind of constrained diversity in terms of its contributors, and socio-cultural specificity in terms of its geographic reach.

Second, language poses one of the major challenges to the assumption that human resource management is a universally applicable concept. Considering difficulties with translation, there is often rudimentary use of sources published in other languages in mainstream English-language IHRM texts. Clark, Gospel and Montgomery (1999) identify two forms of such parochialism in the IHRM texts. First such texts often fail to acknowledge earlier works and methods of cross-national and international study. And a second kind of parochialism relates to the domination of Anglo-Saxon research publications in this field. Although this may appear to be an obvious problem, it is yet the most insidious one as it simply demarcates our knowledge of HRM practice to those geographies where the English language was able to penetrate.

Based on a review of 22 IHRM journals, Özbilgin (2004) argues that although they only provide a partial geography of the international context, IHRM texts still continue to claim 'international' in their titles. Özbilgin and Healy (2003), for example, have noted that HRM practice in the Middle East has remained outside the focus of the IHRM literature. The areas where the English language fails to penetrate converge with geographies of poverty and economic weakness. The ethical challenge that this exclusion poses to academics is twofold: (a) how far does continuing to exclude those regions, which are already underprivileged, from academic imagination contribute to the vicious cycle of their poverty? and (b) could IHRM strip itself of its heritage as an academic field, which deals with issues in a moral or political vacuum, and adopt a more emancipating role?

Third, the difficulty of formulating overarching conceptual frameworks, theoretical models and critical approaches is a recurring theme in IHRM texts. Empirical studies on IHRM are rare, but once made available their assertions find their way to mainstream texts and they are used extensively in teaching and further research. Such studies come with extensive expressions of limitations of method and analysis. However, due to the rarity of their occurrence, great significance is attributed to these studies as their findings are often overstated, misinterpreted or used out of context. Although Hofstede's work in the 1960s and 1970s challenged the assumption that the theoretical frameworks developed in the USA would be universally applicable (Schneider 2001), later treatment of Hofstede's IBM studies, beyond the scope of their intended use, either as a clear indicator of convergence and divergence of management practices or for the purposes of training expatriates, epitomizes this unusual academic phenomenon. In order to address this problem, smaller scale comparative or international projects should also be informing, as these often can offer deep insights and give voice to views and experiences from the margins that larger-scale comparative studies may fail to capture.

Divergence and convergence of IHRM practices in countries with emerging, transitional, developing and developed economies have also been extensively studied in the IHRM literature (Napier 1998). The reasons for divergence of IHRM practices are multifaceted: first, the impact of economic development on the quality of terms and conditions of employment as well as on methods of people management cannot be overstated. Secondly, the heterogeneity in legal, economic and political challenges facing companies in the developed and less-developed parts of the world are fostering divergences at the level of practice. While the main source of convergence rests with the building of economic and political alliances between countries and the spread of advances in communication and transportation technologies which had a moderating impact on radical national differences, divergence prevails due to the aforementioned reasons.

Multinational companies, which set up branches in emerging or less- developed economies, predominantly originate from developed countries. This bodes difficulties in direct transfer of human resource practices, which are developed in advanced economies, to be implemented in countries with developing or less-developed economies, and has further ethical implications for voice and representation of employees in host countries. Therefore both the theoretical and practical imagination of IHRM is severely constrained. Only by a critical recognition of these constraints can academics and practitioners seek to overcome them.

LOCAL VERSUS UNIVERSAL PERSPECTIVES

One of the key themes in the IHRM literature is the choice of using or developing local HRM practices or importing these from other countries. This has been of particular import for MNCs (Jain, Lawler and Morishima 1998). In developing international human resource policy, practitioners are presented with a number of choices. Janssens (2001) identified three such choices in the literature and added a fourth one, which can provide an alternative to others:

1 They may export best practice in HRM from other countries; this is termed as an *exportive approach*.
2 They may adapt to the best practice in HRM in the host country; this is termed aa *adaptive approach*.
3 They may integrate various best practices from different countries; this is termed an *integrative approach*.
4 They may formulate new HRM practices by recognizing and transcending the individual cultures; this approach is termed a *synergistic approach* to IHRM.

These policy choices are used in different combinations in international operations. However, based on an extensive review of IHRM literature in the 1980s and 1990s, Clark *et al.* (2000) identified that there are two key tendencies in IHRM writing. IHRM publications display both parochial and ethnocentric tendencies, and the implication of this at the levels of policy and practice would be a lack of a polycentric knowledge base informing the policy choices of practitioners. Therefore, it is not surprising to find the first two policy choices are more evident in practice than the latter two.

Due to their economic, social, business and ethical implications, the debate on adopting universal or particular approaches, or developing new context-specific ones in IHRM continues to prevail.

MANAGING A DIVERSE WORKFORCE

Following the International Women's Congress in Beijing (1996), over 150 countries undersigned the CEDAW (Convention on Elimination of all forms of Discrimination Against Women). The convention was instrumental in raising awareness and encouraging signatory governments to take effective steps to eradicate sex discrimination. Now there is an increased level of national and international legislation offering protection against discrimination based on sex, race, disability, sexual orientation and other arbitrary factors, particularly in the developed countries. This legal trend is encouraging different forms of workplace diversity to become more visible. However, Özbilgin and Healy (2004) have identified, in their study of professorial careers and gender equality, that equal opportunities by sex can be achieved only if the legal case for equality is complemented by ideological support for equality at the micro, meso and macro levels. The HRM function often assumes a key role in management of workforce diversity and equal opportunities in organizations where there is not a more specialized unit.

IHRM displays a greater interest in management of diversity, since the international level, by definition, embodies a greater level of diversity than the national level. Therefore, several texts and papers on IHRM have recently chosen to address management of diversity as a key theme (Tung 1993; Albrecht and Luthans 2000).

At the international level, Stephen and Black (1991) noted the significance of work–life balance issues with a study on 67 American expatriate managers. They indicated that recognition of career aspirations of not only the expatriates, but also their spouses, who may be trailing them, is an important IHRM consideration. This new awareness has also prompted writers to challenge the 'malestream' nature of the dominant approaches to HRM (Linehan and Walsh 2000). Truss (1999) argued that the interrelationship between HRM and equality and diversity at work should be viewed in the context of other social, political and economic processes.

ETHICAL ISSUES IN IHRM

Winstanley and Woodall (2002) hail the 2000s as the era of the adolescence of ethical considerations in HRM. International HRM is an area ripe with multifaceted ethical concerns: firstly, HRM has been subject to increased levels of ethical scrutiny due to its failure to provide a balanced interface between employers and employees. HRM suggests a highly individualized meritocratic structure of workplace representation where individual employees can influence the terms and conditions of their employment contract based on their individual contribution to the overall performance of the company. This individualized notion of representation poses a challenge to collective understandings of workplace representation and trade unionism. Therefore, this rhetorical formulation bodes ill in practice. In the context of greater economic and political clout of commercial enterprises, individual bargaining power may only remain marginal. Hence it can be argued that the practice of HRM exposes employees to new kinds of uncertainty and employment risk.

International, multinational and transnational companies attract large pools of skilled labour from which to draw their employees. Individual employees' powers of negotiation to affect their conditions are less in these international operations, and therefore the ethical concerns over the diminishing power of employees due to cultural and structural assumptions of HRM are exacerbated in the international context.

Secondly, the driving force behind the expansion of multinational companies has not only been the growth in the global market, but also the search for cheap labour and resources leading to 'social dumping' (for European companies), the avoidance of high labour costs (for North American companies) and the pursuit of less-competitive markets than their highly competitive national market (for Japanese companies) (Jain, Lawler and Morishima 1998). These motives highlight the unidirectional desire of multinational companies from developed countries to take advantage of labour and material resources of developing and less-developed countries. The aforementioned motives coupled with rudimentary levels of legal, political or social policing of MNCs at the international level, their ever-increasing economic and political power and the dependency of developing countries on their investments, collectively contribute to the exploitation of labour by these companies.

The differences between pay and conditions of employment between developed and less-developed countries have been an area of major ethical contention. A similarly significant ethical problem is evident when different national approaches and legal frameworks of equality of opportunity allow MNCs to perpetuate discriminatory practices which are not unlawful or common practice in a host country, even if such practices are unlawful or socially unacceptable in the home country of the company. Ethics is a contemporary theme that has gained significance in the IHRM literature in the last decade. As the imbalances in economic and political power of MNCs in developed and developing countries remain unchallenged, ethical issues pertaining to IHRM are set to burden practitioners.

The dualistic nature of IHRM approaches has been identified as a challenge for practitioners. Echoing the 'hard' and 'soft' HRM debate, the choice between instrumental (focusing on effective deployment of staff in order to achieve organizational objectives) and value-based (focusing on welfare and well-being of staff both as an end in itself and for achieving organizational objectives) approaches to IHRM pose a contemporary challenge for practitioners.

Exploring IHRM in organizational settings around the themes of operations, commitment, learning, flexibility and knowledge transfers, Jackson (2002) identifies that these strategic considerations are indeed informed by both instrumentalist and humanist concerns over the effective use of human resources in cross-cultural contexts. This implies that in an ideal world, IHRM practice should be informed by stakeholder interests, which may range from instrumental deployment of human resources to demonstrating a genuine concern for human welfare and well-being in organizational settings.

The stakeholder approach has many merits in recognizing the divergent nature of interests and expectations placed on an organization from its external and internal environments. However, at the same time, the nature of stakeholder engagement and involvement occurs in a spectrum. While some companies may choose to ignore the voice of various stakeholder groups for the sake of shareholder interests, others may pursue a different line underpinned by a belief that serving stakeholders indeed improves shareholder value in the long term. Even for an organization that seeks to have a stakeholder approach to IHRM, differentiating stakeholder voice from stakeholder noise remains a challenge for management practitioners.

PROFESSIONALIZATION VERSUS INTEGRATION OF IHRM

HRM has been at the crossroads of becoming further professionalized or being assimilated as a line-management responsibility in organizations. The debate on the future of HRM is ongoing, but the current trends indicate that HRM is emerging as a new profession internationally. A similar paradox is evident in the IHRM profession: while IHRM gains currency as a professional area of work, the value and contribution of the corporate IHRM function is questioned. In order to understand what makes IHRM a profession, the notion of professionalization should be defined, and four distinct attributes of a profession can be identified. First, the field of study in which a profession is located embodies an intellectual component. The intellectual component of IHRM is evident in the number of articles and texts published in this field. As Caligiuri (1999) identifies, IHRM has a growing body of academic writing and it has established itself a respectable place between the disciplines of international management and human resource management.

Secondly, emerging professions have extensive requirements of training and experience in order for new members to qualify as new professionals. IHRM is now a common subject taught at undergraduate and postgraduate levels in higher-education institutions which offer the specialization of HRM. Thirdly, the emerging professions have systems and processes for organizing and accrediting members. Institutions such as the Chartered Institute of Personnel and Development in the UK offer professional qualifications and special membership opportunities through a system of accreditation. Finally, the emerging professions have codes of conduct: Growing numbers of international companies and also national institutes of people management in developed countries offer codes of conduct for management of international human resources.

Based on these criteria, IHRM could be termed as an emerging profession. However, IHRM also has its critics. In a controversial article, Foster (2000) contends that the concept of the 'international manager' is merely a myth. He argues that particularly in the UK, the number of international assignments for professional managers have been declining since the 1980s and the psychological and social well-being of managers, contrary to common wisdom, are adversely affected by international assignments. Despite this interesting insight, the reasons which make IHRM an emerging profession continue to justify the existence and contribution of IHRM to decision-making at a managerial level and as a specialized and professional function. For example, Svoboda and Schoreder (2001) examined the development of human resource managers at Deutsche Bank AG, arguing that there are competitive and strategic pressures for human resource managers to professionalize further. They explain that this can be achieved through action and project-oriented learning, new technologies for network-based learning and the use of academic knowledge in order to combine both. However, the debate on eliminating the corporate IHRM function through its integration to line-management roles prevails and warrants further examination.

As an academic subject in its adolescence, IHRM embodies opportunities for the generation of actionable knowledge and critical debate. Although some of these current challenges and puzzles pertaining to IHRM have been examined here, this book has highlighted that IHRM may provide solutions to these challenges and puzzles through creative and thoughtful action informed by an awareness of the dynamic relationships evident in the international, national, organizational and micro-social contexts.

GROUP ACTIVITY

Based on a review of literature, identify the significance of these emerging themes in the practice and theory of HRM in a country of your choice.

Explain your methods for finding the relevant literature and identify useful sources of information.

Case study 10

DIVERSITY MANAGEMENT AT BARCLAYS: a focus on ethnicity

Niccola Swan

In a mature, fiercely competitive financial services market like ours, it would be a dereliction of our duty to close ourselves off from any talent pool based on outdated and frankly immoral notions of race, gender, disability, sexual orientation, age or other barrier.
(Matthew Barrett, CEO, Barclays Plc)

Barclays is a financial-services group engaged primarily in banking, investment banking and asset management with its headquarters in the UK and operations in 60 countries. It is one of the largest financial services groups in the United Kingdom. The group also operates in many other countries around the world and is a leading provider of coordinated global services to multinational corporations and financial institutions in the world's main financial centres. Barclays has been involved in banking for over 300 years and operates in over 60 countries, employing over 78,000 staff globally.

Equality and diversity at Barclays

In 2001, Barclays made a fundamental shift in its approach to equality and diversity, putting it at the heart of business strategy, and mainstreaming the principles into all the organization's activities as a business and an employer. To show it means business, the members of the Group Executive Committee (EXCO) have all personally signed a commitment in the form of the Equality and Diversity Charter to take Barclays to the leading edge worldwide on equality and diversity polices and practices.

The commitment was particularly noteworthy for two reasons. Firstly, the executive consciously undertook to address all diversity issues including disability, race, gender, sexual orientation, religion and age from the outset, an approach which is unusual even amongst leading companies in this area. Secondly, the programme is designed to integrate an equality and diversity rationale into all Barclays activities, with customers, employees, suppliers and community considerations built in. The result is an unprecedented programme of activity, carefully prepared with extensive stakeholder consultation over the proceeding months, which continues to drive change. The text below sets out the work that Barclays have carried out in the field of racial and ethnic equality and diversity in the UK.

Barclays' work on race is an integral part of the group's major drive to achieve equality and diversity, which also includes a focus on issues of gender, sexual orientation, age, religion, disability and working patterns. As a result, race issues are included in a broad range of the company's processes and activities, including performance management, group-wide objectives, executive commitments, training and communications. Detailed below is a range of activities that Barclays has undertaken specifically on race, under the Equality and Diversity programme.

Barclays achieved the Gold Standard in the 2002 BITC (Business In The Community) Race for Opportunity national benchmarking and is working hard to ensure inclusion of people from all ethnic backgrounds. As part of this benchmarking, Barclays was praised for its 'commitment to working on race and diversity as a business agenda'.

Ethnic origin

- The total number of employees from an ethnic-minority background in the UK increased slightly from 5,243 to 5,306 between December 2002 and March 2003.
- The percentage representation remains constant at 8.3% (2004) and compares favourably to the 2001 Census results, where 7.9% of the population in the UK said that they were from an ethnic minority (excluding 'Irish').
- However, it remains the case that ethnic-minority employees are concentrated in the

lower grades, with 81% of ethnic-minority employees in levels *B1–B3*, compared to 69% of white employees. This figure has not changed since December 2002.

■ The number of ethnic-minority senior executive (SX) employees remains at 10 and the percentage is unchanged at 2.4%.

■ The SX feeder level at B7 increased from 58 to 62, which is a slight percentage increase from 3.3% to 3.4% between December 2002 and March 2003.

■ The representation of ethnic-minority employees at B5 and B6 grades remains unchanged at 4.3%.

The target for 2005 is that 3 per cent of senior executive employees will be from an ethnic-minority background and this appears to be achievable given the current rate of progress. It is important, however, that Barclays ensures that the feeder pools are also increasing at an appropriate rate and that the company's own talent pool is also developing, rather than relying on external recruits for senior positions. To that end, the December 2002 Global Diversity Council meeting agreed a target of 5% ethnic-minority representation at the B7 level by December 2005 (Figure 10.1).

Recruitment

The recruitment process has been fully reviewed to ensure it fairly assesses everyone's abilities and potential. As a result of this review certain psychometric tests are no longer used. Ethnic-minority staff have also been trained as assessors, and universities with high proportions of ethnic-minority students have been targeted in the Barclays recruitment round. Members of the Barclays race taskforce attend career fairs and open days at universities to act as role models and encourage ethnic-minority students to apply. In addition, a workshop was held at Bradford University to help explain the application and assessment process to undergraduates. In 2002, 20% of the graduate intake came from ethnic-minority backgrounds, showing that focused work with individual teams is really paying dividends.

For several years, Barclays has been one of the main corporate sponsors of the National Mentoring Consortium (NMC), set up to provide support for ethnic-minority students. In addition to providing finance, Barclays employees have the opportunity to act as mentors to students involved in the NMC, and 57 members of staff were involved in this way in 2002.

Barclays is also involved in London First's

Figure 10.1 *Progress of senior ethnic-minority employees against 2005 targets*

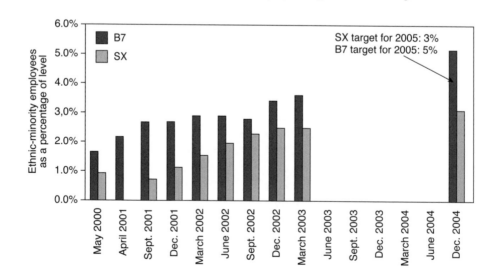

Summer Placement Scheme, which aims to facilitate and support London 'blue-chip' companies who wish to recruit students who live and study in London, many of whom are from an ethnic-minority background. Students are preselected by London First creating an undergraduate/graduate talent pool, from which employers can select individuals for summer work placements.

The careers of several Barclays ethnic-minority employees have been profiled in *Proud*, a magazine targeted at the Black community. A pilot initiative to ensure that the company's employee base reflected the local community in the Bradford region has been successful with interesting consequences for business success in the area. This is a significant achievement and has involved working with the wider community as part of a programme to reflect that local community in the company's employee base.

Development and support

Barclays first cultural network event was hosted by the Group Race Champion, Bob Hunter, Chief Executive of Barclays Private Clients, in October 2002. The event brought over 150 Barclays employees together to discuss whether to establish a permanent cultural diversity network to bring together people interested in race ethnicity issues and help with career development. Plans to launch the first regional network in the London area are now coming together.

Pilot career-development events for ethnic minority employees at a range of levels have taken place with great success. The objective has been to support individuals in their career aspirations and to help provide guidance and techniques on progressing in the organizational culture. Several individuals have had promotions as a result of this training.

There are multifaith quiet rooms in several locations that can be used by employees for prayer and meditation. Barclays also celebrates different religious festivals as part of the organizational commitment to diversity, through internal communications and recognition of different festivals in the branch network. Religious holiday swaps are available in many areas of the group. At the same time, Barclays is piloting bank holiday swaps in the contact centres and this will be rolled out in 2003. The objective of this scheme is to facilitate the swap of currently protected bank holidays, particularly for employees who wish to celebrate religious festivals that don't fall on bank holidays. Feedback has shown that staff are very keen to participate.

Barclays has recently updated its new Asian corporate-wear collection as part of its 2003 range, to keep pace with current fashions and cultural preferences. Creating the new collection involved consultations between staff and fashion consultant Jeff Banks, who drew his inspiration for the garments from all over Asia. This new range is a visual demonstration of the work being undertaken to support the group's equality and diversity ethos and helps to mirror the company's customer base, especially on religious celebration days.

Customer focus

Barclays actively participated in research led by the Bank of England, in partnership with the British Bankers Association and the Commission for Racial Equality, into establishing whether the provision of finance to ethnic-minority businesses is fair and equal. The research did not demonstrate a difference in access to finance, but Barclays nevertheless undertook to ensure this is the case by putting in place further measures to help employees fully understand customers' cultures and expectations.

In addition, Barclays has undertaken research and focus groups into how ethnic-minority customers (personal and small business) see it and the financial services industry in general. Barclays has also undertaken research into the profile and demands of ethnic-minority entrepreneurs in the UK. This research, together with survey materials, forms the base data that the bank needs for both personal and small-business customers, to enable them to track progress and to consider whether setting some objectives will be appropriate. The linkage between customer diversity and employee diversity is well-established at Barclays.

Other initiatives with which Barclays has been involved include:

Executive Professional Network (EPN)

Barclays is a corporate sponsor of the EPN, a networking and socializing forum, which is specifically targeted at black professionals, business owners and those working in professional environments. Their aim is to connect individuals and companies to the culture, lifestyle and employment requirements of black professionals through a wide range of events and initiatives.

In 2002, the company support ensured the continuation of EPN's well-circulated newsletter and assisted them in staging the 2002 'Men & Women of Merit' event. This was very well-attended and awards were presented to individuals to recognize the work they undertake within ethnic communities. Barclays received the Corporate Award for its numerous sponsorships and support within ethnic communities at the EPN 100 'Black Men of London' Annual Gala.

Race on The Agenda (ROTA)

Barclays is a primary sponsor of the work on citizenship in the national curriculum, which has included financial support for the launch of the Business and Education conference, and a series of ongoing projects including a citizenship pack and film, a teachers' support network and revamping the citizenship website. As part of this work, the bank sponsored the ROTA conference, looking at how the citizenship agenda can support the full integration of ethnic-minority children into UK society.

Asian Achievement In Britain (AAIB) – Jewel Awards

AAIB was established in November 2001 to celebrate the success and achievements of the Asian community in Britain today. As a result, AAIB has highlighted successful role models and those companies and organizations that have encouraged and enabled such individuals to succeed in their chosen careers. Barclays supported the AAIB Jewel Awards for Business and Commerce, which

is split into three regional programmes in northern, central and southern Britain.

Respect, anti-racism festival – July 2002

Barclays was one of the sponsors of an anti-racist and multicultural music festival for London which attracted a crowd of 100,000, of all ages, backgrounds and interests, the largest event of its kind in London. This event was attended by Oona King MP, Diane Abbott MP and London Mayor Ken Livingstone.

Dhek Bhal

Barclays is supporting Dhek Bhal, a registered charity based in the centre of Barton Hill an ethnic-minority area of Bristol. The area is predominantly Asian and has many families on low income and unemployment making this an area of deprivation. The aim of Dhek Bhal, which means 'Looking After' in English, is to promote the health and social well-being of South Asian people in Bristol and south Gloucestershire, through a range of services which build on the strength of cultural diversity. Barclays support will provide additional funding for the sitting service to relieve carers of their responsibilities for a few hours each week, with holidays for the carers. A play scheme will also be able to take in additional children from the inner city, and young people from the youth project will be able to film a documentary and launch it on their own website.

Minority Ethnic Carers of Older People

This organization aims to provide a culturally sensitive respite break for minority-ethnic carers, which addresses both their physical needs and well-being. A Barclays donation will help the service become established.

Blackburn with Darwen Education Action Zone

The Education Action Zone is developing a family numeracy project for families living in the Audley area of Blackburn. Audley is ranked 61st on England's ward of deprivations out of 8,414 wards, and in some schools in the zone 95% of pupils are from families speaking English as an additional language. The project will support parents to gain basic numeracy skills to enable them to help their children's learning and increase their confidence in dealing with day-to-day numeracy matters. Parents of younger children will attend sessions during school hours where they will work with qualified tutors to develop a range of skills in a financial context. Barclays funding is helping to cover material and resources, childcare costs where necessary, refreshments, travel and management and administration costs.

Foundation for Young Musicians

The Foundation for Young Musicians is the funding arm of the Centre for Young Musicians (CYM), an organization that offers high-quality instrumental and music training to 2,600 young Londoners who attend state schools. Over 40% are from minority communities. Barclays funding is helping the centre to purchase and replace a number of instruments making music accessible to more youngsters.

Art Asian Trust

Barclays money is being used to help Art Asia hold a concert for anyone in Southampton who is interested in Asian music, thus promoting inclusion within the local area.

Asian Counselling Services

Barclays has enabled this service to replace its only computer and printer which had become broken beyond repair.

Bharat Hindu Samaj

The aims of the Bharat Hindu Samaj are to benefit inhabitants of Peterborough and the neighbourhood, and with the support of Peterborough city council the group has been able to open a community centre, which is open to all. However, the kitchen was in a bad state of repair and the community centre risked losing its kitchen facilities. Food is often a focal point of gatherings held in the centre, and Barclays funding will allow a new kitchen to be built which will meet the necessary Health and Safety standards.

Summer Camps project

Currently under development, Barclays is supporting a summer camps project run by Inspired Futures, with a view to developing a generation of young people with potential to be leaders in their communities, through giving an opportunity to understand the significance of living and working cross-culturally.

Batley High School for boys

Barclays sponsored Batley High School for a project they are working on to create a Heritage Library. The project will help raise key awareness of customs and etiquette, reflecting on Batleys multicultural population.

London Schools and The Black Child Conference

In 2002, Barclays supported the Greater London Authority (GLA), London Schools and the Black Child Conference, hosted by London Mayor Ken Livingstone and Diane Abbott, Hackney MP. The recommendation report produced following the conference was presented to the Education Minister who acknowledged the issues and made a statement of intent and support funding; 2,000 parents, teachers, school governors and policymakers attended.

Improving the poor school records and number of exclusions of many children of African and Caribbean descent in London was a key theme of this groundbreaking Barclays-supported conference. Barclays involvement and sponsorship of this event fits with its current focus on school achievement, social inclusion and regeneration.

Areas of discussion have included the underachievement of black children in London schools, the high number of exclusions, how to achieve excellence within education and reward teachers and children who have excelled. Barclays support was well-received by those who attended from various clusters and businesses, and within this relationship the bank supports and promotes various charities and projects.

Overseas

While the majority of Barclays employees are based in the UK, Barclays has operations across the world, and the group are now extending the Equality and Diversity programme to France, Spain, Germany, Zambia, Ghana and the USA, where work is already well-underway. National definitions of ethnic minorities and cultural attitudes to monitoring and integration differ greatly across these countries, so this is an interesting new area of work for the Barclays programme.

*   *   *

These diverse activities seek to celebrate racial and ethnic diversity, foster equality and challenge discrimination in Barclays Plc. In the words of its CEO, these efforts are not about paying lip-service to equality and diversity:

> This is not about political correctness. Equality and diversity is not a 'nice to do', but a significant part of the answer to our business challenges. From the day I first walked through the door at Barclays I have been determined to ensure that we would stand out from the crowd for the right reasons on this issue. (Matthew Barrett, CEO, Barclays Plc)

Case study discussion topics

1   What are the challenges facing the diversity manager of Barclays Bank? Consider issues pertaining to an international and diverse workforce.
2   If you were a manager with such responsibility, what courses of specific action would you take in order to improve the current state of diversity at Barclays Bank?
3   Justify your plan of action drawing on your readings from earlier sections of this book.

SUMMARY

This chapter has examined the contemporary challenges facing IHRM, providing insights into some of its many puzzles. It is noted that globalization and internationalization of trade have significantly transformed the challenges facing employers in the twenty-first century. Although technological advancements have supported faster transportation of goods, services and information than ever before, and by doing so aided further cross-fertilization of technological innovation and advancements, the new race is for fostering such developments and innovations in the management of people. Such cross-fertilization of management ideas, values and principles in HRM requires comparative insights from a field of study and management practice which has outgrown its infancy.

Bibliography

PERIODICALS OF INTEREST

Academy of Management Executive
Academy of Management Journal
Academy of Management Review
British Journal of Industrial Relations
British Journal of Management
Business Horizons
California Management Review
Career Development International
Columbia Journal of World Business
European Journal of Industrial Relations
European Journal of Work and Organizational Psychology
European Management Review
Gender, Work and Organization
Harvard Business Review
HR Focus
HR Magazine
Human Relations
Human Resource Development International
Human Resource Management
Human Resource Management Journal
International Business Review
International Journal of Human Resource Management
International Journal of Intercultural Training
International Journal of Manpower
International Journal of Manpower
International Journal of Selection and Assessment
International Labour Review
International Management
International Studies of Management and Organization
Journal of Applied Psychology
Journal of Educational Psychology
Journal of European Business
Journal of International Business Studies
Journal of Management Studies
Journal of Organizational Behaviour
Journal of Personality and Social Psychology
Journal of World Business
Management International Review
McKinsey Quarterly
Organization
Organization Studies
Organizational Behaviour and Human Performance
Organizational Psychology
People Management
Personnel Journal
Personnel Psychology
Personnel Review
Psychological Bulletin
Sloan Management Review
Strategic Management Journal
The Financial Times
The Guardian
Work, Employment and Society
Workforce

INTERNET SITES OF INTEREST

World Bank (WB) http://www.worldbank.org/
World Bank Research http://econ.worldbank.org/
International Labour Organization (ILO) http://ilo.org/public/english/employment/strat/index.htm
European Union (EU) http://europa.eu.int/
North American Free Trade Association (NAFTA) http://www.nafta-sec-alena.org/DefaultSite/index.html
United Nations (UN) http://www.un.org/
United Nations Human Development Reports http://hdr.undp.org/
United Nations Development Programme (UNDP) http://www.undp.org/
United Nations Office for Project Services http://www.unops.org/web_forms/welcome.htm
European Industrial Relations Observatory (EIRO) http://www.eiro.eurofound.eu.int/
Chartered Institute of Personnel and Development (CIPD) (UK) http://www.cipd.co.uk/
Investors in People (IiP) (UK) http://www.iipuk.co.uk/
World Trade Organization (WTO) http://www.wto.org/
Organization for Economic Cooperation and Development (OECD) http://www.oecd.org/

ILR Research Portal http://www.ilr.cornell.edu/library/research/researchPortal.html

Society for Human Resource Management (USA) http://www.shrm.org/global/

International Association for Human Resource Information Management (IHRIM) http://www.ihrim.org/

International Public Management Association for Human Resources http://www.ipma-hr.org/

Social Science Information Gateway (SOSIG) HRM Database http://www.sosig.ac.uk/roads/subject-listing/World-cat/hrman.html

The International Industrial Relations Association http://www.ilo.org/public/english/iira/

European Trade Union Congress (ETUC) http://www.etuc.org/

Trades Union Congress (TUC) (UK) http://www.tuc.org.uk/

Union of Industrial and Employers' Confederation of Europe (UNICE) http://www.unice.org/

Association of South East Asian Nations (ASEAN) http://www.aseansec.org/

REFERENCES

ACTU (2003) 'The Future of Australian Unionism',: Australian Council of Trade Unions.

Adler, N. (2002) *International Dimensions of Organizational Behavior*. Canada: Thomson.

Adler, N.J. and Boyacigiller, N. (1996) 'Global Management and the 21st Century', in B.J. Punnett and O. Shenkar (eds) *Handbook for International Management Research*. Cambridge, Mass.: Blackwell, pp. 537–58.

Adler, N.J. (1983) 'Cross Cultural Management: Issues to be Faced', *International Studies of Management and Organizations*, 13(1–2), 7–45.

Adler, N.J. (1984, 1991) *International Dimensions of Organizational Behavior*. Belmont and Boston, Mass.: PWS-Kent.

Adler, N.J. and Ghadar, F. (1990) 'Strategic Human Resource Management: A Global Perspective', in R. Pieper (ed.), *HumanResource Management: An International Comparison*. Berlin, New York: Walter de Gruyter, pp. 235–60.

Albrecht, M. and Luthans, F. (2000) *International Human Resource Management: Managing Diversity in the Workplace*. Oxford: Blackwell.

Appelbaum, E. and Batt. R. (1994) *The New American Workplace*. New York: ILR Press.

Appelbaum, E., Bailey, T., Berg, P. and Kalleberg, A. (2000) *Manufacturing Advantage: Why High Performance Systems Pay Off*. New York: ILR Press.

Armstrong, M. (1992) *Human Resource Management: Strategy and Action*. London: Kogan Page.

Arthur, W. Jr. and Bennett, W. Jr. (1995) 'The International Assignee: The Relative Importance of Factors Perceived to Contribute to Success', *Personnel Psychology*, 48/1, pp. 99–114.

Asdorian, M. (1995) 'Three Tricks of the HR Trade for an International Start-up', *Personnel Journal*, 74, 1.

Australian Bureau of Statistics (2003) 'Population by Age and Sex, Australian States and Territories; June 1997 to June 2002', http://www.abs.gov.au/: Australia Bureau of Statistics.

Bailey, C.T. (1983) *The Measurement of Job Performance*. Hampshire: Gower Publishing.

Banerjee, S.B. (2003) 'Who Sustains Whose Development and the Reinvention of Nature', *Organization Studies*, Jan., 34–61.

Barham, K., and BerthoinAntal, A. (1994) 'Competences for the Pan-European Manager', in P. Kirkbride (ed.), *Human Resource Management in Europe: Perspectives for the 1990s*. London: Routledge.

Barham, K. and Rassam, C. (1989) *Shaping the Corporate Future*. London: Unwin Hyman.

Bartlett, C.A. and Ghoshal, S. (1992) 'What is a Global Manager', *Harvard Business Review*, 70/5, pp. 124–32.

Bartlett, C.A. and Ghoshal, S. (1989) *Managing Across Borders. The Transnational Solution*. Boston: Harvard Business School Press.

Baruch, Y. (2002) 'No Such Thing as a Global Manager' *Business Horizons*, 45/1, pp. 36–42.

Baruch, Y. and Altman, Y. (2002) 'Expatriation and Repatriation in MNC: A Taxonomy', *Human Resource Management*, 41/2, pp. 239–59.

Baruch, Y. (1995) 'Business Globalization – the Human Resource Management Aspect', *Human Systems Management*, 14/4, pp. 313–26.

Baruch, Y. (2004) *Managing Careers: Theory and Practice*. Harrow: FT–Prentice Hall/Pearson Education.

Baruch, Y. and Hind, P. (1999) 'Perpetual Motion in Organizations: Effective Management and the Impact of the New Psychological Contracts on "Survivor Syndrome"', *European Journal of Work and Organizational Psychology*, 8/2, pp. 295–306.

Baruch, Y. Steele, D. and J. Quantrill (2002) 'Management of Expatriation and Repatriation for Novice Global Player', *International Journal of Manpower*, 23/7, pp. 659–71.

BBC (2001a) 'French Court Rules Against M&S', www.news.bbc.co.uk

BBC (2001b) 'M&S Sells French Stores', www.news.bbc.co.uk

Beamish, (1988) *Multinational Joint Ventures in Developing Countries*. London: Routledge.

Bean, R. (1994) Comparative Industrial Relations: an Introduction to Cross-National Perspectives. London: Routledge (2nd edn 1999, International Thomson Business Press).

Beardwell, I. and Holden, L. (eds) (2001) *Human Resource Management: A Contemporary Approach*. Essex: Pearson Education.

Beer, M., Lawrance, P.R., Mills, D.Q. and Walton, R.E. (1985) *Human Resource Management*. New York: Free Press.

Benham, M., and Freeman, C. (2001) 'Rally Piles the Pressure on M&S', *Evening Standard*, London.

Berry, J.W. (1972) 'Radical Cultural Relativism and the Concept of Intelligence', In L.J. Cronbach and P.J.D. Drenth (eds), *Mental Tests and Cultural Adaptation*. Den Haag: Mouton.

Bhagat, R. and Prien, K. (1996) 'Cross-Cultural Training in Organizational Contexts', in D. Landis and R. Bhagat (eds) *Handbook of Intercultural Training*. Thousand Oaks: Sage, pp. 216–30.

Bhagat, R.S. and London, M. (1999) 'Getting Started and Getting Ahead: Career Dynamics of Immigrants', *Human Resource Management Review*, 9, pp. 349–65.

Bhawuk, D. (1990) 'Cross-Cultural Orientation Programs', in R. Brislin (ed.), *Applied Cross-Cultural Psychology*. Newbury Park: Sage, pp. 325–46.

Bird, A. and Beechler, S. (1995) in *Readings and Cases in International Human Resource Management* (eds, M. Mendenhall and G. Oddou). Ohio: International Thomson Publishing, pp. 40–50.

Black, J.S. and Gregersen, H.B. (1999) 'The Right Way to Manage Expats.', *Harvard Business Review*, 77/2, pp. 52–62.

Black, J.S. and Mendenhall, M. (1995) in M. Mendenhall and G. Oddou (eds), *op. cit.*, pp. 178–205.

Black, J.S. *et al.* (1999) *Globalising People Through International Assignments*. Reading: Addison-Wesley.

Black, J., Gregerson, H., and Mendenhall, M. (1992) *Global Assignments*. San Francisco: Jossey-Bass.

Black, S. and Mendenhall, M. (1990) 'Cross-Cultural Training Effectiveness: A Review and a Theoretical Framework for Future Research', *Academy of Management Review*, 15(1), pp. 113–36.

Black, S. and Mendenhall, M. (1989) 'A Practical but Theory-Based Framework for Selecting Cross-Cultural Training Methods', *Human Resource Management*, 28 (4), pp. 511–39.

Blackman, C. (2000) *China Business: The Rules of the Game*, Sydney: Allen & Unwin.

Blakar, R.M. (1984) *Communication: Social Perspectives on Clinical Issues*. Oslo: Universitets-foragiat.

Blake, B., Heslin, R. and Curtis, S. (1996) 'Measuring Impacts of Cross-Cultural Training', in D. Landis and R. Bhagat (eds), *Handbook of Intercultural Training*, Thousand Oaks: Sage, pp. 165–82.

Blunt, P. and Jones, M.L. (1992) *Managing Organizations in Africa*. Berlin: DeGruyter.

Blyton, P. and Turnbull, P. (1998) *The Dynamics of Employee Relations*. Basingstoke: Palgrave Macmillan.

Bock, P. (1970) *Culture Shock: A Reader in Modern Anthropology*. New York: Knopf.

Bonache, J. and Fernandez, Z. (1999) 'Strategic Staffing in Multinational Companies: A Resource Based Approach', in C. Brewster and H. Harris (eds), *International HRM: Contemporary Issues in Europe*. London: Routledge.

Borg, M. and Harzing, A. W. (1995) 'Composing and International Staff', in A.W. Harzing and J.V. Ruysseveldt (eds), *International Human Resource Management*. London: Sage, pp. 179–204.

Borg, M. (1988) *International Transfer of Managers in Multinational Corporations*. Stockholm: Almqvist & Wiksell.

Bourdieu, P. (1998) *Acts of Resistance: Against the New Myths of our Time*. Cambridge: Polity Press.

Boxall, P. and Purcell, J. (2003) *Strategy and Human Resource Management*. New York: Palgrave Macmillan.

Boyatzis, R. (1982) *The Competent Manager: A Model for Effective Performance*. New York: Wiley.

Bradley, H., Erickson, M., Stephenson, C. and Williams, S. (2002) *Myths at Work*. Cambridge: Polity Press.

Brewster C. and Bournois, F. (1991) Human Resource Management: A European Perspective', *Personnel Review*, 20(6), pp. 4–13.

Brewster, C. and Larsen, H.H. (2000) 'Responsibility in Human Resource Management: The Role of the Line' in Human Resource Management in Northern Europe: Trends, Dilemmas and Strategy, edited by Brewster, C. and Larsen, H.H. Oxford: Blackwell

Brewster, C. and Scullion, H. (1997) 'A Review and Agenda for Expatriate HRM', *Human Resource Management Journal*, 7(3), pp. 32–41.

Brewster, C. (1995) 'HRM: The European Dimension', in J. Storey (ed.) *Human Resource Management: A Critical Text*. London: Routledge, pp. 309–31 (3rd edn 2001).

Brewster, C. and Larsen, H. (1992) 'Human Resource Management in Europe: Evidence from 10 Countries', *International Journal of Human Resource Management*, 3(3), pp. 409–34.

Brewster, C. and Scullion, H. (1997) 'A Review and Agenda for Expatriate HRM', *Human Resource Management Journal*, 7(3), pp. 32–41.

Briscoe, D. (1995) *International Human Resource Management*, Englewood Cliffs: Prentice-Hall.

Brislin, R. (1979) 'Orientation Programs for Cross-Cultural Preparation', in A. Marsella, R. Thorpe and I. Ciborowski (eds), *Perspectives on Cross-Cultural Psychology*. New York: Academic Press.

Budhwar, P.S. and Debrah, Y.A. (2001) *Human Resource Management in Developing Countries*, London: Routledge.

Budhwar, P.W. and Sparrow, P.R. (2002) 'Strategic HRM Through the Cultural Looking Glass: Mapping the Cognition of British and Indian Managers', *Organisation Studies*, Jul.–Aug., pp. 107–19.

Burkhart, M. (1999) 'The Role of Training in Advancing a Diversity Initiative', *Diversity Factor*, 8, 1, pp. 2–5.

Caligiuri, P.M. (1999) 'The Ranking of Scholarly Journals in International Human Resource Management', *International Journal of Human Resource Management*, 10, pp. 515–19.

Camdessen, M. (1996) 'The Impact of Globalisation on Workers and Trade Unions'. Paper addressed at the 16th World Congress of the International Confederation of Free Trade Unions (ICFTU), Brussels, 26 June.

Carley, M. (2001) 'Industrial Relations in the EU, Japan and USA, 2000': European Foundation for the Improvement of Living and Working Conditions.

Carrell, M.R., Elbert, N.F. and Hatfield, R.D. (2000) *Human Resource Management: Strategies for Managing a Diverse and Global Workforce*. Florida: Dryden Press.

Cartwright, S. and Cooper, C. (1992) *Mergers and Acquisitions: The Human Factor*. Oxford: Butterworth-Heinemann.

Cattell, R.B. (1940) 'A Culture-Free Intelligence Test', *Journal of Educational Psychology*, 31, pp. 161–79.

Caudron, S. (1994) 'Diversity Ignites Effective Work Teams', *Personnel Journal*, September, pp. pp. 54–63.

Caufield, C. (2001) 'The World Bank', *Foreign Policy in Focus*, at http://www.fpif.org/briefs/vol3/v3n32wb.html (date of access 10 July 2003).

Chen, M. (1995) *Asian Management Systems*, London and New York: Routledge.

Chow, I.H.-S. (2002) 'Organizational Socialisation and Career Success of Asian Managers', *International Journal of Human Resource Management*, 13, pp. 720–37.

Clark, T., Gospel, H. and Montgomery, J. (1999) 'Running on the Spot? A Review of Twenty Years of Research on the Management of Human Resources in Comparative and International Perspective', *International Journal of Human Resource Management*, 10, pp. 520–44.

Clark, T., Grant, D. and Heijltjes, M. (2000) 'Researching Comparative and International Human Resource Management', *International Studies of Management and Organization*, 29, pp. 6–17.

CNN (2001a) 'M&S Offers Hope to French Staff', www.cnn.com

CNN (2001b) 'Talks Over M&S Closures', www.CNN.com

Collier, P. (1998) 'Social Capital and Poverty', Social Capital Initiative Working Paper no. 4. The World Bank Social Development Family Environmentally and Socially Sustainable Development Network.

Conner, J. (2000) 'Developing the Global Leaders of Tomorrow', *Human Resource Management*, 39/2&3, pp. 147–57.

Cooper, C. (2000) 'Freeman's Departure Marks End of an Era for HR at Troubled Marks and Spencer', *People Management*, 28 September.

Cornelius, N. (1999) *Human Resource Management: A Managerial Perspective*. London: International Thomson Business Press.

Cox, P., and Parkinson, A. (2003) 'Values and Their Impact on the Changing Employment Relationship', in G. Hollinshead, P. Nicholls and S. Tailby (eds), *Employee Relations*. London: Prentice-Hall.

Cox, T. (1991) 'The Multicultural Organization', *Academy of Management Executive*, 5, 2, pp. 34–47.

Davis, M.E. and Lansbury, D.R. (1998) 'Employment Relations in Australia' in J.G. Bamber and D.R. Lansbury (eds), *International and Comparative Employment Relations*. London: Sage.

Demirbağ, M., Mirza, H. and Weir, D.T.H. (1995) 'The Dynamics of Manufacturing Joint Ventures in Turkey and the Role of Industrial Groups', *Management International Review*, 35(1), pp. 35–51.

Dessler, G. (2000) *Human Resource Management*. Upper Saddle River: Prentice-Hall.

Dowling, P.J., Schuler, R.S. and Welch, D.E. (1994) *International Dimensions of Human Resource Management*. Belmont, CA: Wadworth (3rd edn 1999).

Dowling, P. and Schuler, R. (1990) *International Dimensions of Human Resource Management*. Boston: PWS-Kent.

Doyle, M. (2001) 'Management Development', in I. Beardwell and L. Holden (eds), *Human Resource Management a Contemporary Approach*. London: Prentice-Hall.

Drucker, P. (1954) *The Practice of Management*. New York: Harper & Row.

Drucker, P.F. (1999) *Management Challenges for the 21st Century*. Oxford: Butterworth-Heinemann.

Earley, C. (1987) 'Intercultural Training for Managers: A Comparison of Documentary and Interpersonal Methods', *Academy of Management Journal*, 30(4), pp. 685–98.

Eaton, J. (2000) *Comparative Employment Relations: An introduction*. Cambridge: Polity Press.

EC (1995) *Employment in Europe*, Office for Official Publications in the European Communities, Luxembourg.

EIRO (1998) 'Works Council Survey Reveals Major Differences in Practice' FR9804101F, European Industrial Relations Observatory.

EIRO (2001a) 'EIRO Annual Review: A Review of Developments in European Industrial Relations', European Industrial Relations Observatory.

EIRO (2001b) 'Globalisation Blamed for Restructuring at Danone and Marks & Spencer', European Industrial Relations Observatory Online, www.eirofound.eu.int

Elashmawi, F. and Philip, R.H. (1993) *Multicultural Management 2000: Essential Insights for Global Business Success*. Houston: Gulf Publishing Company.

ETUC (2003) 'European Trade Union Confederation', http://www.etuc.org

Europa (2003) 'Dialogue with Citizens; Italy: Psychological Tests' in the European Union online, http://europa.eu.int/

Farh, J.L., and Cheng, B.S. (2000) 'Cultural Analysis of Paternalistic Leadership', in J.I. Li, A.S. Tsui and E. Weldon, (eds), *Management and Organizations in the Chinese Context*. London: Palgrave Macmillan, pp. 84–127

Farnham, D. (2000) *Employee Relations in Context*. London: Chartered Institute of Personnel and Development.

Feldman, D.C. and Thomas, D.C. (1992) 'Career Management Issues Facing Expatriates', *Journal of International Business Studies*, 23(2), pp. 271–94.

Ferner, A. (2000) 'The Embeddedness of US Multinational Companies in the US Business System: Implications for HR/IR', Occasional Paper no. 61, Leicester Business School.

Ferner, A. and Hyman, R. (eds) (1998) *Changing Industrial Relations in Europe*, 2nd edn. Oxford: Blackwell.

Ferner, A. (1997) 'Country of Origin Effects and HRM in Multinational Companies', *Human Resource Management Journal*, 7(1), pp. 19–37.

Ferris, G.R., Arthur, M.M., Berkson, H.M., Kaplan, D.M., Harrell-Cook, G. and Frink, D.D. (1998) 'Toward a Social Context Theory of Human Resource Management-Organization Effectiveness Relationship', *Human Resource Management Review*, 8, pp. 235–64.

Fisher, R., and Uri, W. (1981) *Getting to Yes*. Boston, MA: Houghton Mifflin.

Fombrun, C.J., Tichy, N.M. and Devanna, M.A. (1984) *Strategic Human Resource Management*, New York: John Wiley.

Foot, M. and Hook, C. (1996) *Introducing Human Resource Management*. London: Longman.

Ford, J.K., Kraiger, K. and Schechtman, S.L. (1986) 'Study of Race Effects in Objective Indices and Subjective Evaluations of Performance', *Psychological Bulletin*, 99, pp. 330–37.

Foster, N. (2000) 'The Myth of the "International Manager" ', *International Journal of Human Resource Management*, 11, pp. 126–42.

Frost, D. (1999) 'Review Worst Diversity Practices to Learn from Others' Mistakes', *HR Focus*, 76(4), pp. 11–12.

Furnham, A. and Bochner, S. (1986) *Culture Shock*. London: Methuen.

Gentile, M. (1995) 'Managing Diversity', *Harvard Business Review*.

Goldberg, L.R. (1990) 'An Alternative Description of Personality: The Big Five Factor Structure', *Journal of Personality and Social Psychology*, 59, pp. 1216–29.

Gomez-Mejia, L.R., Balkin, D.B. and Cardy, R.L. (2001) *Managing Human Resources*. Upper Saddle River: Prentice-Hall.

Gooley, T.B. (1998) 'NAFTA at Five Years: Uneven Progress', Logistics Management Distribution Report, December 31.

Griffin, R.W. and Pustay, M.W. (1998) *International Business: A Managerial Perspective*, Harlow: Addison-Wesley.

Grobler, P. A., Warnich, S., Carrell, M. R., Elbert, N. F. and Hatfield, R. D. (2002) *Human Resource Management in South Africa*. Cornwall: Thomson Learning.

Grossman, W. and Schoenfeldt, L.F. (2001) 'Resolving Ethical Dilemmas Through International Human Resource Management – A Transaction Cost Economics Perspective', *Human Resource Management Review*, 11, pp. 55–72.

Guardian (2001a) 'France Calls for Protests at M&S Closures', *Guardian*, London.

Guardian (2001b) 'French Say M&S Closure May Have Been Illegal', *Guardian*, London.

Guardian (2001c) 'Sacked European Workers March on M&S in the Rain', *Guardian*, London.

Gudykunst, W., Guzley, R. and Hammer, M. (1996) 'Designing Intercultural Training', in D. Landis and R. Bhagat (eds), *Handbook of Intercultural Training*. Thousand Oaks: Sage, pp. 61–80.

Gudykunst, W., Hammer, M. and Wiseman, R. (1977) 'An Analysis of an Integrated Approach to Cross-Cultural Training', *International Journal of Intercultural Training*, 1, pp. 99–110.

Guest, D.E. (1989) 'Human Resource Management: Its Implications for Industrial Relations', in J. Storey (ed.), *New Perspectives on Human Resource Management*. London: Routledge.

Guillen, M.F. (2001) *The Limits of Convergence: Globalization and Organizational Change in Argentina, South Korea, and Spain*. Princeton, NJ: Princeton University Press.

Guzzo, R.A. Nooman, K.A. and Elron, E. (1994) 'Expatriate Managers and the Psychological Contract', *Journal of Applied Psychology*, 79/4, pp. 617–26.

Hampden-Turner, C., and Trompenaars, F. (1994) *The Seven Cultures of Capitalism, Value Systems for Creating Wealth in the Unites States, Britain, Japan, France, Sweden, and the Netherlands*. London: Piatkus.

Harvey, M. (1989) 'Repatriation of Corporate Executives: An Empirical Study', *Journal of International Business Studies*, 20, pp. 131–44.

Harvey, M. (1996) 'Dual-Career Couples: The Selection Dilemma in International Relocation', *International Journal of Selection and Assessment*, 4/4, pp. 215–27.

Harzing, A.W.K. (1995) 'The Persistent Myth of High Expatriate Failure Rates', *International Journal of Human Resource Management*, 6(2): pp. 457–74.

Harzing, A.-W. and Van Ruysseveldt, J. (eds) (1995) *International Human Resource Management*. London: Sage.

Healy, G. and Özbilgin, M. (2003) 'Same Bed, Different Dreams: Career Development in the Middle East', *Career Development International*, 8, 2, pp. 49–51.

Heenan, D.A. and Perlmutter, H.V. (1979) *Multinational Organizational Development*. Reading, MA: Addison-Wesley.

Hendry, C. and Pettigrew, A. (1986) 'The Practice of Strategic Human Resource Management'. *Personnel Review*, 15(3).

Hladik, K.J. (1985) *International Joint Ventures: An Economic Analysis of US Foreign Business Partnerships*. Lexington: Lexington Books.

Hofstede, G. and Bond, M. (1988) The Confucian Connection: From Cultural Roots to Economic Growth', *Organizational Dynamics*, 4, pp. 5–21

Hofstede, G. (1980) *Culture's Consequences: International Differences in Work-Related Values*, New Jersey: Sage.

Holden, L. (2001) 'International Human Resource Management', in I. Beardwell, and L. Holden (eds), *Human Resource Management: A Contemporary Approach*. Essex: Pearson Education, pp. 633–78.

Hollingsworth, J.R. and Boyer, R. (1997) 'Coordination of Economic Actors and Social Systems of Production', in J.R. Hollingsworth and R. Boyer, (eds) *Contemporary Capitalism. The Embeddedness of Institutions*. Cambridge: Cambridge University Press.

Hollinshead, G., and Leat, M. (1995) *Human Resource Management: An International and Comparative Perspective on the Employment Relationship*. Pitman.

Horwitz, F.M. *et al.* (2002) 'Looking East: Diffusing High Performance Work Practices in the Southern Afro-Asian Context'. *International Journal of Human Resource Management*, 13 (7), pp. 1019–41.

Hu, Y.S. (1992) 'Global or Stateless Corporations Are National Firms with International Operations', *California Management Review*, 34/2, pp. 107–26.

Hunt, J. *et al.* (1987) *Acquisitions: The Human Factor*. London: London Business School and Egon Zehnder International.

Hyman, R. and Ferner, A. (eds) (1994) *New Frontiers in European Industrial Relations*. Oxford: Basil Blackwell.

Ibarra, H. (1993) 'Personal Networks of Women and Minorities in Management', *Academy of Management Review*, 18, 1, pp. 56–88.

ICFTU (2003) 'ICFTU: What it is, What it Does', international Confederation of Free Trade Unions.

Iles, P. and Yolles, M. (2002) 'International Joint Ventures, HRM and Viable Knowledge Migration', *International Journal of Human Resource Management*, 13, pp. 624–41.

ILO (2003) 'About the ILO', International Labour Organization, www.ilo.org

ILO (2003) www.ilo.org/public/english/bureau/exrel/partners/prsp.htm

Irvine, S.H. (1979) 'The Place of Factor Analysis in Cross-Cultural Methodology and its Contribution to Cognitive Theory', in L. Eckensberger, W. Lonner and Y.H. Poortinga (eds), *Cross-Cultural Contributions to Psychology*. Lisse: Swets & Zeitlinger.

Jackson, T. (2002) *International HRM: A Cross Cultural Approach*. London: Sage.

Jahoda, G. (1983) 'The Cross-Cultural Emperor's Conceptual Clothes: The Emic-Etic Issue Revisited', in J.B. Deregowski, S. Dziurzwiec and R.C. Annis (eds), *Cross-Cultural Psychology*. Lisse: Swets & Zeitlinger.

Janssens, M. (2001) 'Developing a Culturally Synergistic Approach to International Human Resource Management', *Journal of World Business*, 36, pp. 429–39.

Jensen, A.R. (1980) *Bias in Mental Testing*. London: Methuen.

Joynt, P. and Morton, B. (1999) 'Introduction: Crossing the Seven Cs', in P. Joynt and B. Morton (eds), *The Global HR Manager: Creating the Seamless Organization*. London: Institute of Personnel and Development.

Kamoche, K. (1993) 'Towards a Model of HRM in Africa', in J.B. Shaw, P.S. Kirkbride and K.M. Rowland (eds), *Research in Personnel and Human Resource Management*. Greenwitch: JAI Press.

Kandola, R.S. and Pearn, M.A. (1992) 'Identfying Competencies', in R. Boam and P. Sparrow (eds), *Designing and Achieving Competency*. London: McGraw-Hill.

Kanter, R.M. (1977) *Men and Women of the Corporation*. New York: Basic Books.

Kaplan, R. and Norton, D. (1996) *The Balanced Scorecard: Translating Strategy into Action*. Boston: Harvard Business School Press.

Kaplan, R. and Norton, D. (2001) *The Strategy Focused Organization*. Boston: Harvard Business School Press.

Kerr, C., Dunlop, J.T., Harbison, F., Myers and C.A. (1960) *Industrialism and Industrial Men: The Problems of Labour and Management in Economic Growth*. New York: Oxford University Press.

KILM (2001–02) '20 Key Indicators', www.ilo.org/public/english/kilm/indicats.htm

KILM (2002) *Key Indicators of the Labour Market 2001–2002*. Geneva: International Labour Office,.

Kirby, D.A. and Fan, Y. (1995) 'Chinese Cultural Values and Entrepreneurship: A Preliminary Consideration', *Journal of Enterprising Culture*, 3(2) 3, pp. 245–60

Klikauer, T. (2002) 'Stability in Germany's Industrial Relations: A Critique on Hassel's Erosion Thesis', *British Journal of Industrial Relations*, 40, pp. 295–308

Kochan, T.A., Katz, H.C. and McKersie, R.B. (1986) *The Transformation of American Industrial Relations*. New York: Basic Books.

Kochan, T. and Dyer, L. (1995) 'HRM: An American View', in J. Storey (ed.) *Human Resource Management: A Critical Text*. London: Routledge, pp. 332–51 (2nd edn 2001).

Kogut, B. and Singh, H. (1988) 'The Effect of National Culture on the Choice of Entry Mode', *Journal of International Business Studies*, 19(3), pp. 411–32.

Kotter, J. (1973) 'The Psychological Contract: Managing the Joining-Up Process', *California Management Review*, 15/3, pp. 91–9.

Kraiger, K. and Ford, J.K. (1985) 'A Meta-Analysis of Ratee Race Effects in Performance Ratings', *Journal of Applied Psychology*, 70, pp. 56–65.

Kurdelbusch, A. (2002) 'Multinantional and the Rise of Variable Pay in Germany', *European Journal of Industrial Relations*, 8, pp. 325–49

Kuwahara, Y. (1998) 'Employment Relations in Japan', in J.G. Bamber and D.R. Lansbury (eds), International and Comparative Employment Relations. London: Sage.

Lane, C. (1989) *Management and Labour in Europe. The Industrial Enterprise in Germany, Britain and France*. Aldershot: Edward Elgar.

Lane, C. (1992) 'European Business Systems: Britain and Germany Compared', R. Whitley (ed.), *European Business Systems. Firms and Markets in Their National Contexts*. London: Sage, pp. 5–45.

Lanier, A. (1979) 'Selecting and Preparing Personnel for Overseas Transfers', *Personnel Journal*, 58, pp. 160–63.

Laurent, A. (1983) 'The Cultural Diversity of Western Conceptions of Management', *International Studies of Management and Organization*, 13(1–2), pp. 75–96.

Laurent, A. (1986) 'The Cross Cultural Puzzle of IHRM', *Human Resource Management*, 25(1), pp. 91–102.

Leat, M. (1998) *Human Resource Issues of the European Union*. London: Pitman.

Leat, M. (2003) 'Multinationals and Employee Relations'' in G. Hollinshead, P. Nicholls and S. Tailby (eds), *Employee Relations*. London: Prentice-Hall.

Lee, E. (1997) 'Globalization and Labour Standards: A Review of Issues', *International Labour Review*, p. 136.

Legge, K. (1989) 'Human Resource Management: A Critical Analysis', in J. Storey (ed.), *New Perspectives on Human Resource Management*. London: Routledge.

Legge, K. (1995) *Human Resource Management: Rhetorics and Realities*. London: Macmillan Business.

Leong, F.T.L. and Hartung, P.J. (2000) 'Adapting to the Changing Multicultural Context of Career', in A.W. Harzing and J.V. Ruysseveldt (eds), *International Human Resource Management*. London: Sage, pp. 212–27.

Levinson, H., Price, C., Munden, K., Mandl, H. and Solley, C. (1962) *Men, Management, and Mental Health*. Cambridge MA: Harvard University Press.

Lewin, K. (1951) *Field Theory in Social Science*, New York: Harper & Row.

Lewis, P., Thornhill, A., and Saunders, M. (2003) *Employee Relations: Understanding the Employment Relationship*. London: Prentice Hall.

Liff, S. (1996) 'Two Routes to Managing Diversity: Individual Differences or Social Group Characteristics', *Employee Relations*, 19, pp. 11–26.

Linehan, M. and Walsh, J. (2000) 'Work-Life Conflict and the Senior Female International Manager', *British Journal of Management*, pp. 11.

Mabey, C., Salaman, G. and Storey, J. (1998) *Human Resource Management: A Strategic Introduction*. Malden MA: Blackwell Publishing.

MacLuhan, M. (1960) *Explorations in Communication*. Boston: Beacon Press.

Marginson, P. and Sisson, K. (1994) 'The Structure of Transnational Capital in Europe: The Emerging Euro-Company and Its Implications for Industrial Relations', in R. Hyman and A, Ferner (eds), *New Frontiers in European Industrial Relations*. Oxford: Basil Blackwell.

Markham, W.T. (1987) 'Sex, Relocation and Occupational Advancement – The "Real Cruncher" for Women, in A.H. Stromberg, L. Larwood and B.A. Gutek (eds), *Women and Work, An Annual Review*, Vol. 2. New Jersey: Sage, pp. 207–32.

Marks, S. (2003) 'History of Marks and Spencer', www.marksandspencer.com

Marks, S.J. (2001) 'Nurturing Global Workplace Connections', *Workforce*, September, pp. 9–12.

Martinez, Z. and Ricks, D.A. (1989) 'Multinational Parent Companies' Influence Over Human Resource Decisions of Affiliates: U.S. Firms in Mexico', *Journal of International Business Studies*, Fall, pp. 465–87.

Maund, L. (2001) *An Introduction to Human Resource Management*, Basingstoke: Palgrave Macmillan.

Maurice, M., Sellier, F. and Silvestre, J.-J. (1986) *Bases of Industrial Power*, Cambridge, Mass.: MIT Press.

Maurice, M., Sorge, A. and Warner, M. (1980) 'Societal Differences in Organizing Manufacturing Units: A Comparison of France, Germany, and Great Britain', *Organization Studies*, 1(1), pp. 59–86.

Mazneski, M.L. (1994) 'Understanding Our Differences', *Human Relations*, 47(5), pp. 531–53.

McCall, G.J. and Simmons, J.L. (1969) *Issues in Participant Observation*. Reading, MA: Addison-Wesley.

McGregor, D. (1957) In Fifth Anniversary Convocation of the M.I.T. School of Industrial Management, pp. 23–30.

McKenna, E. and Beech, N. (1995) *The Essence of Human Resource Management*. London: Prentice-Hall.

McKenna, E. and Beech, N. (2002) *Human Resource Management: A Concise Analysis*. Harlow: FT–Prentice-Hall.

McMahan, G.C., Bell, M.P. and Virick, M. (1998) 'Strategic Human Resource Management: Employee Involvement, Diversity, and International Issues', *Human Resource Management Review*, 8, pp. 193–214.

Mead, R. (1998) *International Management*. Oxford: Blackwell Publishers.

Mendenhall, M. and Oddou, G.R. (1985) The Dimensions of Expatriate Acculturation: A Review', *Academy of Management Review*, 10/1, pp. 39–47.

Mendenhall, M. Dunbar, E. and Oddou, G.R. (1987) 'Expatriate Selection, Training, and Career Pathing', *Human Resource Management*, 26/3, pp. 331–45.

Miller, P. (1989) 'Strategic HRM: What it is and What it isn't'. *Personal Management*, February.

Mok, K.-h., Wong, L. and Lee, G.O.M. (2002) 'The Challenges of Global Capitalism: Unemployment and State Workers' Reactions and Responses in Post-Reform China', *International Journal of Human Resource Management*, 13, pp. 399–15.

Molnar, D.E. and Loewe, G.M. (1997) 'Seven Keys to International HR Management', *Human Resource Focus*, 74, p. 11.

Mondy, R.W., Noe, R.M. and Premeaux, S.R. (1999) *Human Resource Management*. Upper Saddle River: Prentice-Hall.

Morley, M., Mayrhofer, W. and Brewster, C. (2000) 'Communication in Organizations: Dialogue and Impact', in C. Brewster and H.H. Larsen (eds), *Human Resource Management in Northern Europe: Trends Dilemmas and Strategy*. Oxford: Blackwell.

Mutabazi, E. (1994) 'Rhone Poulenc Agrochemicals: A Franco-American Take-Over', in D. Torrington (ed.). *International Human Resource Management: Think Globally, Act Locally*. New York: Prentice-Hall.

Napier, N.K. (1998) 'International Human Resource Management in Developing and Transitional Economy Countries: A Breed Apart?', *Human Resource Management Review*, 8, pp. 39–64.

Nemetz, P. and Christensen, S. (1996) 'The Challenge of Cultural Diversity: Harnessing a Diversity of Views to Understand Multiculturalism', *Academy of Management Review*, 21(2), pp. 434–62.

Ng, S.-h, and Warner, M. (1999) 'International HRM: An Asian Perspective' in P. Joynt and B. Morton (eds), *The Global HR Manager: Creating the Seamless Organization*. London: Institute of Personnel and Development.

Nicholson N. and Johns G. (1985) 'The Absence Culture and the Psychological Contract – Who's in Control of Absence', *Academy of Management Review*, 10, pp. 397–407.

Noble, C. (1997) 'International Comparisons of Training Policies', *Human Resource Management Journal*, 7(1), pp. 5–18.

OECD (Organization for Economic Corporation and Development) (2001) *Economic Outlook*, 2 (70), Paris.

Ohmae, K. (1990) *The Borderless World*. London: Collins.

Olie, R. (1996) 'The "Culture" Factor in Personnel and Organization Policies', in A.-W. Harzing and J. Van Ruysseveldt (eds), *International Human Resource Management*. London: Sage, pp. 124–43.

Özbilgin, M. (2002) 'Inertia of the International Human Resource Management Text in a Changing World', paper presented at the Conference on Human Resource Management in a Changing World, Oxford Brookes University.

Özbilgin, M. and Healy, G. (2003) 'Don't Mention the War! Career Development in the Middle East ', *Career Development International*, 8(7), pp. 325–27.

Özbilgin, M. and Healy, G. (2004) 'Sex Equality in Career Development: The Case of University Professors in Turkey', *Journal of Vocational Behavior*.

Özbilgin, M.F. (2004) 'Inertia of the International Human Resource Management Text in a Changing World: An Examination of the Editorial Board Membership of the Top 21 IHRM Journals', *Personnel Review*, 33(2), pp. 205–21.

Paauwe, J. and Dewe, P. (1995) 'Human Resource Management in Multinational Corporations: Theories and Models', in A.-W. Harzing and J.V. Ruysseveldt (eds), *International Human Resource Management*. London: Sage.

Parkinson, A. (1999) 'Sustaining Constructive Relationships Across Cultural Boundaries', in P. Joynt and B. Morton (eds), *The Global HR Manager: Creating the Seamless Organisation*. London: Institue of Personnel and Development.

Pellegrini, C. (1998) 'Employment Relations in Italy', in J.G. Bamber and D.R. Lansbury (eds), *International and Comparative Employment Relations*. London: Sage.

People Management (2001) 'M&S Defeats French Unions in Court Case Over Consultation: European Works Council Valid Forum for Discussing Redundancies', *People Management*, 10.

Perlmutter, H.V. and Heenan, D.A. (1974) 'How Multinational Should Your Top Managers Be? *Harvard Business Review* (Nov.–Dec.), 52(6), pp. 121–32.

Perlmutter, H.V. (1969) 'The Tortuous Evolution of the Multinational Corporation', *Columbia Journal of World Business*, 4(1), pp. 9–18.

Piore, M. and Sabel, C. (1984) *The Second Industrial Divide: Prospects for Prosperity*. New York: Basic Books.

Poortinga, Y.H. and Malpass, R.S. (1988) 'Making Inferences from Cross-Cultural Data', in W.J. Lonner and J.W. Berry (eds), *Field Methods in Cross-Cultural Research*. Beverly Hills: Sage.

Porter, G. and Tansky, J.W. (1999) 'Expatriate Success May Depend on a "Learning Orientation": Considerations for Selection and Training', *Human Resource Management*, 38/1, pp. 47–60.

Porter, M. (1991) 'Towards a Dynamic Theory of Strategy', *Strategic Management Journal*, 12(S), pp. 95–117.

Porter, M.E. (1989) *The Competitive Advantage of Nations*,Basingstoke: Palgrave Macmillan.

Procter, S. and Mueller, F. (eds) (2000) *Teamworking*. Basingstoke:Palgrave Macmillan.

Punnett, B.J. and Ricks, D.A. (1992) *International Business*. Boston: PWS Kent.

Putnam, R. (1993) 'The Prosperous Community: Social Capital and Public Life', *The American Prospect*, 13, pp. 35–42.

Pye, L.W. (1982) *Chinese Commercial Negotiating Style*. Cambridge: Oelgeschlager.

Reich, R. (1990) 'Who is Us?', *Harvard Business Review*, 62:1 (Jan.–Feb.), pp. 53–65.

Robinson, S.L. and Morrison, E.W. (1995) 'Psychological Contracts and OCB: The Effect of Unfulfilled Obligation on Civic Virtue Behavior', *Journal of Organizational Behavior*, 16/3, pp. 289–98.

Robinson, S.L., Kraatz, M.S. and Rousseau, D.M. (1994) 'Changing Obligations and the Psychological Contract: A Longitudinal Study', *Academy of Management Journal*, 37/1, pp. 137–52.

Rodrigues, C. (1996) *International Management*. Minneapolis/St. Paul: West Publication.

Ronen, S. (1989) 'Training the International Assignee', in Goldstein and Associates (eds), *Training and Development in Organizations*, San Francisco: Jossey-Bass, pp. 417–53.

Rothwell, S. (1992) 'The Development of the International Manager', *Personnel Management*, 24(1).

Rousseau, D.M. (1995) 'Psychological Contracts in Organizations', Thousand Oaks: Sage.

Rowley, C. and Bae, J. (2002) 'Globalization and Transformation of Human Resource Management in South Korea', *International Journal of Human Resource Management*, 13, pp. 522–49.

Royle, T. (2000) *Working for McDonald's in Europe: The Unequal Struggle?* London: Routledge.

Rugman, A.M. and Hodgetts, R.M. (2003) *International Business*. London: Prentice-Hall.

Rugman, A., Kirton, J. and Soloway, J. (1999) *Environmental Regulations and Corporate Strategy: A NAFTA Perspective*. New York: Oxford University Press.

Salamon, M. (1992) *Industrial Relations Theory and Practice*. London: Prentice-Hall (2nd edn 2000).

San Martin, T. and Flinn, L. (2003) 'The Global Workforce: Opportunities and the Value Chain', *Community College Journal*, Dec.–Jan., pp. 11–14.

Schein E.H. (1980) *Organizational Psychology*, 3rd edn. Englewood Cliffs, NJ: Prentice-Hall.

Schell, M.S. and Solomon, C.M. (1997) *Capitalizing on the Global Workforce*. Chicago: Irwin Professional Publishing.

Scheneider, S.C. and Barsoux, J-L. (1997) *Managing Across Cultures*. Harlow: Prentice-Hall.

Schiff, M. (1999) 'Trade, Migration and Welfare: The Impact of Social Capital', Policy Research Working Paper, no. 2044. The World Bank Development Research Group.

Schmitt, N. (1989) 'Fairness in Employment Selection', in M. Smith and I.T. Robertson (eds), *Advances in Selection and Assessment*. Chichester: John Wiley.

Schneider, S. and Barsoux, J.-L. (2003) *Managing Across Cultures*. London: Prentice-Hall.

Schneider, S. (2001) 'Introduction to International Human Resource Management Special Issue', *Journal of World Business*, 36, pp. 341–2.

Schoenberger, E. (1997) *The Cultural Crisis of the Firm*. Oxford: Blackwell.

Schuler, R.S., Jackson, S.E., and Storey, J. (2001) 'HRM and its Link with Strategic Management', *Human Resource Management: A Critical Text*, edited by J. Storey. London: Thomson Learning.

Schuler, R.S. and Jackson, S.E. (1987) 'Linking Competitive Strategies with Human Resource Management Practices', *Academy of Management Review*, 1, pp. 207–19.

Schuler, R.S. and Jackson, S.E. (1999) *Strategic Human Resource Management*. Oxford: Blackwell.

Schuler, R.S. *et al.* (2002) 'International Human Resource Management: Review and Critique', *International Journal of Management Reviews*, 4(1), pp. 41–70.

Scullion, H. (1995) 'International Human Resource Management', in J. Storey (ed.), *Human Resource Management: A Critical Text*. London: Routledge, pp. 352–82.

Selmer, J. (1996) 'Expatriate or Local Boss? HCN Subordinates' Preferences in Leadership Behaviour', *International Journal of Human Resource Management*, 7/1, pp. 165–78.

Selmer, J. (1998) 'Expatriates: Corporate Policy, Personal Intentions and International Adjustment', *International Journal of Human Resource Management*, 9/6, pp. 996–1007.

Shackleton, V. and Newell, S. (1997) 'International Assessment and Selection', in N. Anderson and P. Herriot (eds) *International Handbook of Selection and Assessment*. Chichester: Wiley, pp. 81–95.

Shaw, J.B. and Barrett-Power, E. (1998) 'The Effects of Diversity on Small Work Group Processes and Performance', *Human Relations*, 51(10), pp. 1307–25.

Shenkar, O. and Zeira, Y. (1987) 'Human Resources Management in International Joint Ventures: Directions for Research', *Academy of Management Review*, 12(3), pp. 546–57.

Sievenking, N., Anchor, K. and Marston, R. (1981) 'Selecting and Preparing Expatriate Employees', *Personnel Journal*, 18, pp. 197–202.

Sikking, E. and Brasse, P. (1987) 'Waar Liggen de Grenzen?', in M. Smith and I.T. Robertson (eds), *Advances in Selection and Assessment*. Chichester: John Wiley.

Simons, G. F. *et al.* (1996) *Cultural Diversity: Fresh Visions and Breakthroughs for Revitalising the Workplace*. Princeton: Peterson's/Pacesetter Books.

Slomp, H. (1995) 'National Variations in Worker Participation', in A.-W. Harzing and J. Van Ruysseveldt (eds), *International Human Resource Management*. London: Sage.

Solomon, C.M. (1995) 'Success Abroad Depends on More Than Just Job Skills', *Personnel Journal*, 73/4, pp. 51–4.

Solomon, C.M. (2000) 'The World Stops Shrinking', *Workforce*, 79(1), pp. 11–14.

Sorge, A. (1995) 'Foreword', in A.-W. Harzing and J. Van Ruysseveldt (eds), *International Human Resource Management*. London: Sage, pp. vii–viii.

Sparrow, P. (1998) 'New Organizational Forms, Processes, Jobs and Psychological Contracts: Resolving the HRM Issues', in P. Sparrow and M. Marchington (eds), *Human Resource Management: The New Agenda*. London: Prentice-Hall.

Sparrow, P. (1999a) 'International Recruitment, Selection and Assessment,' in P. Joynt and B. Morton (eds), *The Global HR Manager: Creating the Seamless Organisation*. London: Institute of Personnel and Development.

Sparrow, P. (1999b) 'International Rewards Systems: To Converge or Not to Converge?', in C. Brewster and H. Harris (eds), *International HRM: Contemporary Issues in Europe*. London: Routledge.

Sparrow, P.R. and Hiltrop, J.M. (1997) 'Redefining the Field of European HRM: A Battle Between National Mindsets and Forces of Business Transitions?', *Human Resource Management*, 36/2, pp. 201–19.

Sparrow, P.R. and Hiltrop, J.-M. (1994) *European Human Resource Management in Transition*. London: Prentice Hall.

Staehle, W.H. (1999) 'Human Resource Management and Corporate Strategy', in R. Pieper (ed.), *Human Resource Management: An International Comparison*. Berlin and New York: Walter de Gruyter, pp. 27–38.

Steingruber, W.G. (1997) 'Strategic International Human Resource Management: An Analysis of the Relationship Between International Strategic Positioning and the Degree of Integrated Strategic Human Resource Management', *Journal of International Business Studies*, 28, p. 665.

Stephens, G.K. and Black, S. (1991) 'The Impact of Spouse's Career Orientation on Managers During International Transfers', *Journal of Management Studies*, 28, pp. 417–28.

Storey, J. (1992) *Developments in the Management of Human Resources: An Analytical Review*, Oxford: Blackwell.

Storey, J. (ed.) (1995) *Human Resource Management: A Critical Text*. London: Routledge (3rd edn 2001).

Stroh, L.K. (1995) 'Predicting Turnover Among Repatriates: Can Organizations Affect Retention Rates?', *International Journal of Human Resource Management*, 6/2, pp. 443–56.

Sunoo, B.P. (2000) 'HR Over the Border', *Workforce*, JulY, p. 44.

Svoboda, M. and Schoreder, S. (2001) 'Transforming Human Resources in the New Economy: Developing the Next Generation of Global HR Managers at Deutsche Bank AG', *Human Resource Management*, 40, pp. 261–73.

Tang, J. and Ward, A. (2003) *The Changing Face of Chinese Management*. London and New York: Routledge.

Tatoğlu, E. and Glaister, K.W. (2000) *Dimensions of Western Foreign Investment in Turkey*. London: Quorum Books.

Taylor, S. and Napier, N. (1996) 'Working in Japan: Lessons from Women Expatriates', *Sloan Management Review*, Spring, pp. 76–84.

Taylor, S., Beechler, S. and Napier, N. (1996) 'Toward an Integrated Model for Strategic International Human Resource Management', *Academy of Management Review*, 21, pp. 959–71.

Terborg, J.R. and Illgen, D.R. (1975) 'A Theoretical Approach to Sex Discrimination in Traditionally Masculine Occupations', *Organizational Behavior and Human Performance*, 13, pp. 352–76.

Theuerkauf, I. (1991) 'Reshaping the Global Organization', *McKinsey Quarterly*, 3, pp. 1023–119.

Torres, C. and Bruxelles, M. (1992) 'Capitalizing on Global Diversity', *HR Magazine*, pp. 30–3.

Torrington, D. (1994) *International Human Resource Management: Think Globally, Act Locally*. New York: Prentice Hall.

Trompenaars, F. (1993) *Riding the Waves of Culture*. London: The Economist Books.

Truss, C. (1999) 'Human Resource Management: Gendered Terrain?', *International Journal of Human Resource Management*, 10, pp. 180–200.

Tsui, A.S. and Far, I.L.L. (1997) 'Where Guanxi Matters; Relational Demography and Guanxi in the Chinese Context', *Work and Occupation*, 1(24): pp. 56–79

Tung, R. (1981) 'Selection and Training of Personnel for Overseas Assignments', *Columbia Journal of World Business*, 16, pp. 66–8.

Tung, R.L. (1984) 'Strategic Management of Human Resources in the Multinational Enterprise', *Human Resource Management*, 23, pp. 117–25.

Tung, R.L. (1988) *The New Expatriates: Managing Human Resources Abroad*. New York: Harper & Row.

Tung, R.L. (1993) 'Managing Cross-National and Intra-Nnational Diversity', *Human Resource Management Journal*, 23, pp. 461–77.

Tung, R.L. and Worm, V. (1997) 'East Meets West: North European Expatriates in China', *Business and the Contemporary World*, 9(1), pp. 137–48

Tung, R.L. (1994) 'Human Resource Issues and Technology Transfer', *International Journal of Human Resource Management*, 5(4), pp. 807–25

Tung, R.L. (1996) 'Negotiating with East Asians', in O. Ghauri and J.C. Usunier (eds), *International Business Negotiations*. Oxford, UK: Pergamon, pp. 369–81.

UNCTAD (1999) *World Investment Report 1999. Foreign Direct Investment and the Challenge of Development; Overview*, New York: United Nations.

Von Glinow, M.A. (2002) 'Best practices in IHRM: Lessons learned from a ten-country/regional analysis', *Human Resource Management*, 41:1, pp. 3–4.

Walton, R.E. (1987) *Managing Conflict, Interpersonal Dialogue and Third-party Roles*. Reading, MA: Addison-Wesley.

Warner, M. (2002) 'Globalization, Labour Markets and Human Resources in Asia-Pacific Economies: An Overview', *International Journal of Human Resource Management*, 13, pp. 384–98.

Warson, A. (1999) 'Marks & Spencer, Other U.K. Firms Exit Canada', in *Shopping Centres Today*.

Wasti, S.A. (1998) 'Cultural Barriers in Transferability of Japanese and American Human Resource Practices to Developing Countries', *International Journal of Human Resource Management*, 9(4), pp. 608–15.

Weightman, J. (2001) *Managing People*. London: Chartered Institute of Personnel and Development.

Welch, D. (1994) 'Determinants of International Human Resource Management Approaches and Activities', *Journal of Management Studies*, 31, pp. 139–54.

Welch, J. (1999) 'Marks and Spencer Axes its Graduate Programme', *People Management*, 3, June, p. 14

Wentling, R.M. and Palma-Rivas, N. (1998) 'Current Status and Future Trends of Diversity Initiatives in the Workplace', *Human Resource Development Quarterly*, 9, 3, pp. 235–54.

WFPMA (2003) World Federation of Personnel Management Association, www.wfpma.com/wfpma.html

Whitley, R. (1992) 'Societies, Firms and Markets: The Social Structuring of Business Systems', in R. Whitley (ed.), *European Business Systems. Firms and Markets in Their National Contexts*. London: Sage, pp. 5–45.

Willey, B. (2003) *Employment Law in Context: An introduction for HR Professionals*. London: Prentice-Hall.

Winstanley, D. and Woodall, J. (2002) 'The Adolescence of Ethics in Human Resource Management', *Human Resource Management Journal*, 10, pp. 45–8.

Womack, J.P., Jones, D.T. and Roos, D. (1990) *The Machine that Changed the World*. New York: Rawson Associates.

Wong, G.Y.Y. and Birnbaum-More, P.H. (1994) 'Culture, Context and Structure: A Test on Hong Kong Banks', *Organization Studies*, 15(1), pp. 99–123.

World of Work (2001) 'KILM 2001', Dec. 41, pp. 11–13.

World of Work (2002a) 'World Commission on the Social Dimension of Globalization Meets', June 43, pp. 22–3.

World of Work (2002b) 'Conference Tackles Globalisation, Personal Security, Poverty and Job Creation', Sep.–Oct., 44, pp. 22–5.

World of Work (2002c) 'World Commission on the Social Dimension of Globalization Holds Third Meeting', Dec., 45, p. 29.

Yang, M. M.-h. (1994) *Gifts, Favours, and Banquets: The Art of Social Relationships in China*. Ithaca, NY: Cornell University Press.

Yao, E.L. (1987) 'Cultivating "Guanxi" (Personal Relationships) with Chinese Partners'. *Business Marketing*, 72(1), pp. 62–6.

Yin, R.K. (1994) *Case Study Research: Design and Methods*. Beverly Hills, CA: Sage.

Zakaria, N. (2000) 'The Effects of Cross-Cultural Training on the Acculturation Process of the Global Workforce', *International Journal of Manpower*, 21, pp. 492–510.

Zetlin, M. (1994) 'Making Tracks', *Journal of European Business*, 5/5, pp. 40–7.

Glossary of Terms

Ahu Tatlı

Access discrimination: discrimination experienced at the point of recruitment.

Adaptive approach: the human resource management approach advocating the adaptation to the best practice in the host country.

Aix model of HRM: the approach that originated from France and underlines the significance of social and educational systems in the management of human resources.

'Best-fit' approach: a rather particularistic analysis of the relationship between management of human resources and corporate strategy. According to this approach every context has its own peculiarities which should be considered as reference points by human resource strategists, and both corporate strategy and human resource strategy need to be harmonized with the context-specific characteristics of the internal and external business environment.

'Best-practice' approach: the approach that advocates the adoption of universal principles with respect to human resource management strategies regardless of the context. According to this perspective, 'best practices' in the area of strategic human resource management should guide the strategic human resource decisions elsewhere and this would produce similar successful results for firms.

Business strategy: see **Corporate strategy**

Competitive advantage: a firm's possession of several assets and resources that provide it with a competitive edge in the external business environment.

Convergence approach: one of the dominant approaches in international management research which argues that business practices around the world would become similar, converge towards the most efficient, namely the United States model, as technology imposes similar structures and work organization. This approach is also called the 'universalist paradigm' (see also **Divergence approach**).

Corporate strategy: an integrated body of plans that covers all aspects of business activities and aims to achieve corporate objective. It is also referred to as business strategy.

Corporatist approach: the approach to industrial relations that seeks the close involvement of government, trade unions and employer organizations in centralized decision-making on fiscal and policy decisions which relate to employment matters. This is also known as the 'tripartite' approach.

Criterion bias: the discrepancy between measures for work performance and the employee's real value for the organization.

Culturalist approach: one of the dominant approaches in international management research which explains the differences in managerial behaviour as mainly stemming from variations in national culture. This perspective attempts to explain variances in work organization, managerial behaviour and HR/personnel practices by referring to uniqueness of values, ideas and beliefs in each national culture.

Culture shock: an emotional reaction or stress reaction that is associated with the early and profound experiences in a new culture and includes individuals' lack of points of reference, social norms and rules to guide their actions and understand others' behaviour due to the lack of familiarity with both the physical setting and the social environment.

Direct discrimination: unfair treatment towards a person due to a reason directly related to his or her membership or belonging to a particular group.

Discriminating effect: the situation when the characteristics upon which the decision is based correlates with irrelevant characteristics in such a way as to render the procedure discriminatory towards certain groups or individuals, although the process is free of direct and indirect discrimination.

Discrimination: the act of distinguishing between individuals or groups based on objective or subjective criteria. Although the technical meaning of discrimination is neutral, its general meaning has the negative connotation of unfair behaviour towards an individual or group. It then refers to disadvantaging an individual or a group on the basis of arbitrary criteria of labelling.

Divergence approach: one of the dominant approaches in international management research which advocates the necessity of research to find the context-specific practices and approaches in view of the contextual and cultural differences that prevail in the international context. This approach is also referred to as the 'contextual paradigm' (see also **convergence approach**).

Employers' associations: representative bodies for employers whose main functions, in general, are lobbying the government; representing employers in discussions with trade unions and the government; providing advice and guidelines to employers on employment-relations issues; representing employers at employment tribunals; and providing guidelines on 'best practice' in employment relations.

Ethnocentric approach: the international management approach which involves transferring home-country applications directly to subsidiaries in host countries.

European Union (EU): in 1957 six European countries, Belgium, France, Italy, Luxembourg, the Netherlands and West Germany, came together in formulating the Treaty of Rome which created the European Economic Community (EEC), the forerunner of the current EU. Broadly, the major objectives were to create a Europe that was economically more interdependent, thereby rendering war between European countries less likely, and to create a large economic bloc in order to trade more effectively to compete internationally. In 1967, the EEC was renamed as the European Community (EC). The Maastricht Treaty of the European Union, agreed in 1991, paved the way for the Community to gain a social dimension and to become the European Union (EU).

Expatriate: a home-country employee who takes up employment in an overseas subsidiary of a company, for a considerable period of time.

Exportive approach: the human resource management approach advocating the export of best practice from other countries.

Financial control: the form of control where interdependence between strategic business units (SBUs) are loose; SBUs are, to a large extent, separated from the centre; operating decisions are decentralized; and the main type of control exercised by the corporate office on SBUs is 'budgetary'.

Geocentric orientation: an organizational configuration which has a worldwide perspective rather than a local (ethnocentric) or a polycentric orientation.

Global Manager: a manager in a company that operates across borders. Alternatively, the 'global manager' may be defined as an state of mind, which embodies an openness and willingness to cross borders as part of a career experience.

Global mind-set: the readiness and willingness to work within a global environment, to accept differences, and benefit from such diversity.

Global workforce: the human capital available in the international arena and across national borders.

Globalization: the worldwide process of increase in the pace of flow of capital, labour, goods and services across national boundaries. The process is generally associated with the liberalization of economic policies, that is the opening of trade and capital markets, increase in foreign investment; emergence of new international business blocs; increased mobility of labour across national borders; and increased competition in the international context.

Glocal: being global in strategy, but adaptive to the local environment, finding the right balance across different operations, and setting a policy that will take into account the strategy of the organization as well as local requirements.

Hard human resource management: the HRM perspective that considers employees as one of the key resources of organizations. It is argued in this tradition that human resources should be used effectively in order to achieve organizational goals (see also **Soft human resource management**).

Harvard model: the approach which suggests that human resource management decisions should be informed by both stakeholder interests and also a set of situational factors. The model illustrates the influence of situational factors on stakeholder interests, and their impact on human resource policy choices which are destined to deliver a raft of predetermined human resource outcomes such as commitment, competence, congruence and cost-effectiveness. The Harvard model emphasizes the human element in human resource formulations.

Home country: the country where the main operation was established, where the headquarters of the international or multinational firm is situated, and where strategies are defined and where the control is. It is also referred to as 'mother company' (see also **Host countries**).

Host countries: the countries where the home company operates (see also **Home country**).

Human resource management: a range of management activities which aim to achieve organizational objectives through effective use of employees.

Human resource strategy: a plan that defines how the human resources would be utilized in order to achieve the objectives of the firm. It includes decisions regarding the selection, recruitment, development, deployment and training of human resources.

Indirect discrimination: introduction of an arbitrary criteria in employment which has a disproportionately negative impact on a group or a cluster of individuals. It may occur when some requirements of employee selection, such as height or an age restriction, disproportionately exclude a particular group, or certain minority ethnic groups or women.

Institutionalist perspective: one of the dominant approaches in international management research which suggests that business organizations are 'embedded' in their own national systems, and organizational behaviour is determined by the social-institutional environment of nation states at sub- or supra-national levels. According to this perspective, the different national development paths followed by countries mean different national forms of business organization and business systems, as the sum of intertwined structures and institutions shape the internal organization of firms and the nature of markets and competition.

Instrumental approach: the IHRM approach that focuses on effective deployment of staff in order to achieve organizational objectives (see also **Value based approach**).

Instrumental collectivism: workers' affiliations to trade unions primarily to protect their terms and conditions of employment (see also **Solidaristic collectivism**).

Integrative approach: the human resource management approach advocating the integration of various best practices from different countries.

International human resource management: a range of people-management functions, processes and activities which involve consideration of more than one national context.

International joint ventures: subsidiaries of MNCs where the equity ownership is shared between a local and a foreign partner, with the percentage ownership of partners defined for individual studies, ranging from 5–20 per cent minimum to 80–95 per cent maximum.

International Labour Organization (ILO): founded in 1919 following the Treaty of Versailles which brought about the League of Nations, the ILO is the specialized agency of the UN which seeks to promote social justice through establishing and safeguarding internationally recognized human and labour rights. It brings together governments, employers and workers of its 176 member states in common action to improve social protection and conditions of life and work throughout the world.

International Monetary Fund (IMF): the IMF is an international organization of 184 member countries. It was established to promote international monetary cooperation, exchange stability, and orderly exchange arrangements to foster economic growth and high levels of employment, and to provide temporary financial assistance to help ease balance of payments adjustments in countries which experience financial difficulty.

Japanese model: the Japanese approach was introduced in the 1980s and emphasized how quality considerations can be integrated into people-management techniques.

Labour-force participation rate: a measure of the extent of an economy's working-age population that is economically active.

Labour productivity: output per unit of labour input.

Managing conflict: finding a resolution or controlling a conflict so that its negative consequences are decreased. An essential precondition of engaging in this process is a commitment to the ongoing relationship despite the differences and discomfort it causes.

Managing diversity: the approach that aims to build specific skills, create policies and draft practices that get the best from every employee; to establish a heterogeneous workforce to perform to its potential in an equitable work environment.

Matching models' of HRM: another name for the Harvard, Michigan and New York models because of their common aim to match the human resources strategy with that of the corporation.

Michigan model: the approach which illustrates that in order to improve their performance, companies must build a direct link between their corporate and human resource strategies and structures. It promotes an instrumental use of human resources in order to realize corporate objectives. The Michigan model accentuates the strategic resource aspect of human resources.

MIT model: the approach that advocates the 'new industrial relations' model, which assumes that joint consultation between employees and employers, and increased levels of cooperation and flexibility in the workplace, will provide companies with adaptability and representation.

New York model: the approach which focuses on the theme of strategic relevance of HRM. The model has introduced and illustrated the concept of 'strategic fit' between corporate and human resource strategy.

North American Free Trade Agreement (NAFTA): NAFTA is the regional economic bloc between the USA, Canada and Mexico. NAFTA adds a new institutional layer alongside domestic rules and regulations affecting trade. Since it took effect in 1994, its most obvious impact has been on accelerating trade volumes between the three countries.

Organizational flexibility: the capacity of the firm's human resources to adapt to internal and external changes.

Polycentric approach: the international management approach which involves adopting host-country applications.

Professional associations for human resource managers: organizations representing HR professionals. In most cases their functions include regulating the professionalization of human resources, offering advice, networking possibilities, support, education and training to their members and other national and industrial agencies about management of people.

Psychological contract: the informal, unspoken and reciprocal agreement between individual workers and their organization, consisting of the mutual expectations between employer and employee and based on mutual trust and respect.

Regiocentric orientation: the organizational configuration that attempts to compromise and divide the operation into several regions.

Resource based view: one of the recent approaches to strategic HRM which argues for the importance of the management of firms' internal resources such as management quality and organizational culture, in increasing business performance.

Reversed cultural shock: the experience of a person returning to his or her home country and home organization both due to the change in his or her own behaviours and perceptions, and changes that may have occurred in the home country and the organization while she or he was away.

Social capital: the form of capital consisting of networks, norms and trust that manifests itself in the quality of coordination and cooperation in organizations.

Social dumping: the process in which international, transnational and multinational firms move their facilities across national borders in pursuit of cheaper labour and lower working standards in order to gain competitive advantage. The process has negative implications for the standards of life both in home and host countries as this movement pushes the standards of pay and conditions of work towards a lower common denominator in the international scene.

Soft human resource management: the HRM perspective that considers employees first and foremost as human beings who contribute to the organization (see also **Hard human resource management**).

Solidaristic collectivism: workers' affiliation to trade unions based on their belief in the role of trade unions as the collective voice of labour (see also **Instrumental collectivism**).

Strategic business unit: a division of a firm which is responsible for a discrete area of business consisting of a group of interrelated products.

Strategic direction: the decisions that are made in line with corporate strategy and related to the type and location of a firm's business operations.

Strategic fit: the extent to which strategic choices regarding the key dimensions of a business are compatible with each other.

Strategic international human resource management: management of the human resource functions, processes and activities that involve consideration of more than one national context, in such a way as to integrate different levels of corporate management with HRM, and to situate the organization in the wider sectoral, national and international context.

Strategy: a plan which is designed for a particular purpose and that associates the available resources with future objectives.

Synergistic approach: the approach advocating the formulation of new human resource management practices by recognizing and transcending individual cultures.

Synergistic control: a form of control that targets both horizontal networking and organizational integration at the same time.

Third country nationals: people who move from a third country, an altogether different country from the home or host country, to work for the company (see also **Home country** and **Host countries**).

Trade unions: the organizations that consist of, and act on behalf of, workers who are their members. Alternatively, trade unions can be defined as the mechanism which provides a collective voice for employees; in that sense, the role of trade unions is wider than representing their members at the local workplace level and includes representing them at a societal level.

Travelling manager: a manager who operates across borders as a routine, but has a base in one country, usually the country where the core operation and the headquarters are located.

Tri-partite approach: see **Corporatist approach**.

Value based approach: the IHRM approach that focuses on the welfare and well-being of staff both as an end in itself and for achieving organizational objectives (see also **Instrumental approach**).

Warwick model: the approach which provides a number of key attributes and indicators of people management and highlights the differentiation between personnel and human resource management approaches.

Works councils: representative committees that are formed by the election of members from the local workforce. The functions of works councils are to encourage worker involvement in decision-making by informing and consulting representatives on issues of business concern. Works councils are mainly a European phenomenon where they are supported by legislation at both national and European level.

World Bank (WB): established in 1944, the WB is one of the specialized agencies of the United Nations and is made up of 184 member countries. The 'World Bank' is the name that has come to be used for the International Bank for Reconstruction and Development and the International Development Association. It provides low-interest loans, interest-free credit and grants to developing countries.

World Trade Organization (WTO): the WTO is the only global international organization dealing with the rules of trade between nations. The goal is to help producers of goods and services, as well as exporters and importers, conduct their business.

Index

consultation, 68–9, 157, 169
    joint, 5, 70, 190
    laws, 158
    rights, 70–1
    role in HRM, 59
    skills, 153
    with trade unions, 154, 158
convergence and divergence
    approaches, 50–53, 55, 62, 67
    in HRM systems, 17, 45, 47, 57, 162–3
corporatist approach, 64, 69, 150, 187
corporate strategy, 42, 56, 82–5, 87, 89, 92, 102,
        146, 149, 187, 191
    international, 56
cultural sensitivity, 155
culturalist approach, 53, 55
culture
    assimilation, 118
    business, 128
    corporate, 44, 84, 94, 95–6, 97, 100
    diversity of, 9, 11, 43, 96, 127, 132–3, 158–9
    global-oriented, 139
    local, 97, 135
    management, 84
    managerial, 130–2, 143
    national, 44, 53, 91, 93, 96, 100, 129, 131
    organizational, 7, 17, 55, 56, 90, 93, 95–6, 99,
        113–14, 123, 126, 136
    shock, 115–17, 120
    strong, 83
    workplace, 88

D
Denmark, 21, 33, 39, 67
developed countries, 37, 55, 57, 166
    development of HRM, 6
    less-developed countries, 3, 17, 165
    MNCs, 163, 164, 165
    see also industrialized counties
developing countries, 37, 55–6, 94, 165, 191
    business environment, 57
    development of HRM in, 6–7, 21
    employment, 38
    labour productivity in, 30, 32
    production plants, 93
Dhek Bhal, 170
discriminating effect, 104–5, 188
discrimination, 64, 104–164
    access, 104, 187
    definition of, 105, 188
    effect, 105, 107, 188
    direct, 105, 187
    indirect, 105, 189
    laws, 111
    sex, 163–4
discrimination-free
    performance appraisal, 106
    selection process, 106, 109
dismissal, 71, 150
diversity, 9, 43, 94–5, 103, 109

business case for, 109
    cultural, 7, 82, 89, 90, 92–4, 96, 102
    ethnic, 61
    gender, 61
    managing, 20, 43, 83, 94–6, 103–4, 113
    national, 95
    policy, 61
    training, 103–4, 110–15

E
employee voice, collective, 67–8, 161, 191
employment relations
equal opportunities, 36, 39, 86, 164
    employer, 86
    policies and practices, 68
    by sex, 86, 164
    in the workplace, 64
equality, 30, 40, 84, 164, 167, 169, 171–2
    ethnic, 167
    gender, 164
    legal case for, 164
    mainstream, 86
    between men and women, 86
    of opportunity, 36, 165
    racial, 169
ethnic minority, 64, 105, 167–9, 170–1, 189
ethnicity, 105, 167, 169
ethnocentric approach, 2, 56, 90, 96–7, 134–5,
        149, 163
ETUC (European Trade Union Confederation),
        69
European Commission, 39
European Community (EC), 39, 188
European Court of Auditors, 39
European Court of Justice, 39, 150
European Economic Community (EEC), 39, 188
European Parliament, 39, 157
European Union (EU), 16, 29, 38, 39–40, 41, 47,
        48, 67, 139, 188
    budget, 39
    Council of the, 39
    equal opportunities, 86
    institutions, 39
    legislation, 40, 70, 86
    member states, 36, 86
    nationals, 41
    workforce, 40
Executive Professional Network (EPN), 170
expatriates, 8–9, 18, 44, 48–9, 97, 126, 131–48,
        164
    failure, 97, 133–4
    management of, 7, 48–9, 139
    managers, 48, 97, 103, 104, 115–17, 124, 126,
        128, 135
    stress, 119–21
    training, 103–4, 117–19, 162
    transfer of, 44, 97
expatriation, 19, 97, 117–18, 128–9, 133–8
    failure rate of, 133
    managing, 125, 135–6, 139–43